Lecture Notes in Computer Science   2213

Edited by G. Goos, J. Hartmanis, and J. van Leeuwen

T0230296

Springer
Berlin
Heidelberg
New York
Barcelona
Hong Kong
London
Milan
Paris
Tokyo

Marten J. van Sinderen
Lambert J.M. Nieuwenhuis (Eds.)

Protocols for Multimedia Systems

6th International Conference, PROMS 2001
Enschede, The Netherlands, October 17-19, 2001
Proceedings

 Springer

Series Editors

Gerhard Goos, Karlsruhe University, Germany
Juris Hartmanis, Cornell University, NY, USA
Jan van Leeuwen, Utrecht University, The Netherlands

Volume Editors

Marten J. van Sinderen
Lambert J.M. Nieuwenhuis
University of Twente, Department of Computer Science
Centre for Telematics and Information Technology (CTIT)
P.O. Box 217, 7500 AE Enschede, The Netherlands
E-mail: sinderen@ctit.utwente.nl
bart@cs.utwente.nl

Cataloging-in-Publication Data applied for

Die Deutsche Bibliothek - CIP-Einheitsaufnahme

Protocols for multimedia systems : 6th international conference ;
proceedings / PROMS 2001, Enschede, The Netherlands, October 17 - 19, 2001.
Marten J. van Sinderen ; Lambert J. M. Nieuwenhuis (ed.). - Berlin ; Heidelberg ;
New York ; Barcelona ; Hong Kong ; London ; Milan ; Paris ; Tokyo : Springer, 2001
    (Lecture notes in computer science ; Vol. 2213)
    ISBN 3-540-42708-2

CR Subject Classification (1998): C.2.2, C.2.5, H.5.1

ISSN 0302-9743
ISBN 3-540-42708-2 Springer-Verlag Berlin Heidelberg New York

Springer-Verlag Berlin Heidelberg New York
a member of BertelsmannSpringer Science+Business Media GmbH

http://www.springer.de

© Springer-Verlag Berlin Heidelberg 2001
Printed in Germany

Typesetting: Camera-ready by author, data conversion by PTP-Berlin, Stefan Sossna
Printed on acid-free paper   SPIN: 10840842   06/3142   5 4 3 2 1 0

Preface

This conference in Enschede, The Netherlands, is the sixth in a series of international conferences and workshops under the title Protocols for Multimedia Systems, abbreviated as PROMS. The first PROMS workshop took place in June 1994 in Berlin, Germany, followed by workshops in Salzburg, Austria (October 1995) and Madrid, Spain (October 1996). In 1997, PROMS formed a temporary alliance with Multimedia Networking, a conference previously held in Aizu, Japan, in 1995. This led to the international conference on Protocols for Multimedia Systems – Multimedia Networking, PROMS-MmNet, that took place in Santiago, Chile (November 1997). Since then PROMS has been announced as an international conference, although informal contacts and interactive sessions – as in a workshop – were retained as a desirable feature of PROMS. After a gap of three years, PROMS was organized in Cracow, Poland (October 2000), for the fifth time. We consider it a challenge to make this sixth edition of PROMS as successful as the previous events.

The goal of the PROMS series of conferences and workshops is to contribute to scientific, strategic, and practical cooperation between research institutes and industrial companies in the area of multimedia protocols. This is also the goal of PROMS 2001. The basic theme of this conference continues to be multimedia protocols, both at the network and application level, although the increasing interest in wireless, mobility, and quality-of-service as interrelated topics with relevance to multimedia are reflected in the current program.

This year, 43 research papers were submitted from academic and industrial institutions all over the world, which confirms the international character of work in this area. Every submitted paper was reviewed by at least three reviewers. Thanks to the first class reviews from our program committee members and additional reviewers, and with the help of the online conference tool ConfMan, we were able to select 18 high-quality papers for presentation at the conference. These papers are grouped as follows in sessions for the single track technical program: (1) QoS in the Internet, (2) Multimedia streaming, (3) Multimedia multicast, (4) Wireless networks and host mobility, (5) TCP/IP optimization, and (6) Service development and deployment. The technical program is complemented with two invited presentations: "From Mars to Your TV at Home - Selected Internet Developments" by Erik Huizer and "Which Way to the Wireless Internet ?" by Andrew Campbell.

Also part of this conference, but not reflected in these proceedings, is a tutorial program, scheduled before the technical program. We are pleased that we could attract Alan Parkes, Frank Eliassen, and Thomas Plagemann who were willing to share their overviews and insights on "Approaching Multimedia Content Description" (Parkes) and "Multimedia Middleware" (Eliassen/Plagemann).

We would like to thank the tutorial and invited speakers for their contribution to PROMS 2001. We are grateful for the efforts of the program committee members. With the help of additional reviewers, they managed to produce reviews on all submitted research papers while observing the tight deadlines that were imposed by the organizers. They also contributed to the paper selection process that resulted in the strong technical program of this conference. We appreciate the useful advice of the organizer of the previous conference, Zdzislaw Papir. We gratefully acknowledge the cooperation with ACM SIGCOMM and SIGMM, and the COM Chapter of IEEE

Benelux Section. We are also grateful for the financial support of our industrial sponsors, of the Faculty of Computer Science of the University of Twente, and of the Centre of Telematics and Information Technology of the University of Twente. Finally, we wish to thank the people from our local organizing committee, Marloes Castañeda, Annelies Klos, Giancarlo Guizzardi, and Christian Tzolov. We really appreciated your help!

July 2001   Marten van Sinderen
                                                              Bart Nieuwenhuis

Organization

Conference Chairs

Marten van Sinderen   U. of Twente, The Netherlands
Bart Nieuwenhuis   KPN Research / U. of Twente, The Netherlands

Program Committee

Arturo Azcorra	Carlos III U., Spain
Hans van den Berg	KPN Research / U. of Twente, The Netherlands
Andrew Campbell	Colombia University, USA
Michel Diaz	LAAS-CNRS, France
Henk Eertink	Telematica Instituut, The Netherlands
Frank Eliassen	U. of Oslo, Norway
Luís Ferreira Pires	U. of Twente, The Netherlands
Francisco Fontes	Portugal Telecom Inovação, SA, Portugal
Geert Heijenk	Ericsson Eurolab, The Netherlands
Ulrich Hofmann	U. Salzburg, Austria
David Hutchison	Lancaster U., UK
Wim Jonker	KPN Research / U. of Twente, The Netherlands
Dimitri Konstantas	U. of Twente, The Netherlands / U. of Geneva, Switzerland
Claudia Linnhoff-Popien	Institut für Informatik, Germany
Laurent Mathy	Lancaster U., UK
Bart Nieuwenhuis	KPN Research / U. of Twente, The Netherlands
Sergio Palazzo	U. of Catania, Italy
Zdzislaw Papir	AGH U. of Technology, Poland
Thomas Plagemann	U. of Oslo, UniK, Norway
Radu Popescu-Zeletin	GMD-FOKUS, Germany
Dick Quartel	U. of Twente, The Netherlands
Jean-Luc Raffy	Institut National des Telecommunications, France
Jeroen Schot	Lucent Technologies, The Netherlands
Marten van Sinderen	U. of Twente, The Netherlands
Johan Zuidweg	Tecsidel, Spain

Local Organization

Marloes Castañeda	U. of Twente, The Netherlands
Annelies Klos	U. of Twente, The Netherlands
Giancarlo Guizzardi	U. of Twente, The Netherlands
Christian Tzolov	U. of Twente, The Netherlands

Referees

Arturo Azcorra	Carlos III U., Spain
Hans van den Berg	KPN Research / U. of Twente, The Netherlands
Andrew Campbell	Colombia University, USA
Veronique Baudin	LAAS-CNRS, France
Robert Chodorek	AGH U. of Technology, Poland
Nikolay Diakov	U. of Twente, The Netherlands
Michel Diaz	LAAS-CNRS, France
Henk Eertink	Telematica Instituut, The Netherlands
Jacco Brok	Lucent Technologies, The Netherlands
Frank Eliassen	U. of Oslo, Norway
Luís Ferreira Pires	U. of Twente, The Netherlands
Francisco Fontes	Portugal Telecom Inovação, SA, Portugal
Clever Guareis de Farias	U. of Twente, The Netherlands
Geert Heijenk	Ericsson Eurolab, The Netherlands
Ulrich Hofmann	U. Salzburg, Austria
Thierry Gayraud	LAAS-CNRS, France
David Hutchison	Lancaster U., UK
Wim Jonker	KPN Research / U. of Twente, The Netherlands
Dimitri Konstantas	U. of Twente, The Netherlands / U. of Geneva, Switzerland
Alberto García-Martínez	Carlos III U., Spain
Patrick Bush	Lucent Technologies, The Netherlands
Tom Kristensen	U. of Oslo, Norway
Claudia Linnhoff-Popien	Institut für Informatik, Germany
Rui Lopes	Lancaster U., UK
Kjetil Lund	U. of Oslo, Norway
Laurent Mathy	Lancaster U., UK
Bastien Peelen	Lucent Technologies, The Netherlands
Marek Natkaniec	AGH U. of Technology, Poland
Bart Nieuwenhuis	KPN Research / U. of Twente, The Netherlands
Pascal Berthou	LAAS-CNRS, France
Sergio Palazzo	U. of Catania, Italy
Zdzislaw Papir	AGH U. of Technology, Poland
Arjen de Heer	Lucent Technologies, The Netherlands
Thomas Plagemann	U. of Oslo, UniK, Norway
Ignacio Soto	Carlos III U., Spain
Radu Popescu-Zeletin	GMD-FOKUS, Germany
Dick Quartel	U. of Twente, The Netherlands
Jean-Luc Raffy	Institut National des Telecommunications, France
Martin Molina	LAAS-CNRS, France
Jeroen Schot	Lucent Technologies, The Netherlands
Marten van Sinderen	U. of Twente, The Netherlands
Ing Widya	U. of Twente, The Netherlands
Johan Zuidweg	Tecsidel, Spain

Supporting and Sponsoring Organizations

ACM SIGCOMM
ACM SIGMM
IEEE Benelux Section, COM Chapter
KIvI
NGI
University of Twente, Computer Science Faculty
University of Twente, CTIT

Table of Contents

Globule: A Platform for Self-Replicating Web Documents

Guillaume Pierre and Maarten van Steen

Vrije Universiteit Amsterdam
Department of Mathematics & Computer Science
{gpierre,steen}@cs.vu.nl

Abstract. Replicating Web documents at a worldwide scale can help reduce user-perceived latency and wide-area network traffic. This paper presents the design of Globule, a platform that automates all aspects of such replication: server-to-server peering negotiation, creation and destruction of replicas, selection of the most appropriate replication strategies on a per-document basis, consistency management and transparent redirection of clients to replicas. Globule is initially directed to support standard Web documents. However, it can also be applied to stream-oriented documents. To facilitate the transition from a non-replicated server to a replicated one, we designed Globule as a module for the Apache Web server. Therefore, converting Web documents should require no more than compiling a new module into Apache and editing a configuration file.

1   Introduction

Large-scale distributed systems often address performance and quality-of-service (QoS) issues by way of caching and replication. In the Web, attention has traditionally concentrated on caching and in much lesser extent to replication. Recently, Web hosting services such as Akamai and Digital Island have started to emerge as the solution to achieve scalability through replication. In this approach, content is replicated to places where user demand is high. Content itself can vary from simple static pages to bandwidth-demanding video streams.

Web hosting services have the advantage over static mirroring of Web sites in that decisions on *what* content to replicate, and *where* replicas should be placed can be made automatically. However, current solutions generally do not differentiate how copies are to be kept consistent. In other words, once the decision is made to replicate, the same replication protocol is applied in all cases. In essence, no distinction is made between the type of content, nor are different access patterns taken into account. In many cases, static HTML documents are treated the same as large files containing, for example, audio- or videodata.

Many protocols have been proposed to achieve caching or replication, each of which presents specific advantages and drawbacks. However, as we have shown in a previous article, there is no single policy that is best in all cases [11]. This statement is true even for simple Web documents that are constructed as a static collection of logically related files. Typically, files in such documents contain HTML text, images, icons, and so on. When dealing with complex documents, such as those also containing streaming data,

M.J. van Sinderen and L.J.M. Nieuwenhuis (Eds.): PROMS 2001, LNCS 2213, pp. 1–11, 2001.

or which are (partly) generated on request, differentiating policies becomes even more important.

As a consequence, we can expect to see a myriad of protocols that need to co-exist in a single system. One approach is to build multiprotocol servers, preferably following techniques that allow future extension. However, we believe such an approach is not sufficient. As an alternative, we propose to establish integration by following an object-based approach, in which a document is encapsulated in an object that is fully responsible for its own distribution. In other words, an object should not only encapsulate its state and operations, but also the implementation of a replication or distribution policy by which that state is delivered to clients.

To examine the feasibility of our approach we have been concentrating on Web documents, which we represent as distributed, self-replicating objects. Our approach allows a document to monitor its own access patterns and to dynamically select the replication policy that suits it best. When a change is detected in access patterns, it can re-evaluate its choice and switch policies on the fly [12].

Although we have demonstrated the potential merits of self-replicating documents, we have not yet addressed their practical implementation. There are two problems that need to be addressed. First, Web servers need to be adapted so that they can support adaptive per-document replication policies. Second, servers need to cooperate to allow replicas to be dynamically installed and removed, and to redirect clients to the nearest replica. One additional requirement that we feel is justified, is that adaptations should fit into the current Web infrastructure, requiring minimal modifications to existing servers and no modification at all to clients.

This paper presents the design of Globule, a platform for hosting adaptive Web documents that encapsulate their own distribution and replication protocol. It is designed as a module for the popular Apache server. Making use of our approach should require no more than compiling a new module into Apache and editing a configuration file. Globule handles all management tasks: discovering and negotiating with remote sites for hosting replicas; replicating static and some dynamic documents; and transparently redirecting clients to their closest replica.

The paper is structured as follows: Section 2 describes our document and server models; Section 3 details the architecture of the system, and Section 4 shows how such a system can be implemented as an Apache module. Finally, Section 5 presents related work and Section 6 concludes.

2   General Model

Our system is made of servers that cooperate in order to replicate Web documents. This section describes our document and server models.

2.1   Document Model

In contrast to most Web servers, we do not consider a Web document and its replicas only as a collection of files. Instead, we take a more general approach and consider a document as a physically distributed object whose state is replicated across the Internet.

The fact that the object's state is distributed is hidden from clients behind the object's interfaces. There is one standard interface containing methods such as put() and get() to allow for delivering and modifying a document's content. Special interfaces may be provided as well. For example, a document containing multimedia data may offer an interface for setting a client's QoS requirements before delivery takes place.

Our system is based on Globe, a platform for large-scale distributed objects [18]. Its main novelty is the encapsulation of issues related to distribution and replication *inside* the objects. In other words, an object fully controls how, when, and where it distributes and replicates its content. We have even designed documents that can dynamically select their own replication policy. Our "documents-are-objects" model is also a key to replicating dynamic or streaming documents.

Adaptive Replicated Web Documents. We have shown in previous papers that significant performance improvements can be obtained over traditional replicated servers by associating each document with the replication strategy that suits it best [11,12]. Such per-document replication policies are made possible by the encapsulation of replication issues inside each document.

The selection of the best replication policy is realized internally to each document by way of trace-based simulations. Replicas transmit logs of the requests they received to their master site. At startup or when a significant access pattern modification is detected, the master re-evaluates its choice of replication strategy. To do so, it extracts the most recent trace records and simulates the behavior of a number of replication policies with this trace. Each simulation outputs performance metrics such as client retrieval time, network traffic and consistency. The "best" policy is chosen from these performance figures using a cost function. More details about these adaptive replicated documents can be found in [12].

Replicating Dynamic Web Documents. Many documents are not made from static content, but are generated on the fly. For each request, a Web server executes a request-specific piece of code whose output is delivered to the client. This code can in turn access external resources such as databases, execute shell commands, and issue network requests for generating a *view* of the dynamic document.

Replicating dynamic documents requires replicating the code as well as all data necessary for its execution (databases, etc.). This can be done by encapsulating the code and the databases in replicated distributed objects. Every request sent to the database is intercepted by the encapsulating object before being executed. Following the object's replication policy, if the request is likely to modify the internal state of the database, then it is propagated and applied to the other replicas in order to maintain a consistent state [18].

Our object model does not differentiate between static and dynamic documents. Therefore, dynamic documents are considered as objects implementing the same interface as static documents, but they differ in their implementation: static documents use always the same implementation to access various internal states, whereas dynamic documents differ in both their internal states and method implementations.

The main issue with respect to dynamic documents arises when converting existing dynamic documents into objects. The Web server must be able to determine automatically which resources, files or databases are accessed by each dynamic document in order to include them inside the object. This can be difficult for documents such as CGIs, where the server delegates request handling to an arbitrary external program. However, a large portion of dynamic documents such as PHPs and ASPs are in fact scripts interpreted by the Web server itself. In this case, the server knows the semantics of the document, and can often automatically detect which resources are required by the document.

Dynamic documents that the server can not analyze cannot be encapsulated into objects. Therefore, they are not replicated in our approach. In these cases, client requests are directed to the master site.

2.2   Cooperative Servers

One important issue for replicating Web documents is to gain access to computing resources in several locations worldwide (CPU, disk space, memory, bandwidth, etc.). On the other hand, adding extra resources locally is cheap and easy. Therefore, the idea is to trade cheap local resources for valuable remote ones. Servers automatically negotiate for resource peering. The result of such a negotiation is for a "hosting server" to agree to allocate a given amount of its local resources to host replicas from a "hosted server." The hosted server keeps control on the resources it has acquired: it controls which of its clients are redirected to the hosting server, which documents are replicated there and which replication policies are being used.

Of course, servers may play both "hosting server" and "hosted server" roles at the same time: a server may host replicas from another server, and replicate its own content to a third one. We use these terms only to distinguish roles within a given cooperation session.

Servers communicate with each other in an NNTP-like fashion. Each server is configured to communicate with a few other servers, which jointly communicate with more servers. This server network allows information to be spread efficiently among the whole group: messages are propagated from host to host through the entire network. Each message carries a unique identifier, so that duplicate message transmission can be avoided.

This communication channel allows servers to broadcast data such as their name, location and publicly available resources such as available storage capacity, network bandwidth, available Apache modules and database software.[1] When a server searches for a new hosting server in a certain area, it uses its local list of server locations to choose a site which would be suitable. It then contacts it directly and starts a negotiation phase. This negotiation can, for example, determine the price asked for accessing the required resources [3,19].

Other types of data that flow through the network of servers are information about disconnected nodes (which may be caused by a failure or simply by a server deciding to leave the group). That way, hosted servers are informed when their hosting servers become unreachable, so they can stop redirecting clients to them.

---

[1] Note that this channel only propagates servers' meta-information. Actual content delivery is realized by means of separate document-specific channels.

2.3 Security Issues

The proposed system presents obvious security risks. A malicious server could accept to host Web document replicas, and deliver modified versions to the users. It could also accept replicas and refuse to answer any request directed to them, causing a "denial of service." More subtle attacks could be, for example, to allocate less resources to replicas than was negotiated.

We propose to solve this problem by using a peer-to-peer trust model. Each server associates a recommendation to a number of nodes, representing the trust it has that these sites are honest. Recommendations can be either positive, meaning that the recommended site is probably honest, or negative, meaning that the site is probably malicious. Recommendations are made public using the information propagation technique presented above. Based on the full set of recommendations, each node autonomously decides whether it trusts or distrusts each of the cooperative servers.

Although this scheme cannot provide complete certainty about a node being good or bad, it generally allows to discriminate good nodes from bad ones. It also tolerates a relatively high number of wrong recommendations (good recommendations for a bad node or *vice versa*). Discussing the full details of our trust model is beyond the scope of this paper, and can be found in [13].

Another issue is to protect servers against malicious dynamic documents, which could be used to run unauthorized code on remote platforms. This problem will be solved with classical techniques such as executing remote code in a sandbox or a remote playground [8].

3   System Architecture

Figure 1 shows Globule's architecture. It provides several distinct features: negotiating with remote servers for resource allocation and resource management, document replication and consistency, and automatic client redirection.

3.1 Delegated Resource Management

When a server notices that replicating the content of a specific document would improve the quality of service for that document's clients, it identifies one or more locations where replicas would be needed. Those locations are determined, for example, as the Autonomous Systems from which most of the requests originate.[2] It then locates suitable hosting servers in those locations and negotiates resource allocation, as was discussed in Section 2.2.

When a hosted server has acquired appropriate resources on a hosting server, it can use those resources to create a replica and redirect clients to that replica. Its only obligation is to not exceed the amount of resources that it has been allocated. This rule is enforced by the hosting server: to prevent excessive use of storage space, a replacement module similar to those of caches is associated to the set of replicas from this hosted

---

[2] Usually, a small number of origin Autonomous Systems account for a large fraction of the requests, as shown for example in [11].

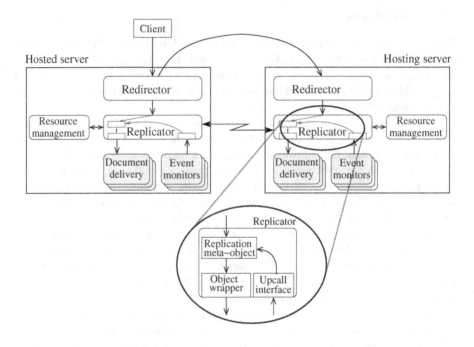

Fig. 1. General Architecture

server. If a hosted server tries to use more resources than it has been allocated, the hosting server will automatically delete other replicas from the same server.

A hosting server, having allocated resources for several different hosted servers, manages each resource pool separately. Therefore, it must have several replacement module instances, each of which enforces resource limitations to one of the hosted servers. This mechanism is similar to those of partitioned caches [9].

Even though resource limitation is enforced by the hosting server, the hosted server remains in control of its allocated resources. It does so by attaching priority flags to its documents, indicating how important each replica is. When making replacement decisions, the hosting server takes these priorities into account in addition to standard parameters such as the frequency of requests and replica size. The more important a replica, the less likely it is to be removed.

Similar mechanisms can be setup to enforce limitations in resources such as bandwidth usage (for which Apache modules are readily available). Such limitations are of primary importance when considering multimedia documents, as their requests may easily prohibit processing requests for other documents at the hosting server.

Basically, one can associate bandwidth usage limitations to the replicas from a given hosted server. When the request stream for a specific set of documents from a hosted server exceeds the negotiated bandwidth, data transmission to the requesting clients is slowed down forcing those clients to share the allocated bandwidth. This algorithm is very similar to handling reserved bandwidth in routers.

This bandwidth management technique seems adequate to smooth occasional load peaks. However, slowing down connections is acceptable only as long as it remains exceptional. If a server must slow down connections on a regular basis, it will trigger a re-evaluation of the placement and replication policy, possibly leading to the creation of more replicas in its neighborhood (see Section 2.1).

3.2 Document Replication

As is also shown in Figure 1, a replica is made of two separate local objects: a document's content which is available in the form of delivery components capable of producing documents, and a replication meta-object which is responsible for enforcing the document's replication policy. Each object can either reside in memory or be marshaled to disk. State transitions between memory and disk are dictated by the per-hosted-server resource limitation module described in Section 3.1.

All replication meta-objects implement a standard interface, but they can have various implementations depending on the replication policy they represent. They maintain information about the object's consistency, such as the date of last modification and the date of the last consistency check.

Each time a request is issued to a document, the server transmits the characteristics of the request to the replication meta-object. Based on its implementation, the meta-object responds by indicating how to treat the request: reply immediately based on the local replica, or require to first check for freshness, etc. The server is in charge of actually performing the operation.

Once the replication meta-object has authorized the request, the Web server uses one of its standard document delivery modules to respond. These can be modules that deliver static documents, or modules that generate a document on request.

Certain replication policies require taking actions at other times than request time, such as prefetching large documents, periodically checking for a document's freshness, sending invalidations to replicas when the master copy is updated, and processing incoming invalidations. To do so, meta-objects can register to local services for being invoked when certain events take place. For example, a meta-object can request to be woken up periodically or when a given file is updated.

3.3 Client Redirection

Each document is assumed to have a home server. This server is responsible for automatically redirecting clients to their most suitable replica. Knowing the location of clients and replicas, such a selection can be reduced to a shortest path problem [14]. Each incoming client is associated with its Autonomous System. Knowing the locations of replica sites and the map of network connections between autonomous systems, each client is directed to a server such that the number of autonomous systems on the path between the client and the replica server is minimized. If necessary, more criteria can be used in the selection of a replica site, such as the load of each replica site and the intra-AS network distances.

Mechanisms to effectively redirect clients to replicas can be classified in two categories [2]:

– HTTP redirection: when it receives an HTTP request, the server sends a redirection response, indicating from which URL the document should be retrieved. This scheme is very simple, but it is not transparent. That is, browsers display the URL of the mirror site instead of the home site. This may become a problem if, for example, a user bookmarks a mirror page. Later on, when he tries to access the page again, this mirror may have been removed.
– DNS redirection: before accessing a page, a browser needs to request the DNS to convert the server's name into an IP address. After locating an authoritative server for the given domain, the client's DNS server contacts it for actually resolving the name. DNS redirection requires the authoritative server to send customized responses depending on the location of the client [17]. Small TTL values are associated to responses, so that client DNS caches are updated often. A customized authoritative DNS server is necessary, but no other DNS server needs to be modified. This method is fully transparent to the user, since URLs do not need to be modified. On the other hand, it has a coarse granularity: it is not possible to replicate only part of a server, since all requests to this server will be sent to the mirrors.

We decided to use DNS redirection, as did most of the content distribution networks, such as Akamai. However, our system's architecture does not depend on this decision; we may later decide to use another mechanism, for example when the HTTP standard will feature more powerful redirection mechanisms.

As we discuss in next section, we will implement a customized DNS server *inside* the Globule Apache module. This allows for easier administration as well as for tight coupling between the replication and redirection modules.

4   Integration into the Apache Web Server

In order to allow for easy deployment, we decided to develop Globule as an Apache module. This way, turning a normal Apache server into a replication-aware server would require only compiling a new module into the server and editing a configuration file.

The Apache Web server is built from a modular design, which enables one to easily add new features [7]. It decomposes the treatment for each request into several steps, such as access checking, actually sending a response back to the client, and logging the request.

Modules can register handler functions to participate in one or more of these steps. When a request is received, the server runs the registered handlers for each step. Modules can then accept or refuse to process the operation; the server tries all the handlers registered for each step until one accepts to process it.

Many third party modules have been developed to extend Apache in a number of ways, such as the PHP server scripting language and a streaming MP3 delivery module.

The architecture of Apache provides us all the tools necessary to implement Globule: a replication module can, for example, intercept a request before being served by the standard document delivery modules to let the replication meta-objects check for consistency. Likewise, servers can communicate with each other by HTTP.

Although Apache has been originally designed to handle only the HTTP protocol, its newest version allows one to write modules that implement other protocols. An appropriate module could therefore turn Apache into a DNS server. We plan to use this feature for redirecting clients to mirrors.

5 Related Work

5.1 Content Distribution Networks

Many systems have been developed to cache or replicate Web documents. The first server-controlled systems have been push-caches, where the server was responsible of pushing cached copies close to the users [5]. More recently, content distribution networks (CDNs) have been developed along the same idea. These systems rely on a large set of servers deployed around the world. These servers are normal caches, configured as surrogate proxies. The intelligence of the system is mainly concentrated in the DNS servers which are used to direct clients to a server close to them. Consistency is realized by incorporating a hash value of document's content *inside* its URL. When a replicated document is modified, its URL is modified as well. This scheme necessitates to change hyperlink references to modified documents as well. In order to deliver only up-to-date documents to users, this system cannot use the same mechanism to replicate HTML documents; only embedded objects such as images and videos are replicated.

Globule presents three major differences with CDNs. First, since its consistency management is independent from the document naming scheme, it can replicate all types of objects. Second, contrary to CDNs which use the same consistency policy for all documents, Globule selects consistency policies on a per-document basis so that each document uses the policy that suits it best. This is of particular interest when replicating heterogeneous sets of documents such as static and dynamic pages, and streaming documents. Finally, the system does not require one single organization to deploy a large number of machines across the Internet: Globule users automatically trade resources with each other, therefore incrementally building a worldwide network of servers at low cost.

5.2 Peer-to-Peer Systems

Globule can be seen as a peer-to-peer system [10]. Most of these systems, such as Gnutella, are used to locate files at user's locations without the need for a centralized server. Other peer-to-peer applications allow, for example, for distribution of parallel computations on users' machines, such as the SETI@home project.

Globule qualifies as a peer-to-peer system because it makes nodes from different administrative domains cooperate to provide a service that no single server could ever achieve. Moreover, its architecture is entirely decentralized, which means that no central server is necessary. The protocol for propagating meta-information among the network of servers is also similar to the protocol for searching a file among a Gnutella network.

The main difference between Globule and other peer-to-peer systems relies in the nature of the inter-node cooperation. Resources being exchanged in Gnutella are files whereas Globule servers exchange storage space and network bandwidth.

5.3 Streaming Media Replication

Replicating streaming documents is a very different issue than replicating regular Web documents. Although we do not consider this class of documents as our primary application target, we believe that our approach could be beneficial in this area as well.

On the one hand, consistency is often not a major issue, since these documents are hardly ever updated. On the other hand, since they are quite big (typically between 1 MB and 100 MB), partial replication often offers better cost-benefit ratio than total replication. Prefix caching (i.e., replicating only the beginning of each file) can help reducing the startup delay and smooth the subsequent bandwidth requirement between the server and the cache [4,16]. The utility of such prefix caching is reinforced by the fact that many users stop movie playback after only a few seconds [1]. Another possibility for partial replication is video staging, where only the parts of the variable-bit-rate video stream that exceed a certain cut-off bandwidth are replicated [20]. Replication of layered encoded video can also be realized by replicating only the first N layers [6]. However, the authors note that this last technique is of interest only if at least some clients use the ability of viewing a low-quality version of the video.

Redirecting clients to appropriate replicas is more difficult with streaming documents than with Web documents. Streaming sessions last longer and use more resources at the replica site, in particular in terms of network bandwidth and disk I/O. This leads to complex scheduling and resource reservation problems at the server or at the replicas. However, many solutions have been proposed that range from clever scheduling policies to mechanisms for redirecting a client to another server during a streaming session [15].

Clearly, streaming documents place different requirements on wide-area content delivery platforms than Web documents. Specific mechanisms are being developed to handle them efficiently. Moreover, these mechanisms do not apply to all situations, depending on the interactive or non-interactive nature of the documents, their compression formats, and the usage pattern of users.

We believe that our adaptive per-document replication scheme would be well suited to handle the variable requirements of video-on-demand applications. Future research will investigate the interest of our approach for wide-area delivery of streaming documents.

6 Conclusion

We have presented Globule, a platform for Web document replication. Globule integrates all necessary services into a single tool: dynamic creation and removal of replicas, consistency management, and automatic client redirection. Globule will be implemented as a module for the Apache server.

The architecture presented in this article is still work in progress, but we hope to release a first prototype soon. Two problems have been left for future work. First, security: the administrator of a server would like to make sure that remote servers which accepted to host his replicas will do it without modifying documents, for example. We plan to use a trust model to solve this. Second, details of server-to-server negotiation still have to be figured out.

When the Globule project is completed, we expect to provide a free cooperative platform for Web document replication that will match the ever-increasing quality of service expectations that users have.

References

1. Acharya, S., Smith, B.: MiddleMan: A video caching proxy server. In: Proc. 10th International Workshop on Network and Operating System Support for Digital Audio and Video (NOSSDAV), Chapel Hill, NC (2000)
2. Barbir, A., Cain, B., Douglis, F., Green, M., Hofmann, M., Nair, R., Potter, D., Spatscheck, O.: Known CDN request-routing mechanisms. Internet Draft (2001)
3. Buyya, R., Abramson, D., Giddy, J.: An economy driven resource management architecture for global computational power grids. In: Proc. International Conference on Parallel and Distributed Processing Techniques and Applications (PDPTA), Las Vegas, NA (2000)
4. Gruber, S., Rexford, J., Basso, A.: Protocol considerations for a prefix-caching proxy for multimedia streams. In: Proc. 9th International World Wide Web Conference, Amsterdam (2000)
5. Gwertzman, J., Seltzer, M.: The case for geographical push-caching. In: Proc. 5th Workshop on Hot Topics in Operating Systems (HotOS), Orcas Island, WA, IEEE (1996)
6. Kangasharju, J., Hartanto, F., Reisslein, M., Ross, K.W.: Distributing layered encoded video through caches. In: Proc. 20th INFOCOM Conference, Anchorage (AK), IEEE (2001)
7. Laurie, B., Laurie, P.: Apache: The Definitive Guide. 2nd edn. O'Reilly & Associates, Sebastopol, CA. (1999)
8. Malkhi, D., Reiter, M.: Secure Execution of Java Applets using a Remote Playground. IEEE Transactions on Software Engineering 26 (2000) 1197–1209
9. Murta, C.D., Almeida, V., Meira, Jr, W.: Analyzing performance of partitioned caches for the WWW. In: Proc. 3rd Web Caching Workshop, San Diego, CA (1998)
10. Oram, A., ed.: Peer-to-Peer: Harnessing the Power of Disruptive Technologies. O'Reilly & Associates, Sebastopol, CA. (2001)
11. Pierre, G., Kuz, I., van Steen, M., Tanenbaum, A.S.: Differentiated strategies for replicating Web documents. Computer Communications 24 (2001) 232–240
12. Pierre, G., van Steen, M., Tanenbaum, A.S.: Self-replicating Web documents. Technical Report IR-486, Vrije Universiteit, Amsterdam (2001)
13. Pierre, G., van Steen, M.: A trust model for cooperative content distribution networks. Technical report, Vrije Universiteit, Amsterdam (2001) In preparation.
14. Qiu, L., Padmanabhan, V., Voelker, G.: On the placement of Web server replicas. In: Proc. 20th INFOCOM Conference, Anchorage (AK), IEEE (2001)
15. Schulzrinne, H., Rao, A., Lanphier, R.: Real time streaming protocol (RTSP). RFC2326 (1998)
16. Sen, S., Rexford, J., Towsley, D.: Proxy prefix caching for multimedia streams. In: Proc. 19th INFOCOM Conference, New York, NY, IEEE (1999)
17. Tang, W., Du, F., Mutka, M.W., Ni, L.M., Esfahanian, A.H.: Supporting global replicated services by a routing-metric-aware DNS. In: Proc. 2nd International Workshop on Advanced Issues of E-Commerce and Web-Based Information Systems, San Jose, CA (2000) 67–74
18. van Steen, M., Homburg, P., Tanenbaum, A.S.: Globe: A wide-area distributed system. IEEE Concurrency 7 (1999) 70–78
19. Wolski, R., Plank, J.S., Brevik, J., Bryan, T.: Analyzing market-based resource allocation strategies for the computational grid. Technical Report CS-00-453, University of Tennessee, Knoxville (2000)
20. Wang, Y., Zhang, Z.L., Du, D.H., Su, D.: A network-conscious approach to end-to-end video delivery over wide area networks using proxy servers. In: Proc. 18th INFOCOM Conference, San Francisco, CA, IEEE (1998) 660–667

Architecture of QOSMIC — A QoS Manager for Internet Connections

Franco Tommasi[1], Simone Molendini[2], Antonio Vilei[1], and Andrea Sponziello[1]

[1] University of Lecce, Department of Innovation
[2] ISUFI, Innovative Materials and Technologies Area

{simone.molendini,franco.tommasi}@unile.it,
{vilei, asponzy}@libero.it

Abstract. RSVP is an Internet protocol designed to reserve network resources. Availability of optimized free implementations of RSVP daemon and the development of extensions designed to improve RSVP's behaviour have increased the attention towards the protocol. Though RSVP has been designed to fulfill QoS needs of multimedia applications, development of compliant applications is slowed by complexity of logic behind the access to QoS. This paper describes the current problems related to the deployment of RSVP into multimedia applications and the QOSMIC architecture in support to multimedia applications that tries to solve these problems. The QOSMIC elements allow a user to reserve resources without requiring the update of multimedia applications neither on the client side nor on the server one, allow a receiving user to require RSVP Path messages needed to start reservations and allow a centralized management of QoS. A test implementation of QOSMIC is also briefly described.

1 Introduction

RSVP (Resource ReSerVation Protocol) is a IETF (Internet Engineering Task Force) proposed standard protocol [8] designed to exchange information about the reservation of resources in the Internet. As the demand for a Quality of Services Internet goes up, more and more attention is being paid to RSVP as a mean to fulfill it. In the last years the availability of optimized free implementations of the RSVP daemon [9] and the development of extensions [2] designed to improve RSVP's behaviour have increased the attention towards the protocol. Moreover some works [1][3] regard to RSVP as a signalling QoS protocol between end-users and ingress points of a DiffServ Area. Though protocols were designed to fulfill the QoS needs of multimedia applications, the development of compliant applications is somewhat slowed by the complexity of the logic behind the access to QoS. We think that the development of QoS managers is a fundamental step in the migration process towards QoS, because they cover the signalling gap between applications and the network offer.

This paper is organized as follows: this Section chiefly describes the current problems related to the deployment of RSVP into multimedia applications. Section 2 presents

M.J. van Sinderen and L.J.M. Nieuwenhuis (Eds.): PROMS 2001, LNCS 2213, pp. 12-22, 2001.

the elements of the QOSMIC architecture that tries to solve these problems. Section 3 explains the use of QoS protocols in the context of the QOSMIC architecture. Section 4 briefly describes the implementation of the elements we have developed.

1.1 RSVP for RSVP-Less Applications

A great part of the current multimedia applications would benefit from Quality of Service, but they don't use it. The RSVP/IntServ basic approach requires that these applications should perform RSVP signalling on their own. A standard RSVP API has been defined to support applications as an interface to the RSVP daemon; the RAPI [7] is discussed with greater detail in the Section 4.1. The Microsoft GQoS (Generic Quality of Service) [11] provided with Winsock 2 is a support to QoS with an higher level of abstraction because programmers may abstract from a specific signalling protocol. All these approaches require that programmers would update the network support of their applications to support RSVP. As a matter of facts, very few of such applications deploy QoS. Some router vendors (e.g. Cisco) have overcome the lack of native RSVP support in applications allowing the router to work as an RSVP proxy. In this paper we discuss a client/server architecture that transparently manages QoS on behalf of applications (at least legacy ones) that don't support RSVP signalling. Our approach is different from Cisco's, because it doesn't require the routers to work as RSVP proxies. There is no need to configure the routers (not everybody could have the permissions) and this gives more flexibility.

1.2 Receiver Oriented Reservations

One winning feature of RSVP is that it is a receiver oriented reservation protocol. According to the RSVP reservation paradigm, a sender application transmits to the receiver a Path message that creates an RSVP state into routers. The responsible for the reservation of resources is the receiving application that transmits a Resv message to the sender application which has the scope of a single TCP/UDP flow. Resv messages travel back to the sender using the RSVP state created by the Path messages. The receiver-oriented design allows receiving applications to reserve only the needed amount of resources, when a reservation is needed, i.e. when the receiver application detects an insufficient level of QoS (datagrams are lost due to network congestion.)

Before reserving resources, a receiver needs that the sender has transmitted a Path message. A kind of signalling outside the scope of RSVP is needed then to allow the receiver to request Path messages. The sender may decide to reveal existing flows and to send Path messages to all the receivers. This solution has an important drawback: RSVP state is know to be a complex one, and the routers are able to manage a limited number of RSVP sessions. Thus, this limit could be quickly reached because of a number of Path states that are not followed by an effective reservation. The RSVP extensions defined in [2] might significantly alleviate this problem but they will not solve it. Thus, a mechanism that could allow a receiver to ask a sender for a Path message is needed.

1.3 Use of Policy Data

The IntServ/RSVP [6] architecture requires that each RSVP message must pass a policy control in order to be processed (otherwise it is rejected to its sender). In order to allow a policy decision, RSVP messages must carry a POLICY_DATA object with domain-specific policy information. It is hard to imagine that each application would communicate on its own with its ISP to receive a correct POLICY_DATA. It is easier to use a single QoS client which do support applications for this task.

1.4 Admission Control

At the moment, the architecture does not fully support admission control: QOSMIC is being used at University of Lecce, and admission control is not a fundamental problem. However, we are working to add admission control feature to this architecture.

1.5 Exchange of Agreement-Specific Information

Network resources are precious ones. In any commercial environment it is very likely that a form of charging would be associated to the access to QoS, because it allows a prioritized access to network's links. A user contracts then an agreement with his ISP which specifies the levels of QoS he may require and the related charge. This is an information contained in a so-called Service Level Agreement, SLA. It is not the scope of this document to deepen the form of such SLAs and the structure of charging mechanisms. An information exchange is needed between the user and its ISP to report the user's will of starting reservations and the ISP's notification of any kind of charging. Part of these information are ISP-specific ones: instead of duplicating all these features in all the QoS applications would be simpler to concentrate them into an ad-hoc QoS Manager. The protocol we use to this purpose (the QOSMIC Logging Protocol) is designed in an extensible way, allowing the transport of ISP-specific information.
We assume that to the purpose of QoS reservations the user accesses the Internet through the same ISP providing to him/her the multimedia stream. To this purpose the user has stipulated an SLA. In the following of this paper, we will then assume that all the entities involved in the architecture belong to the same ISP.

2 Architecture of QOSMIC

The QOSMIC architecture is a client/server one that implements two basic functions. The first one allows the user to log onto the ISP's policy server to identify himself and to communicate his IP address. The second one allows the user to reserve QoS towards the streaming server. We have then three involved entities (refer to Fig. 1): the user, responsible to log and reserve resources, the policy server, responsible for verifying logged users, and the streaming server that transmits the flow. We also describe benefits and concerns related to the use of a QoS sender proxy in the QOSMIC architecture.

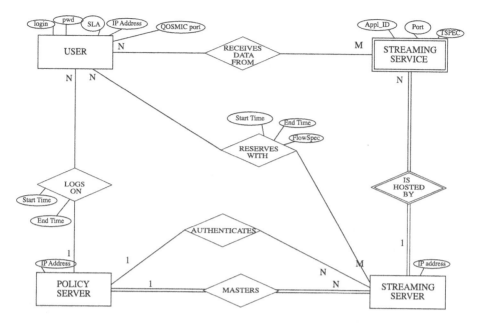

Fig. 1. Conceptual representation of the QOSMIC architecture: Entity-Relationship

2.1 The Client

The user works at a client host. The QOSMIC client, running on this host, actually reserves resources on behalf of the user. The QOSMIC client (refer to Fig. 2) contains a "QLP Client Module" (QLM Client in Fig. 2), a "QoS Selector" and a "QOSMIC Master".

QLP Client Module makes the user log onto its ISP's Policy Server in a transparent way and enables him to use QoS services. QLP is the QOSMIC Logging Protocol used by the QLP Client Module at the client and by the QLP Server Module (QLM Server in Fig. 2) at the policy server. The client uses the QLP protocol to transmit to the Policy Server the user's login and password and its IP Address. QLP server's IP address and port are configured information at the QOSMIC client. After having successfully logged, the user may start a streaming client to receive an audio/video stream. In the case that the Streaming Server is at the ISP it has logged into, the QOSMIC Client will receive a Path message from that server. The QOSMIC Client may now send a Resv message to the streaming server. Path and Resv messages are received and sent by means of the QOSMIC Master module. The QoS Selector is the module responsible (perhaps interacting with the user) of the choice of the IntServ QoS parameters characterizing the reservation.

We just mention that the user is free to ignore the Path message without performing any reservation. In the case that the user logs into the policy server after the beginning of the streaming, the QOSMIC master will receive the PATH message a few seconds (at most 30 seconds, if the network doesn't loose any Path) after the log.

2.2 The Streaming Server

A server runs a QOSMIC Server whose primary task is to send an RSVP Path message to a possible user. The QOSMIC Server (refer to Fig. 2) contains a "Flow Handler" module and a "PEP" module.

The Flow Handler module catches up all the TCP/UDP flows transmitted by the server. It works interacting with the server's kernel, and may reveal any new connection using one of the following methods, in order of decreasing efficiency:

1) Trapping at a kernel level all opened connections
2) Periodically polling onto the OS's connections list
3) Capturing incoming packets and filtering TCP's SYN packets or UDP's packets containing a new IP address/port pair.

The first solution (the most difficult to implement) is the best one because it has minimal impact on streaming server performances.

After having identified a new connection, the Flow Handler verifies that the destination port has been bound as a streaming one. Then it creates a new RSVP sender-side session.

The PEP module is the policy client according to COPS protocol specifications (refer to section 3.3 for details about PEP and PDP in COPS). The PEP module queries the PDP module at the Policy Server. If the decision returned from the PDP is a positive one, that is the user connected to the streaming server has an IP address known to the Policy server, the RSVP module is enabled to send the Path message to the client.

2.3 The Policy Server

The Policy Server allows trusted users to reserve resources. The Policy Server (refer to Fig. 2) contains a "QLP Server Module" (QLM Server in Fig. 2) and a "PDP" module.

The Policy Server performs two main tasks. At first, the QLP Server Module accepts logins by users and registers their IP address and QOSMIC transport port. It then acts as the PDP server for the domain: it will receive requests to install and transmit RSVP messages from the PEPs in the domain (refer to section 3.3 for details about PEP and PDP in COPS). As a special case, it will receive from the streaming server the request to transmit a Path message. The Policy Server will extract the destination IP address (from the SESSION object of the message) and, if belonging to a logged user, it allows the server to transmit the message. The PDP and the QLP Server processes need then to share information related to logged users - at least the list of their IP addresses.

2.4 QoS Sender Proxy

Since now, we have assumed that the QOSMIC server were running on the streaming server. This is a strong assumption, but is possible to remove it adding a QoS sender proxy to the QOSMIC architecture. A QoS sender proxy is a router along the path between the user and the streaming server. It sends Path messages on behalf of the streaming server and receives Resv messages from the user. Thus, the reservation is actually made only along this piece of the path. This may be not a problem in the case the QoS sender proxy is near to the streaming server, perhaps its first hop, in the case they both are connected with well-provisioned links. Many different servers of a stub area may use the same proxy (a QoS-dedicated host).

No dramatic changes are required to the architecture described above, in order to use a proxy. The only significant change is due to the fact that no data flows are directed to it, so it must filter all UDP/TCP packets to identify new streams.

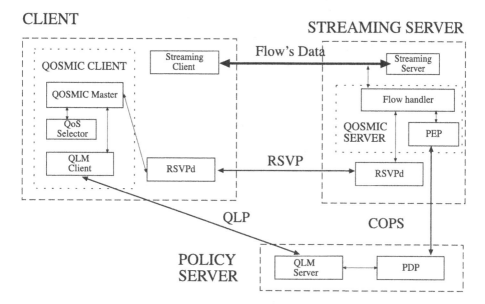

Fig. 2. The Client, the Streaming Server and the Policy Server in the QOSMIC architecture

3 QOSMIC Protocols

We describe in this section the new QLP protocol designed for the architecture and the use in the QOSMIC architecture of existing, well-estabilished IETF protocols.

3.1 Functional Specifications of QLP — The QOSMIC Logging Protocol

We have designed a new logging protocol to exchange policy information between the QOSMIC client and the QOSMIC Logging Protocol server (QLP server) running at the policy server. The QLP client connects to the QLP server opening a TCP connection to the IP address/transport port specified in the agreement contracted with the ISP. It then sends the basic parameters of the contract in a tagged textual form, specifying its login and password. After having verified the correctness of the log in, the QLP server registers the user's login, and his IP address. This last information will be used to send RSVP Path messages to it once the user connects to a streaming server. The QLP server then transmits to the user a reply message whose basic function is to acknowledge the successful login.

The connection the user has established with the policy server is a stateful one, that is it is not closed after this first exchange. Periodically the user transmits keep-alive messages, and the server answers with keep-alive replies. The keep-alive period is chosen by the QLP server and sent to the user within the acknowledgment message; a possible value may be 5 minutes. After two times this value, if no Ack or Ak reply message is received the QLP client or server may assume that the connection has been lost. During the connected time the user is enabled to receive Path messages from streaming servers he connects to, and to reserve resources along the path. Charging is not started on logging and it does not depends on logging time. It is actually applied once reservations are requested by the user.

All the functionalities we have described since now are mandatory, in the sense that they are needed to keep the QOSMIC architecture consistent. It is possible that the QLP server may transmit to the user additional information. For example, at logging time the QLP server may transmit to the QLP client the URL of a Web site containing a list of services the user may connect to. At the log-out time, the client may also ask to the server a sort of bill of the session, that is the server returns to it a list of the performed reservations specifying the amount of time these reservations took place and the related charge due to the ISP.

3.2 Use of RSVP — The Resource Reservation Protocol

The basic reservation is acted by RSVP - the IETF proposed standard resource reservation protocol. In this paper we consider one-to-one kind of reservations only, though RSVP allows many-to-many reservations.

There are two fundamental RSVP message types: Resv and Path. Each RSVP sender host transmits RSVP "Path" messages downstream along the unicast route provided by the routing protocol, following the paths of the data. These Path messages store "path state" in each node along the way which is used to route the Resv messages hop-by-hop in the reverse direction. A Path message contains the following information: the SESSION/SENDER_TEMPLATE pair of objects that identifies the UDP/TCP flow, the previous hop address used for the proper reverse routing of Resv messages, an ADSPEC used to collect QoS parameters along the path and a TSPEC object that contains a sender's specification of the traffic the receiver will reserve for.

After the receipt of a Path message, the QOSMIC client verifies the existence and the kind of QoS services along the network using the information lead by the ADSPEC object. It will then use the information into the TSPEC object to set the amount of resources to request to the network. This object characterizes   (specifying the parameters of the Token Bucket data structure) the flow. That is, the QOSMIC client will reserve a QoS level of resources for no more than the amount specified by the TSPEC: any exceeding amount of resources is a waste of them because not used by the data flow. The QOSMIC client may decide to reserve an amount of resource lower than suggested by the the TSPEC, in the case a lower charge is allowed and desired.

Each QOSMIC client sends then an RSVP reservation request (Resv) message upstream towards the senders. This message follows exactly the reverse of the path the data packets will use, upstream to the sender host. It creates and maintains "reservation state" in each node along the path, and do effectively start the reservation. The Resv message is finally delivered to the sender host itself.

3.3 Use of COPS — The Common Open Policy Server

The COPS protocol [4] is a product of the RAP Working Group of the Internet Engineering Working Group. COPS is a simple client/server model for supporting policy control over QoS signalling protocols such as RSVP [5]. It can be used to exchange policy information between a policy server (Policy Decision Point or PDP) and its clients (Policy Enforcement Points or PEPs) that are RSVP routers/hosts. The model does not make   any assumptions about the methods of the policy server, but is based on the server returning decisions to policy requests. The protocol employs a client/server model where the PEP sends requests, updates, and deletes to the remote PDP and the PDP returns decisions back to the PEP. The PEP is responsible for initiating a persistent TCP connection to a PDP. The PEP uses this TCP connection to send requests to and receive decisions from the remote PDP. Communication between the PEP and remote PDP is mainly in the form of a stateful request/decision exchange. The TCP connection between the PDP and the PEP is an authenticated one. Each QoS signalling protocol is a client and is assigned a client number: RSVP is the client number 1. To distinguish between different kinds of clients, the type of client is identified in each message, because different types of clients may have different client specific data and may require different kinds of policy decisions. According to COPS specifications each RSVP node (routers and end hosts) may be PEPs though an RSVP node may be a Policy Ignorant Node - PIN. Each PEP must require to the PDP, for each received message, the authorization to process the message, to allocate related resources (for Resv messages only) and to send messages derived by the processing of the message. The PEP transmits to the PDP, among other objects, the whole RSVP message the policy decision is required for.

In the QOSMIC architecture, at least two network nodes must be PEP ones. They are the streaming server and the user's access router. Each time a new outgoing streaming flow is identified, the streaming server must decide whether to send a Path message to the receiver or not. The server locally installs a Path state, and requests to the domain's PDP the authorization to transmit the Path. To this purpose, it creates a PATH message and uses the built-in PEP module to pass a COPS REQUEST message to the Policy server, acting to this purpose as a PDP. This REQUEST message contains the PATH message (that on its turn contains the user's IP address) and specifies a context of "Outgoing message". This context is used to request the permission to transmit RSVP messages. The authenticating server at the PDP verifies only that the user's IP address belongs to a logged user. In this case, it answers with COPS DECISION message containing an "Install" decision and the QOSMIC proxy sends a PATH to the user. In the case the answer is a "Reject" one, no PATH message is sent.

After having received the Path, the user may transmit a Resv message to request resources. This Resv is policed by its ISP's first router (the access router) which on its turn asks to the PDP the permission to reserve resources and to forward the message upstream. The Resv message contains a POLICY_DATA object of the kind of AUTH_USER ones [12]. These objects may contain an authentication string of the form of a Kerberos ticket, a X509 certificate or a PGP certificate. It depends upon the kind of authentication server installed at the PDP what kind of authentication scheme to choose. This piece of information is transmitted to the user at the time of the stipulation of the agreement and inserted by the QOSMIC client into each Resv message.

This kind of authentication only securely identifies users, at the time of reserving resources, and eventually starts billing. Policing of Path messages is only a means to reduce the number of Path states installed into the network's routers and can't be considered, on its own, a secure policy method.

4 Implementation of QOSMIC

We describe in this sections some details regarding the QOSMIC implementation. We have developed a QOSMIC client for Windows NT and both QOSMIC server and QLP server for Linux Redhat 7.0 kernel 2.2.16.

4.1 The RAPI Standard Interface to RSVP

Both the QOSMIC client and server use the standard RAPI [7] to access RSVP. RAPI stands for RSVP API. It is an application program interface that programmers can use to make rsvp-compliant applications. There is no need for the programmer to write complex network routines, because RAPI works as a broker between the application and the RSVP daemon. RAPI and RSVP daemon are logically independent, so they can be changed independently. RSVP signalling is performed by the RSVP daemon. The main advantage of RAPI is that applications can run in user space but RSVP network code must be run in kernel space instead. Writing code that runs in kernel space is difficult and requires good programming skill. Furthermore it would be a bad idea to include RSVP signalling code directly in the applications: in fact every application should replicate the same signalling facilities. RAPI gives an easy interface to QoS facilities.

RAPI interface:

Session handling is performed by these functions:
- rapi_session(): register a session to the local RSVP daemon
- rapi_sender(): send a PATH message for the specified session
- rapi_reserve(): send a RESV message for the specified session
- rapi_release(): send a PATHTEAR/RESVTEAR message
Notification about RSVP state change and about error conditions is performed by the functions:
- rapi_getfd(): return the file descriptor where an event comes from
- rapi_dispatch(): call the callback function for a given event
Formatting functions:
- rapi_fmt_flowspec(): format the RSVP FLOWSPEC object
- rapi_fmt_tspec(): format the T_SPEC object
- rapi_fmt_adspec(): format the RSVP ADSPEC object
- rapi_fmt_filt_spec(): format the RSVP FILTER_SPEC object

4.2 User Interface

We suppose that the user owns a local copy of the SLA and that this SLA contains, among QoS-related parameters, the IP address and transport port of the QOSMIC policy server. That is, after connecting to Internet, the user starts its QOSMIC client and choses one SLA among all those he has contracted. The QOSMIC client automatically logs onto the related QLP server, and reports the return state. The QLP server also returns the Web URL where the client downloads from a list of services available in the next hours. The user may then open a stream by simply clicking over this entry (a link with the multimedia application is started); after receiving the Path from the server the QOSMIC client sends the Resv. According to this (test) version the Resv automatically uses a FLOWSPEC specifing the same amount of resources defined by the TSPEC object in the Path, that is we have used a void QoS selector module. After using QoS and logging out, the QOSMIC client shows the list of used reservations (refer to Fig. 3), together with their charge, as billed by the server.

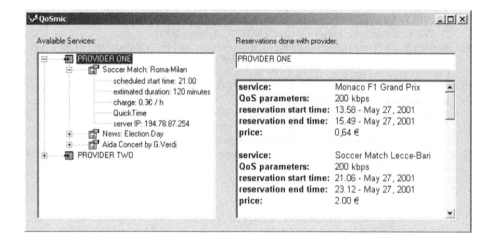

Fig. 3. Interface of the QOSMIC client under Windows

5 Conclusions and Future Work

In this paper we have described the QOSMIC architecture that allows users to transmit and receive RSVP messages on behalf of their applications, that centralizes policy information exchange, and exchanges with the ISP information related to the type of available services and their charge. We are working on admission control feature. Further work is needed to add to the QLP security features, as well as to clearly separate protocol-critical data and ISP-specific data. Multicast streams support is a fundamental feature in a streaming context; we will adapt in the future the architecture to support such transmissions. It would be useful that QOSMIC could monitor the effective quality of received stream (via monitoring of RTP sequence numbers) to dynamically adapt the reservation level according to the received quality. We have also developed and tested a prototype of such QOSMIC manager.

References

1. Baker F., Iturralde C., Le Faucheur F., Davie B., "Aggregation of RSVP for IPv4 and IPv6 Reservations", Work in progress, draft-ietf-issll-rsvp-aggr-04.txt, April 2001.
2. Berger L., Gan D., Swallow G., Pang P., Tommasi F., Molendini S., "RSVP Refresh Overhead Reduction Extensions", RFC2961, April 2001.
3. Bernet Y., Ford P., Yavatkar R., Baker F., Zhang L., Speer M., Braden R., Davie B., Wroclawski J., Felstaine E., "A Framework for Integrated Services Operation over Diffserv Networks" , RFC2998, November 2000.
4. Boyle J., Cohen R., Durham D., Herzog S., Rajan R., Sastry A., "The COPS (Common Open Policy Service) Protocol", RFC2748, January 2000.
5. Boyle J., Cohen R., Durham D., Herzog S., Rajan R., Sastry A., "COPS usage for RSVP". RFC2749, January 2000.
6. Braden R., Clark D., Shenker S., "Integrated Services in the Internet Architecture: an Overview", RFC1633, June 1994.
7. Braden R., Hoffman D., "RAPI -- An RSVP Application Programming Interface", Work in progress, draft-ietf-rsvp-rapi-00.txt, December 1997.
8. Braden R., Zhang L., Berson S., Herzog S., Jamin S. , "Resource ReSerVation Protocol (RSVP) -- Version 1 Functional Specification", RFC2205, September 1997. Herzog S., "RSVP Extensions for Policy Control". RC2750, January 2000.
9. Karsten M., Schmitt J., Steinmetz R., "Implementation and Evaluation of the KOM RSVP Engine", Proceedings of the 20th Annual Joint Conference of the IEEE Computer and Communications Societies (INFOCOM'2001).
10. Mankin A., Baker F., Braden B., Bradner S., O`Dell M., Romanow A., Weinrib A., Zhang L., "Resource ReSerVation Protocol (RSVP) -- Version 1 Applicability Statement Some Guidelines on Deployment", RFC2208, September 1997.
11. Microsoft Corporation, "The Microsoft QoS Components", http://www.microsoft.com/TechNet/win2000/qoscomp.asp
12. Yadav S., Yavatkar R., Pabbati R., Ford P., Moore T., Herzog S., "Identity Representation for RSVP", RFC2752, January 2000.

A QoS-Driven ISP Selection Mechanism for IPv6 Multi-homed Sites

Marcelo Bagnulo, Alberto Garcia-Martinez, David Larrabeiti, and Arturo Azcorra

Departamento de Ingeniería Telemática
Universidad Carlos III, Madrid. Spain.
{marcelo, alberto, dlarra, azcorra}@it.uc3m.es

Abstract. A global solution for the provision of QoS in IPng sites must include ISP selection based on per-application requirements. In this article we present a new site-local architecture for QoS-driven ISP selection in multi-homed domains, performed in a per application basis. This architecture proposes the novel use of existent network services, a new type of routing header, and the modification of address selection mechanisms to take into account QoS requirements. This proposal is an evolution of current technology, and therefore precludes the addition of new protocols, enabling fast deployment. The site-local scope of the proposed solution results in ISP transparency and thus in ISP independency.

1. Introduction[1]

As more organizations depend on critical applications built over the Internet, access links are becoming a vital resource for them. Consequently, many organizations are improving fault tolerance and QoS over their Internet connection through *multi-homing*, i.e. the achievement of global connectivity through several connections, possibly supplied by different Internet Service Providers (ISPs). Focusing on QoS, some mechanism is required to allow QoS policies to gain control over the path followed by packets, enabling for example, to route traffic generated by critical applications (i.e. real time or multimedia applications) through links providing a proper service in terms of bandwidth, delay, etc., while non critical traffic (i.e. ftp, www) is routed without interfering premium traffic.

IPv6 aggregatable global unicast address delegation rules [1] constrains multi-homed sites to obtain one prefix per connecting ISP when current provider-based aggregation, aimed to provide routing scalability is used. Therefore, the site will have as much prefixes as ISPs. Address selection mechanisms impact on ISP selection and thus on the QoS obtained since source address selection will determine the return path of sent packets.

---

[1] This research was supported by the LONG (Laboratories Over Next Generation networks) project, IST-1999-20393.

M.J. van Sinderen and L.J.M. Nieuwenhuis (Eds.): PROMS 2001, LNCS 2213, pp. 23-34, 2001.

In this article, we will present an architecture designed to provide QoS-driven ISP selection on a per-application basis, taking into account coherence between forward and backward paths. The solution presented relies on a host mechanism that builds packets appropriately to enable the network components to route it through the selected ISP.

The remainder of the paper is structured as follows: in section 2 an introduction to IPv6 multi-homing is presented, along with a discussion of multi-homing requirements. In section 3, the problem addressed in the article is thoroughly characterized and the proposed architecture is detailed, describing the network and host mechanisms, and their interaction for achieving QoS-enabled ISP selection. Finally, section 4 is devoted to conclusions and future work.

2. Introduction to IPv6 Multi-homing

Multi-homing deployment has been fostered since Internet connectivity has become a critical resource. Increasing QoS requirements, including those regarding to reliability, and the proliferation of Internet providers, are raising demand for appropriate multi-homing architectures.

In IPv4 solutions, ISPs propagate reachability routes to the multi-homed sites over the network. However, the actual IPv6 framework cannot directly apply the IPv4 solution, since one of the main concerns of IPng is routing system scalability, based on hierarchical routing, which restricts route propagation. Therefore, the IPv6 community has addressed the problem of defining specific mechanisms to allow IPv6 site multi-homing, taking into account the routing particularities above mentioned. Some of the results of this effort are described in this section, and include a draft detailing the requirements that IPv6 multi-homing proposals should fulfill [2] (issued by a recently created IETF group on IPv6 multi-homing, *multi6*), and a set of different architectures that has been proposed for IPv6.

2.1. Multi-homing Requirements

The initial requirements identified for multi-homing are [2]:

- *Redundancy and reliability*: A multi-homing architecture is built to improve Internet connection reliability, so fault tolerance is a key issue in any proposed mechanism. Failures that should be coped with include physical and logical link breakdowns, routing protocol malfunction, and ISP or exchange crash.
- *Load sharing*: Distribution of load among available links is another key issue in a multi-homed environment. Distribution criteria include:
  - Performance improvement in situations such as long-term congestion.
  - Cost optimization: Depending on the SLA agreed, cost and quality of different connections may vary among ISPs. Cost-aware selection mechanisms are needed to fulfill the requirements of multi-homed organizations.

- *Simplicity* is a relevant condition if the architecture is meant to be deployed. The fewer the changes in existing protocols and mechanisms that are introduced, the faster the solution would be developed.

- *Scalability* has been a major concern in IPv6 definition so proposed multi-homing architectures must adhere to this policy. In particular, routing scalability provided by ISP-based aggregation must be preserved. Other scalability issues such as the manageability of the solution should also be considered.

Note that the requirement of QoS-driven ISP selection is included among the multi-homing requirements, in the *load-sharing* item discussion.

2.2. Review of Proposed Solutions for Multi-homing Issues

We can find several proposals aiming to solve different multi-homing challenges. We will introduce some of them that we have considered close to our study.

2.2.1. IPv4 Multi-homing Proposals

Initial IPv4 approaches to the multi-homing problem were based on the ability of CIDR for prefix propagation [3]. The most common solutions are based on the injection of routing information regarding the site prefix into the Internet. Since this approach does not impose the addition of new prefixes, address scarcity is not fostered. The main drawback of these approaches is that they contribute to the undesirable explosion of the number of entries in the routing tables of the default free zone (DFZ) of the Internet [4].

A more scalable approach is presented in [5], with several prefixes assigned to the multi-homed site, one per each ISP. In normal operation no extra routing information is advertised to the DFZ, and non-hierarchical route injection only occurs in case of link failure. The main drawback of this mechanism, given the lack of IPv4 addresses, lies in the requirement of assigning several prefixes to each site.

2.2.2. IPv6-Compatible Multi-homing Proposals

As we have seen, IPv4 solutions, that are based on routing information injection, collide with the IPv6 provider-based aggregation paradigm. We will briefly present some new IPv6-oriented solutions.

Multi-homing support at exit routers, presented in [5] and developed for IPv6 in [6], is an optimization of the last IPv4 mechanism described, eliminating the need for route information injection even in the case of link failure. This solution is aimed to provide link fault tolerance through multi-homing. Provider-based aggregation is assumed, so each ISP delegates one prefix to the considered site. Link fault tolerance is achieved through tunnels between site egress routers (RA, RB) and ISP border routers (BRB, BRA) as it is depicted in figure 1. In normal operation tunneled paths are advertised with a low priority, to guarantee that traffic is routed through direct links whenever possible. In case of link failure, the link that is down is no longer advertised as a valid route, so tunneled path becomes the preferred route (in spite of its low priority).

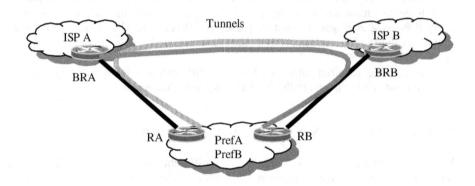

Fig. 1. Multi-homing at exit routers

Multi-homing with router renumbering [7] is intended to avoid the usage of ISP delegated prefixes when the delegating ISP is down. The proposal uses the Router Renumbering protocol [8] as a mechanism to deprecate addresses delegated by the unreachable ISP in routers. Routers perform deprecation of host addresses using Router Advertisement. While this solution is a good option for long-term failures, established communications cannot be preserved after the failure event. A better approach could be an hybrid one, i.e. to use Router Renumbering for long-term failures and a tunneling scheme, such as the one described before, for established communications.

There are other proposed solutions, which involve the usage of mobile IP protocols [7], the modification of the TCP handshake protocol to include a set of possible source and destination addresses [9] or the report of link failure through explicit routing information [10].

We should stress that the proposed solutions focus on fault tolerance, taking into account even long term failures and the preservation of established TCP connections in case of failure. Load balancing could be enabled in some cases, but QoS driven ISP selection has not been considered.

3. QoS-Driven ISP Selection

We will present now a proposal for an ISP selection mechanism based on QoS criteria. First the problem is delimited, and the intended solution scope is stated. Later the proposed architecture is described and finally the main components are detailed.

3.1 Problem Delimitation

The topology we are going to consider for illustrating the problem is depicted in figure 2.

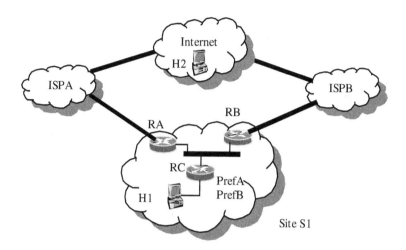

Fig. 2. Problem topology

As we can see in the figure above, we are considering a site (S1), composed of several sub-networks, that obtains external connectivity through two different ISPs, ISPA and ISPB. Note that even if we are considering the case of only two ISPs, the solution presented is valid for more ISPs, and this limitation is introduced only to facilitate comprehension.

Each one of the connected ISPs, delegates one prefix to S1, so that the hosts belonging to S1 may have addresses containing prefix PrefA::/nA and prefix PrefB::/nB. In order to enable the reception of packets from a given ISP, any host must have one address with the corresponding prefix of that ISP.

To properly delimitate the problem, we could divide the problem into the following two cases:

- *Internally initiated traffic:* Suppose that a host (H1) that belongs to S1 needs to communicate with a remote host (H2). Based on site-local routing policies, the host and/or the network should be able to decide which ISP will carry the outbound packet, and this selection should be based on QoS requirements that could be specified on a per application basis.
  Note that the route from the Internet towards the destination host is determined by the destination address returned by DNS, and by the external routing policies[2]. However, intra-site mechanisms can influence on intra-site routing and ISP selection.

---

[2] The Routing Header option can be used to specify routes, but global topology information is required for making routing decisions, information that is not generally available in hosts.

The ISP used in the return path for the outbound traffic is determined by the source address included in the outbound packet, more specifically by the prefix used (PrefA::/nA or PrefB::/nB), so there should be a relation between the selected exit path and the source address included in the packet, in order to provide a coherent path for outgoing and incoming packets belonging to the same data stream.

- *Externally initiated traffic:* The ISP included in the path for inbound connections is determined by the prefixes of the addresses returned by DNS, PrefA::/nA or PrefB::/nB. This issue is out of the scope of this work.

3.2. An Architecture for a QoS-Based ISP Selection Mechanism

In this paper we present a solution that allows the selection of the ISP used for coursing locally initiated traffic (i.e. traffic initiated by H1). The ISP selection is based in the QoS policies defined within a site and it is done on a per application basis (H1 can select ISPA for some applications and ISPB for others).

The solution for the stated problem should involve both host and network. A basic justification for this statement is the following: Intra-site route selection is performed by network devices, because the host does not have all the routing information needed for that decision (and it is not desirable that it had it). However, the host is involved in the route selection, since the return path is determined by the source address included by the host. So we will next present the two main components of the solution: network elements and host mechanism.

3.2.1. Network Elements for QoS-Based ISP Selection

A mechanism intended to force routing through a specific ISP in multi-homed sites is suggested in [11]. The main idea is to include a routing header with an intermediate anycast address identifying selected ISP routers, in order to force the packet path through the chosen ISP. In this section we describe a different approach, based in a mechanism for path selection that achieves ISP transparency through the usage of a self-destructive routing header. We will end with a comparison between the mechanisms proposed and other possible approaches.

ISP transparent path selection. ISP selection can be performed by means of selecting the appropriate exit router, in the case that each ISP connection were supported in a different router. Note that supporting both ISP connections on a single router introduces a single point of failure, which precludes the fault tolerance ability of multi-homing architectures, so we will focus on the first case. Besides, when all the packets are routed to a single exit router, ISP selection can be implemented locally in the border device.

When different routers support ISP connections, exit router selection can be done using a Routing Header that includes a site-local address assigned to one of the router interfaces. In the case that there was more than one exit router connected to the same ISP, this address would become an anycast address, because we should assign it to all the connecting routers.

Self-destructive routing header. Routing header information is no longer useful once the exit router is reached. Furthermore, considering that the address included in this particular routing header has site-local scope, it becomes meaningless once the packet is out of the site. So a new type of routing header is proposed, possibility that is considered in [12]. This type of routing header is self-destructive, meaning that once it has reached the intermediate destination (exit router in our case) this particular routing header is removed from the packet. This reduces the overhead introduced by the ISP selection mechanism in the most critical links in terms of bandwidth, the WAN links.

One concern about the stated solution could be the overhead introduced by routing headers, even considering that routing headers are only present inside the local site. Note that the packets routed through one of the ISPs do not need to include the routing header, since it could be the site's default exit router.

The main advantages of the proposed solution are described next:

- ISP transparence: In previous proposals, the routing header was used to force a path including the ISP routers anycast address; as a consequence, processing of the routing header requires ISP routing resources. In this proposal, the processing of the routing header is done by the site exit router, which combined with the self destructive routing header makes path selection completely transparent to the ISP. This presents several benefits:

  - Improved scalability: as one ISP connects many sites with the Internet, interpretation of routing headers could be a heavy task. If it is done at site exit routers, scalability is preserved.

  - No bandwidth overhead caused by ISP selection on WAN links, because the self-destructive routing header ensures that no useless routing header information is transmitted over these links.

- ISP independence. There is no need for ISP cooperation, such as support for the all routers anycast address in the ISP network.

- This solution is based in existing protocols, so it is fast and easy to implement.

- This solution is deployed completely at network level, without NAT or proxy services that could compromise performance.

3.2.2. Host Mechanism for QoS-Based ISP Selection

As we have seen before, once the ISP to be used is decided, the host must include in all packets the appropriate routing header, in order to force routing through the selected ISP, and the according source address to ensure a coherent return path. In the following paragraphs we are going to detail how source address and routing header are determined. We first introduce the non QoS-enabled source address selection algorithm described in [13] and then we present a novel extended mechanism performing the desired behavior.

3.2.2.1 Source Address Selection Algorithm

The source address selection mechanism relies on a set of rules to obtain the most appropriate source address for a given destination address and a defined policy. For further reading on this issue the reader is referred to [13].

The policy table is a longest prefix match table that takes an address (source or destination) as input, and returns two values: a label value and a precedence value. The label value is used to match destination addresses with source addresses. The precedence value is used to select destination address among a set of available destination addresses, and it is not needed for our study so it will not be introduced. The suggested default policy table is included in Table 1.

Table 1. Default policy table

Prefix	Precedence	Label
::1/128	50	0
::/0	40	1
2002::/16	30	2
::/96	20	3
::ffff:0:0/96	10	4

The process of source address selection is as follows: Once a packet is to be sent to a destination address, the host routing mechanisms will select the interface used for delivering the packet. After this, source address selection is started. The source address selection algorithm has as inputs a destination address (D) and the first two source addresses (SA and SB) from a proposed candidate source address set, and it returns the source address that fits best with the destination address. Successive pair-wise comparisons are performed throughout all addresses in the candidate set to obtain the best one. The algorithm is implemented as an ordered set of rules; if a rule selects one of the two addresses, no further rules are processed. Here we list the proposed rules (Sx refers to any SA and SB)

- Rule 1: Prefer same address: If Sx=D then prefer Sx
- Rule 2: Prefer appropriate scope: If SB has a larger scope than SA (i.e. SA is a site local address and SB is a global address) and D has a larger scope than SA then prefer SB; otherwise, prefer SA.
- Rule 3: Avoid deprecated addresses.
- Rule 4: Prefer home address: This applies to mobile IP environments so it will not be discussed here.
- Rule 5: Prefer outgoing interface: If SA is assigned to the interface that will be used to send the packet towards D, and SB is not, then prefer SA.
- Rule 6: Prefer matching label. Obtain label for SA, SB and D from policy table and compute the following condition: if label(SA)=label(D) and label(SB)<>label(D) then prefer SA.

- Rule 7: Prefer public address: if SA is a public address and SB is a temporary address, then prefer SA (public and temporary addresses are discussed elsewhere [14])
- Rule 8: Use longest matched prefix of Sx with D.

3.2.2.2 Proposed Host Mechanism

The only modifications required to allow QoS-enabled source address selection are related with the policy table. In particular, port information (to identify the application) and an intermediate address (to force routing path) are included in the table. Also the policy table search algorithm must be adapted to included the added information. The address selection rules, however, do not have to be modified.

Policy table modifications. Port information must be included in order to be able to make application based source address selection. Besides, we also include exit router addresses in another column to be used as intermediate addresses in the routing process. The new policy table will then have the aspect illustrated in Table 2.

To perform a lookup in the table, an address and optionally a port are required as inputs, and the outputs are a label value, a precedence value and an intermediate routing address when available. The lookup algorithm first performs longest prefix match among the matching port entries, and, if no matching port is found, longest prefix match is performed with entries that do not have a specified port.

Table 2. QoS-enabled policy table

Port	Prefix	Precedence	Label	Intermed. Add.
P1	0::/0	60	100	
	::1/128	50	0	
	::/0	40	1	
	2002::/16	30	2	
	::/96	20	3	
	::ffff:0:0/96	10	4	
	PrefA::H1/128	5	100	RA

Resulting behavior. Consider that a multi-homed site (figure 2) is connected to ISPA through exit router RA, and to ISPB through exit router RB. The site obtains prefix PrefA::/nA from ISPA and prefix PrefB::/nB from ISPB. Suppose that a host (H1) of the considered site needs to send QoS-demanding traffic, with destination port P1, to several destination addresses through ISPA, and best-effort traffic through ISPB. In order to ease the explanation, suppose that host H1 has only one interface with two assigned addresses, PrefA::H1 and PrefB::H1, besides link-local and site-local addresses. The host policy table included in table 2 accomplish the desired behavior:

Applying the defined policy table, when an application needs to communicate to a remote host D with an application listening at port P1, the policy table will return the following values:

- For destination address D and port P1, it will return a label value equal to 100, because destination address and entry ports match.
- For source address PrefA::H1, it will return a label value equal to 100, and RA as the intermediate address for the routing header.
- For source address PrefB::H1, it will return a label value equal to 1, because longest prefix match is applied.

Final label matching leads to a resulting packet with PrefA:H1 as source address, RA as destination address and PA as destination port, and a routing header containing address D. This packet will then exit through ISPA, and response packets will also be routed through ISPA because their destination address will be PrefA:H1.

Note that all the previously described process is carried out only if the first five rules specified in the source address selection algorithm do not apply. We will next justify that rule 6, where the host part of the QoS-driven ISP selection mechanism resides, is reached when it is needed.

-   Rule 1: Same address only applies when the target host is the local host, so no ISP selection is needed.
-   Rule 2 assures that ISP selection is aimed only to traffic addressed to destinations outside the site; therefore no ISP selection is performed with site local or link-local connections. Mechanism will only work for global addresses, which is the intended behavior. To avoid being routed through exit routers when systems of the same site use ports associated with QoS delivery service, site-local addressing should be deployed.
-   Rule 3 enables compatibility with the fault tolerance features provided by multi-homing through the Router Renumbering mechanism. So when there is a failure in an ISP, address deprecation through Router Renumbering and Router Advertising precludes the selection of addresses delegated by crashed ISP, without need to modify existing policy tables on hosts.
-   Rule 4 does not applies.
-   Rule 5. The interface selection in the host routing mechanism for a given destination could force selection in rule 5 if the chosen interface has not been assigned at least one address from all ISPs. Then, if one interface has an address with prefix PrefA::/nA, it must also have an address with prefix PrefB::/nB and vice versa to ensure proper functioning.

4. Conclusions and Future Work

We have presented a QoS-driven ISP selection mechanism, which allows to force routing through a selected ISP of both inbound and outbound packets of on a per application basis. The selection of ISP is based on site local policies implemented in hosts through a modified policy table. The overall behaviour of the mechanism can be summarized as follows: When an application running on a local host needs to communicate with another application listening in a particular port of the remote host, the source address selection algorithm uses the policy table to provide an intermediate address and a source address. The intermediate address forces outbound packets to pass through the ISP assigned for that application, and the corresponding source address ensures that response packets will be routed across the same ISP. Once the host transmits the packet, the network routes it to the selected ISP exit router. When the router receives the packet, it updates destination address accordingly and removes the routing header, according to the behaviour of a newly defined routing header type.

A key advantage of the presented mechanism is the provision of QoS on a per application basis, without introducing a new protocol, based only on the modification of an existing mechanism. Changes only affect hosts, so deployment is eased. Since only network-level processing is performed, performance will not be impaired by this mechanism. Another significant advantage is ISP transparence, which allows enabling ISP selection without ISP cooperation as a result of the site-local nature of the proposed solution. Moreover, ISP performance is not affected by site multi-homing. It is also important to note compatibility with existing multi-homing mechanisms, such as *multi-homing support at exit routers* or *multi-homing with Router Renumbering*, allowing a complete solution providing a fault tolerant and QoS aware multi-homing architecture. We want to stress that this is the first proposal achieving per application QoS-driven ISP selection. Moreover, this capacity is achieved in an ISP transparent manner.

Further work remains to be done. Manual policy table configuration has a high management cost, and opposes to the IPv6 autoconfiguration-enabling spirit. Therefore, automatic distribution mechanisms should be developed in order to provide convenient policy management. Another future working issue is the evaluation of a possible optimization for the overhead in bandwidth and processing introduced by the routing header usage. A possible improvement is the inclusion of a routing header only in the first packet of a connection, along with an IPv6 header flow label. Routing of subsequent packets of the connection will be based on the flow label.

References

[1]   Deering, S., Hinden, R., O'Dell, M.: RFC 2374 - An IPv6 Aggregatable Global Unicast Address Format. July 1998.
[2]   Black, B., Gill, V., Abley, J.: Requirements for IP Multihoming Architectures, draft-ietf-multi6-multihoming-requirements-00, February 2001.
[3]   Fuller, V., Li, T., Yu, J., Varadhan, K.: RFC 1519 - Classless Inter-Domain Routing (CIDR): an Address Assignment and Aggregation Strategy. September 1993.
[4]   Huston, G.: Analysing the Internet BGP Routing Table. Internet Protocol Journal. Cisco 2001.
[5]   Bates, T., Rekhter, Y.: RFC 2260 - Scalable Support for Multi-homed Multi-provider Connectivity. January 1998.
[6]   Hagino, J.: IPv6 multihoming support at site exit routers. draft-ietf-ipngwg-ipv6-2260-01. April 2001.
[7]   Dupont, F.: Multihomed routing domain issues for IPv6 aggregatable scheme. draft-ietf-ipngwg-multi-isp-00. September 1999.
[8]   Crawford, M.: RFC 2894 - Router Renumbering for IPv6. August 2000.

[9]   Tattam, P. Preserving active TCP sessions on multihomed IPv6 networks. IPng Working Group Meeting Minutes. Tokio, September 1999.

[10] Bragg, N.: Routing support for IPv6 Multi-homing. draft-bragg-ipv6-multihoming-00. November 2000.

[11] Johnson, D., Deering, S.: RFC 2526 - Reserved IPv6 Subnet Anycast Addresses. March 1999.

[12] Deering, S., Hinden, R.: RFC 2460 - Internet Protocol, Version 6 (IPv6) Specification. December 1998.

[13] Draves, R.: Default Address Selection for IPv6. draft-ietf-ipngwg-default-addr-select-04. May 2001.

[14] Narten, T., Draves, R.: RFC 3041 - Privacy Extensions for Stateless Address Autoconfiguration in IPv6. January 2001.

Broadcasting Multimedia Channels in Future Mobile Systems

Cristian Hesselman and Henk Eertink

Telematica Instituut, P.O. Box 589, 7500 AN Enschede, The Netherlands
{hesselman, eertink}@telin.nl

Abstract. In this paper, we present ongoing work on an application-level platform that assists in broadcasting multimedia streams in heterogeneous mobile systems. Our work revolves around the notion of a technology domain, which is a set of resources that serve mobile clients connecting to the mobile system through a specific wireless technology. We consider the policies that technology domains use to (a) manage the availability of content channels and their perceptual quality levels, and (b) to manage the adaptation strategy that clients must follow in switching between quality levels. We discuss our future work in these areas, which will focus on adaptation as a result of clients roaming between different technology domains.

1. Introduction

In a Future Mobile System (FMS), applications will run on top of an IP-based network infrastructure that uses a wide variety of wireless network technologies and serves many different mobile devices [1]. An FMS will be operated by various administrative authorities [2] that enable mobile users to roam in an unrestricted manner [3-7].

In this paper, we present ongoing work on an application-level platform [8] that assists in broadcasting multimedia streams in an FMS (cf. [9]). Our model of an FMS revolves around the notion of a technology domain. A technology domain consists of a set of resources at the edge of an FMS that serve mobile clients connecting to the FMS through a specific wireless technology [2]. Technology domains manage the availability of content channels (e.g., the eight o'clock news of a certain television network) and their perceptual quality levels (e.g., videophone or TV quality [10]) through channel policies. Similarly, they manage the strategy that clients must follow in switching from one quality level to another through adaptation policies [11]. Our work concentrates on adaptation as a result of clients roaming between different technology domains [3-6].

The rest of this paper is organized as follows. In Section 2, we introduce the high-level notion of a broadcast channel that we use in our work. In Section 3, we present our view of an FMS in terms of technology domains. We consider the channel and adaptation policies that technology domains use in Sections 4 and 5, respectively. We conclude with a summary and a brief outlook on our future work in Section 6.

M.J. van Sinderen and L.J.M. Nieuwenhuis (Eds.): PROMS 2001, LNCS 2213, pp. 35-43, 2001.
© Springer-Verlag Berlin Heidelberg 2001

2. Channels

A *channel* broadcasts multimedia content (e.g., a soccer match) from one server to a number of (mobile) clients. A channel consists of a small number (up to 3 or 4) of *differentiated channels* (diff channels) that the server simulcasts [12]. The diff channels of a channel contain the same content, but are optimized for different coarse-grained classes of clients (e.g., clients with small displays). At the application-level, a server compresses and packetizes each diff channel using various types of encoders (e.g., MPEG-4 [13]) and packetizers (e.g., RTP [14]) to attain good client coverage. The output of these two operations consists of a set of *streams* for each encoder-packetizer combination. The number of streams depends on whether the server packetizes the audio and video parts of a diff channel together, and on whether or not the involved encoder is a layered one [15-17]. A client can receive several streams of a channel at a time, but we assume that they must belong to the same diff channel.

As an example, consider the channel of Figure 1. The content that it carries is a class on Object Oriented Programming (OOP). The server uses two diff channels for the OOP channel, one of which has additional contrast to better suit (mobile) clients with small screens. The server encodes and packetizes the high-contrast stream into four streams using two encoder-packetizer combinations. One of these combinations involves MPEG-4 (encoding) and RTP (packetization) and results in three layered MPEG-4/RTP streams. Client 2 in Figure 1 is a PDA that subscribes to one or more of these streams to receive the high-contrast diff channel.

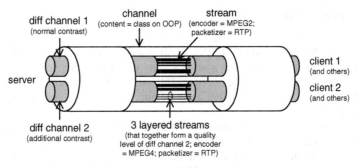

Fig. 1. Example of a channel.

In our model, servers associate *perceptual quality levels* [10] with each diff channel they transmit. These quality levels can for instance be based on perceived quality assessments [11, 18]. For each combination of encoder and packetizer, a server also defines which streams a client must receive to attain which quality level [15-17].

Servers provide information on the channels they support so that clients can determine which diff channels and which of their quality levels they can receive. This information pertains to the content a channel carries, the properties and perceptual quality levels of its diff channels, the encoding and packetization properties of its streams, their relation to the quality levels of a diff channel (e.g., the number of streams a client needs to receive to attain a certain quality level), and the IP-level QoS requirements of streams (e.g., in terms of bandwidth and loss characteristics). A server can for instance describe the perceptual quality levels of a stream in the form of parameters such as frame rate and pixel count [19]. Alternatively, they may be expressed in the form of well-known labels such as 'videophone' or 'TV' quality [10]. For ease of notation, we will use the latter option in this paper.

Channels may be aggregated into *multi-channels* if there exist multiple servers that simultaneously transmit the same content. For instance, there could be multiple servers that transmit a soccer match. We assume however that clients only receive streams of one channel of a multi-channel (e.g., the soccer match transmitted by CNN) at a time. Observe that multi-channels are identified by the content they carry. Individual channels are identified by the content they carry and the server that transmits them. We will not consider multi-channels any further in this paper.

3. Domains

We model the infrastructure of an FMS in terms of *administrative domains*. An administrative domain consists of a set of resources (hosts, networks, routers, and gateways) that is owned and governed by a single administrative authority (based on [20, 21]). We think of an administrative domain as an autonomous system that operates its resources according to a set of policies [21]. Our work concentrates on edge domains that (at a minimum) provide client devices with wireless IP-level connectivity to an FMS (e.g., the campus, Computer Science and Electrical Engineering domains of Figure 2). We focus on domain policies that manage application-level resources such as channels, diff channels and streams. In this context, we particularly zoom in on policies that deal with Quality of Service (QoS) and mobility issues (see Sections 4 and 5).

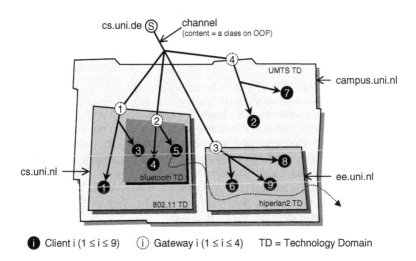

Fig. 2. Broadcasting an audio-video channel in a multi-domain FMS.

Our model distinguishes one or more *technology domains* within each administrative domain. A technology domain consists of the subset of resources and policies of an administrative domain that serve client devices connecting to the FMS through a specific link-level technology. In our work, these are typically wireless technologies such as UMTS, 802.11, and HIPERLAN2.

The radio front-end of a technology domain typically forms a separate subnet that covers a certain geographical area. This area is determined by the location of the administrative domain (e.g., a university campus in the Netherlands) and the coverage characteristics of the associated network technology (e.g., short-range for Bluethooth, medium-range for 802.11, and long-range for a UMTS technology domain) [2]. The back-end resources of different technology domains in the same administrative domain may overlap. For instance, an 802.11 and a Bluetooth technology domain may share routers, fixed network links and gateways. Figure 2 shows several examples of technology domains (e.g., the 802.11 technology domain in the Computer Science administrative domain). In this example, we assume that the campus domain (campus.uni.nl) forms an overlay [1, 4] for the Computer Science and Electrical Engineer domains (cs.uni.nl and ee.uni.nl, respectively). We will explain the other objects that appear in Figure 2 in the next section.

4. Channel Policies

A technology domain uses a *channel policy* to define which channels (e.g., the class on OOP from server S in Figure 2) and diff channels (e.g., the high-contrast one only) are available to clients in a technology domain, at which perceptual quality levels (e.g., videophone and VCR quality), and under which conditions. The latter may for instance depend on the time of day (e.g., resource hungry quality levels are only available off rush hour) or on the types of clients that are present in the technology domain at a particular point in time (e.g., there is a majority of devices with a small display). A channel policy also prescribes which types of streams (in terms of encoding and packetization formats) must be used under which conditions.

We use an *application-level gateway* [10, 11, 17, 22-26] to *enforce* the channel policies of a technology domain. A gateway (logically) belongs to one technology domain and intercepts a channel before it reaches any of the client devices in the technology domain. This means that clients always receive a channel from a gateway in one of the technology domains they can connect to and do not directly connect to a server [15, 16, 27]. Our approach is therefore breaks the Internet's end-to-end paradigm. Unfortunately, technology domains would be unable to locally enforce their channel policies without an intermediate gateway. The exception to this rule are clients that reside in the same technology domain as the server. In this case, we expect the server to enforce the channel policy. Figure 2 shows four gateways (one for each technology domain) that intercept the OOP channel.

A gateway *may* modify a channel if it does not conform to the channel policy of a technology domain. A gateway does not make any modifications to a channel if the channel is already in line with the policy. In this case, the gateway simply relays the channel to the clients in the technology domain.

A gateway may change a channel in several ways [10] to have it meet a certain channel policy. It may for instance reduce the perceptual quality of a diff channel (e.g., by dropping frames) to reduce the bandwidth it consumes. In this case, the gateway essentially defines and creates its own quality levels. A gateway may also change the encoding of a stream [22, 25] if the clients in the technology domain do not support the encoding that the server uses. Although technology domains are free to support as many domain-specific quality levels and streams as they see fit, we envision that they will only make a small number of them available simultaneously for reasons of scalability.

We expect that servers will indicate to what degree they allow gateways in the FMS to alter their streams. Some servers may for instance be very strict (e.g., a server of a television network) and will not allow gateways to make any changes to their (copyrighted) content. Other servers (e.g., the tele-learning server S of Figures 1 and 2) might allow this, but may want to put restrictions on the perceptual quality levels to which a stream may be lowered. They may also want to limit the set of encoding formats to which streams may be transcoded, how many times a stream may be modified, and so on. Yet other servers might not care about modifications at all and allow gateways to change their streams as they see fit. Observe that in this paper we only allow gateways to alter streams. We do not consider clients that modify a stream other than in terms of depacketization and decompression operations.

The effects of a channel policy (e.g., the availability of certain high-end perceptual quality levels) should be restricted to the corresponding technology domain. To accomplish this, we have proposed that gateways transmit streams onto IP multicast groups that are scoped [28] to the gateway's technology domain [29]. Clients in the technology domain can subscribe to one or more of these multicast groups (streams) to attain a quality level that is appropriate for them. As we will see in Section 5, this approach also allows us to combine QoS adaptation and handoff control.

Clients use a service discovery mechanism (e.g., a well-known multicast group [22, 23]) to learn about the technology domains they can use to connect to an FSM. For instance, client 5 (Figure 2) can use the Bluetooth and 802.11 domains of cs.uni.nl, and the UMTS domain of campus.uni.nl. Clients interact with these technology domains to determine which channels, diff channels, streams, and perceptual quality levels they can receive from each technology domain. The inputs of this negotiation process consist of the channel policies of the involved technology domains (e.g., of the 802.11 technology domain), the capabilities of the client (e.g., the properties of client 5's display and its encoder support), and the available resources on the paths from the client to the various gateways (e.g., gateways 1, 2 and 4 for client 5). The result consists of a set of scoped multicast groups from one of the technology domains that the client must join to attain a quality level associated with a channel of its choice.

5. Adaptation Policies

Technology domains use an *adaptation policy* to define at which points a client in a technology domain should initiate and complete a change to which other perceptual quality level (e.g., when to drop back from VCR to videophone quality) [11], and under which conditions (e.g., depending on the time of day). This may be a quality level of the same diff channel that the client currently receives, or a quality level of one of the other diff channels in a channel (cf. Figure 1).

Adaptation may be required for various reasons, including roaming, RF interference, increased traffic load [30, 31], network congestion [15, 16, 27], or a channel policy evaluating to false (which could for instance trigger the removal of a quality level that some clients are receiving at). Our work concentrates on adaptation as a result of a client roaming between different technology domains, either within the same or across different administrative domains [7]. Application-level adaptation policies are also discussed in [11], but for the purpose of configuring per-stream rate controllers.

Since channels are scoped to technology domains at the FMS' edges (see Section 4), a roaming client (e.g., client 5 in Figure 2) may have to hand off to a scoped channel in another technology domain when it crosses a technology domain boundary. A *handoff policy* is a special type of adaptation policy that defines when a mobile client should initiate and complete such an inter-tech handoff. We have outlined several application-level handoff policies in [29] that are based on the packet loss characteristics of the paths between a client and the gateways it can reach. These policies can be used for inter-tech handoffs in an overlay situation. Work on IP-level handoff policies for similar purposes can be found in [32].

Before a client can execute a handoff, it must first discover if the channel (i.e., content) it is currently receiving is available in the technology domains that are potential targets for handoff. For each domain where this is the case, the client must also figure out which diff channels, quality levels, and streams it can use. This procedure is similar to the one we discussed at the end of Section 4. The result consists of a set of diff channels and quality levels for each technology domain the client can handoff to. In case of a tie, policies of the end-user should ensure that a handoff can commence automatically ("user involvement with minimal user interaction" [32]). As an example, consider client 5 (Figure 2) roaming from the Bluetooth domain into the 802.11 domain. Before the client can execute a handoff, it must first determine if the OOP channel it is receiving is available in the 802.11 domain. Assuming this is the case, the client has to figure out which diff channels, quality levels, and streams it can use. If there are multiple possibilities, the end-user policies must resolve the tie. The end-user could for instance favor the videophone quality level of the 802.11 domain over its TV quality level because the former consumes less energy [32]. Alternatively, client 5 may consider subscribing to OOP channels other than the one in the 802.11 domain (e.g., the UMTS technology domain of campus.uni.nl). This situation for instance occurs when the OOP channel is not available in the 802.11 domain. Another possibility would be that client 5 considers the OOP diff channels and quality levels that are available in the 802.11 domain unacceptable.

The handoff targets in our model (a diff channel, a quality level, and its associated streams) map to a set of scoped multicast groups in the target technology domain (see Section 4). The client therefore subscribes to the multicast groups in the target technology domain to execute the handoff. To smooth the handoff [11] and to handle ping-pongs [3] between the current and the target technology domains, the client may buffer the streams it receives from the gateway in the target domain. When it is done buffering, it puts the streams in the target domain on screen and leaves the multicast groups in the old technology domain.

Finally, it is important to observe that our solution operates at the application-level and combines QoS adaptation and handoff control (cf. [11]). Similar application-level approaches exist for Internet Telephony [33, 34] and H.323 [35, 36]. They can be used for inter-technology and inter-domain roaming as well, but as far we know they only deal with mobility management (including handoff control) and do not consider QoS-related issues ([36] briefly mentions it, but gives no details). Also note that the indirection provided by IP multicast frees us from having an invariant IP address for mobile clients (UDP communications only). In fact, a client in our model gets a new IP address (e.g., through DHCP [37]) every time it crosses a boundary of a technology domain. We are thus not required to use Mobile IP [38]. Although IP multicast has been used to support IP-level mobility [4, 6, 39-41], we are not aware of any work that uses IP multicast for combined QoS adaptation and handoff control at the application-level.

6. Summary and Future Work

We have presented a model for broadcasting multimedia content in an FMS. The model revolves around the notion of a technology domain. A technology domain manages the channels, diff channels, streams, and perceptual quality levels it offers to clients through a channel policy. Similarly, it manages the adaptation behavior of clients in case of an inter-tech handoff by means of a handoff policy.

Our future work will be on discovering the channels, diff channels, perceptual quality levels and streams that are available in the technology domain into which a client roams. This will involve negotiation protocols that take channel and handoff policies, as well as capabilities and available resources of mobile clients and wireless networks into account.

Acknowledgements. The authors would like to thank Ing Widya and Erik Huizer for their valuable comments on this work.

References

1. M. Haardt, W. Mohr, "The Complete Solution for Third-Generation Wireless Communications: Two Modes on Air, One Winning Strategy", IEEE Personal Communications, Dec. 2000
2. DOLMEN Consortium, "Open Service Architecture for Mobile and fixed environments (OSAM)", Final Release, Version 4.0, July 1998
3. K. Pahlavan, P. Krishnamurthy, A. Hatami, M. Ylianttila, J. Makela, R. Pichna, J. Vallström, "Handoff in Hybrid Mobile Data Networks", IEEE Personal Communications, April 2000
4. M. Stemm, R. Katz, "Vertical Handoffs in Wireless Overlay Networks", ACM Mobile Networking, Special Issue on Mobile Networking and Internet, Spring 1998
5. J. Meggers, A. Park, R. Ludwig, "Roaming between GSM and Wireless LAN", ACTS Mobile Summit, Granada, Spain, Nov. 1996
6. E. Brewer, R. Katz, Y. Chawathe, S. Gribble, T. Hodes, G. Nguyen, M. Stemm, T. Henderson, E. Amir, H. Balakrishnan, A. Fox, V. Padmanabhan, S. Seshan, "A Network Architecture for Heterogeneous Mobile Computing", IEEE Personal Communications, Oct. 1998

7.   G. Markoulidakis, G. Lyberopoulos, D. Tsirkas, E. Sykas, "Inter-Operator Roaming Scenarios for Third Generation Mobile Telecommunication Systems", 2nd IEEE Symposium on Computers and Communications (ISCC'97), Alexandria, Egypt, July 1997

8.   B. Aiken, J. Strassner, B. Carpenter, I. Foster, C. Lynch, J. Mambretti, R. Moore, B. Teitelbaum, "Network Policy and Services: A Report of a Workshop on Middleware", RFC 2768, February 2000

9.   R. Keller, T. Lohmar, R. Tönjes, J. Thielecke, "Convergence of Cellular and Broadcast Networks from a Multi-Radio Perspective", IEEE Personal Communications, April 2001

10. N. Yeadon, F. Garcia, D. Hutshison, D. Shepherd, "Filters: QoS Support Mechanisms for Multipeer Communications", IEEE Journal on Selected Areas in Comm., Sept. 1996

11. R. Liao, A Campbell, "On Programmable Universal Mobile Channels in a Cellular Internet", 4th ACM/IEEE International Conference on Mobile Computing and Networking (MOBICOM'98), Dallas, October, 1998

12. X. Wan, H. Schulzrinne, "Comparison of Adaptive Internet Multimedia Applications", IEICE Transactions on Communications, June 1999

13. R. Koenen, "MPEG-4 — Multimedia for Our Time", IEEE Spectrum, Feb. 1999

14. H. Schulzrinne, S. Casner, R. Frederick, V. Jacobson, "RTP: A Transport Protocol for Real-Time Applications", RFC 1889, Jan. 1996

15. S. McCanne, V. Jacobson, M. Vetterli, "Receiver-driven Layered Multicast", Proc. of ACM SIGCOMM, Stanford, USA, August 1996

16. L. Wu, R. Sharma, B. Smith, "Thin Streams: An Architecture for Multicast Layered Video", 7th Intl. Workshop on Network an Operating Systems Support for Digital Audio and Video (NOSSDAV97), St. Louis, USA, May 1997

17. A. Balachandran, A. Campbell, M. Kounavis, "Active Filters: Delivering Scaled Media to Mobile Devices", 7th Int. Workshop on Network and Operating System Support for Digital Audio and Video (NOSSDAV'97), St. Louis, USA, May 1997

18. A.Watson, M. Sasse, "Measuring Perceived Quality of Speech and Video in Multimedia Conferencing Applications", Proc. ACM Multimedia '98, Sept. 1998, Bristol, England

19. OMG Telecommunications Domain Task Force, "Control and Management of A/V Streams", ftp://ftp.omg.org/pub/docs/formal/00-01-03.pdf

20. TINA Glossary, http://www.tinac.com

21. D. Comer, "Internetworking with TCP/IP", Prentice Hall, 1995

22. E. Amir, S. McCanne, R. Katz, "An Active Service Framework and its Application to Real-time Multimedia Transcoding", Proc. of ACM SIGCOMM'98, Vancouver, Canada, Sept. 1998

23. K. Jonas, M. Kretschmer, J. Moedeker, "Get a KISS – Communication Infrastructure for Streaming Services in a Heterogeneous Environment", Proc. of ACM Multimedia'98, Bristol, UK, Sept. 1998

24. B. Zenel, D. Duchamp, "A General Purpose Proxy Filtering Mechanism Applied to the Mobile Environment", Proc. 3rd ACM/IEEE International Conference on Mobile Computing and Networking, Budapest, Hungary, Sept. 1997

25. E. Amir, S. McCanne, H. Zhang, "An Application Level Video Gateway", Proc. of ACM Multimedia, San Fransisco, USA, Nov. 1995

26. I. Kouvelas, V. Hardman, J. Crowcroft, "Network Adaptive Continuous-Media Applications Through Self Organised Transcoding", Proc. Network and Operating Syst. Support for Digital Audio and Video (NOSSDAV'98), July 1998, Cambridge, UK

27. S. Cheung, M. Ammar, X. Li, "On the use of destination set grouping to improve fairness in multicast video distribution", proceedings IEEE Infocom '96, San Francisco, USA, March 1996, pp. 553-560

28. D. Meyer, "Administratively Scoped IP Multicast", RFC 2365

29. C. Hesselman, H. Eertink, A. Peddemors, "Multimedia QoS Adaptation for Inter-tech Roaming", Proc. of the 6th IEEE Symosium on Computers and Communications (ISCC'01), Hammamet, Tunisia, July 2001
30. A. Campbell, "A Research Agenda for QOS-aware Mobile Multimedia Middleware", NSF Wireless and Mobile Communications Workshop, Virginia, USA, March 1997
31. D. Chalmers, M. Sloman, "A Survey of Quality of Service in Mobile Computing Environments", IEEE Communications Surveys, http://www.comsoc.org/pubs/surveys, 2nd Quarter 1999
32. H. Wang, R. Katz, J. Giese, "Policy-Enabled Handoffs Across Heterogeneous Wireless Networks", 2nd IEEE Workshop on Mobile Computing and Applications (WMCSA 1999), New Orleans, USA, February 1999
33. E. Wedlund, H. Schulzrinne, "Mobility Support Using SIP", 2nd ACM/IEEE Int. Conf. on Wireless and Mobile Multimedia (WoWMoM'99), Seattle, USA, Aug. 1999
34. W. Liao, "Mobile Internet Telephony Protocol (MITP): an Application-Layer Protocol for Mobile Internet Telephony Services", Proc. IEEE ICC'99, Vancouver, Canada, June 1999
35. W. Liao, "Mobile Internet Telephony: Mobile Extensions to H.323", Proc. IEEE INFOCOM'99, New York, USA, March 1999
36. D. Park, W. Yoon, D. Lee, "An Efficient Handoff Management for Mobility Support to H.323", International Workshop on Mobile Multimedia Communications (MoMuC'00), Tokyo, Japan, Oct. 2000
37. R. Droms, "Automated Configuration of TCP/IP with DHCP", IEEE Internet Computing, July-August 1999
38. J. Solomon, "Mobile IP — The Internet Unplugged", Prentice Hall, 1998
39. A. Helmy, "A Multicast-based Protocol for IP Mobility Support", ACM Second International Workshop on Networked Group Communication (NGC 2000), Palo Alto, USA, November 2000
40. C. Tan, S. Pink, K. Lye, "A Fast Handoff Scheme for Wireless Networks", Proc. 2nd ACM Workshop on Wireless Mobile Multimedia (WoWMoM'99), Seattle, Aug. 1999
41. J. Mysor, V. Bharghavan, "A new multicasting-based architecture for internet host mobility", Proc. ACM/IEEE Mobicom, Sept. 1997

Providing VCR Functionality in Staggered Video Broadcasting*

Jin B. Kwon and Heon Y. Yeom

School of Computer Science and Engineering
Seoul National University
Seoul, South Korea 151-742
{jbkwon,yeom}@dcslab.snu.ac.kr

Abstract. A true video-on-demand(TVOD) system lets users view any video program, at any time, and perform any VCR functions, but its per-user video delivery cost is too expensive. A near video-on-demand(NVOD) is a more scalable approach by batching multiple clients to a shared stream or broadcasting videos. Staggered video broadcasting, one of NVOD techniques, broadcasts multiple streams of the same video at staggered times, with one stream serving multiple clients. In order to provide subscribers with a high-quality VOD service, it is desirable to add VCR functionality such as fast forward and fast backward, but it is not easy to provide VCR functionality in NVOD, especially video broadcasting system where any dedicated or interaction channel is not available.

In this paper, we analyze the conditions necessary to provide VCR functions and then propose a reception schedule which satisfies these conditions, with minimal resource requirements. Since our proposed scheme receives video frames as a unit it can keep up rapidly with a changing VCR action pattern. It is demonstrated that the scheme provide VCR functionality consistently through simulations.

1 Introduction

Video-On-Demand (VOD) service enables a subscriber to watch a video of his choice whenever he wants. In True-VOD (TVOD) systems, each subscriber is served by an individually allocated channel. Although TVOD can respond to requests immediately, server network bandwidth runs out rapidly. Thus, unicast VOD systems are expensive due to their low scalability. It is known that the majority of the requests are for a small group of videos and that the popularities of these videos follow the Zipf distribution[9,10]. The network I/O bottleneck presented by TVOD may be eliminated by employing a multicast facility of modern communication networks[1,8,16,20] to share a server stream among multiple clients. These services are referred to as Near-VOD (NVOD) service.

There are two basic approaches to NVOD provision. One is called *scheduled multicast* and the other *periodic broadcast*. In conventional scheduled multicast[4,

---

* This work wass supported by the Brain Korea 21 Project in 2001

M.J. van Sinderen and L.J.M. Nieuwenhuis (Eds.): PROMS 2001, LNCS 2213, pp. 44–58, 2001.

5,7,9,10,21], the server collects user requests (i.e., a *batch*) during a specific time period. Clients requesting the same video within the same period will receive the video stream over a single multicast channel. When a server channel becomes available, the server selects a batch to multicast according to some scheduling policy. For instance, the *Maximum Queue Length* (MQL)[9] selects the batch with the highest number of pending requests to serve first. Periodic Broadcasts, as the name suggests, broadcasts videos periodically and can service an unlimited number of clients simultaneously with bounded service latency [9]. That is, a new stream corresponding to a video starts every d seconds, and the server channels are individually allocated to each video. Periodic broadcast schemes guarantee the maximum *service latency* experienced by any client to be less than d seconds, and allocate one or more channels to each video. Periodic broadcast bounds the service latency, bypasses the need to process individual user requests, and eliminate the need for an upstream channel. Thus, periodic broadcast is more scalable than TVOD or other NVOD techniques. Due to these benefits, a number of periodic broadcast schemes have been recently presented[3,9,12,13,14,17,18,19, 22]. In *staggered broadcasting*[9], several channels broadcast a video periodically with staggered start times. In this case the maximum service latency is the length of video divided by the number of the channels allocated for the video. Most proposed schemes aim at minimizing the system required resources for a given maximum service latency, or minimizing the maximum service latency for a given system resource, such as server network bandwidth, client I/O bandwidth, client disk space, etc. Recently, videos have been fragmented into separate segments and each segment then transmitted repeatedly over a different channel. Periodic broadcast schemes can be divided into *pyramid-based* schemes and *harmonic-based* schemes. The pyramid-based schemes[3,12,13,22] divide each video into segments of "increasing size" and transmit the segments over "equal bandwidth" channels. On the other hand, the harmonic-based schemes[14,17,18] divide each video into segments of "equal size" and transmit the segments over "decreasing bandwidth" channels.

Digital television(DTV) technology appears commercially today in digital video broadcasting systems, such as digital satellite, Cable TV(CATV), and terrestrial broadcasting. The key benefit of DTV is the high transport efficiency - digital compression packs five or more times as many channels in a given distribution-network bandwidth. This makes it possible to delivery more content and pay-per-view events with multiple closely spaced start time(i.e., staggered broadcasting). This trend makes periodic broadcast more feasible than scheduled multicast. In order to provide subscribers with a high-quality video service, it is desirable to add VCR functions such as fast forward or fast backward to NVOD services. Since TVOD allocates a channel to each client, it is relatively easy to provide such VCR functions. However, in NVOD it is not easy to provide VCR functions due to the characteristics of the multicast. Several schemes have been proposed to deal with the problem of providing VCR functions in NVOD systems[2,5,6,7,15]. However, most of these have addressed VCR functions in scheduled multicast systems and depend on both a client buffer and "interactive" channels to provide VCR functions. Client buffering techniques can be applied to the periodic broadcast model, but interactive channels are not available. Fei et al. proposed a scheme to provide VCR functions in a staggered broadcast[11]. However, the scheme cannot guarantee VCR functions. In other words, it cannot determine whether a requested VCR action can be provided. Moreover, the scheme cannot rapidly adapt to the user's pattern of VCR actions because of its *segment-level* reception schedule.

In this paper, we present the conditions required for providing consistent VCR actions in NVOD systems using staggered broadcasting, and then propose a reception schedule for staggered broadcasting which requires minimal resources while satisfying the conditions.

The remainder of this paper is organized as follows. First, we introduce some previously published related work in Sect. 2. And, in Sect. 3 we present the conditions for continuous VCR functions theoretically, and propose a reception schedule for staggered PB, while satisfying these conditions. Section 4 demonstrates the effectiveness of the proposed schemes through simulations, and Sect. 5 summarizes the performance of our scheme and includes a discussion on some other issues. The paper concludes with Sect. 6.

2   Related Work

NVOD satisfies the requests of several clients with one channel and thus circumvents the the need for individual subscriber service. Although it is desirable to provide VCR functionality for high-quality service, it is difficult in NVOD systems since clients do not have dedicated channels. Several schemes have been proposed to deal with the problem of providing VCR functions in NVOD systems[2,5,6,7,15]. Almeroth and Ammar incorporated the VCR functions into NVOD systems and introduced the concept of discontinuous VCR actions. The scheme uses client buffering to provide VCR functions and proposes that *emergency interactive channels* be used when the client buffer contents are insufficient for the desired interaction. The SAM (*Split And Merging*) protocol[15] uses a synch-buffer and special interactive channels, called I-stream, to provide VCR functions. Abram-Profeta and Shin improved the SAM protocol by changing the shared synch-buffers to separate buffers at each client, thus making the system more scalable[2].

Most of these proposed schemes have addressed VCR functions in scheduled multicast models and depend on both the client buffer and interactive channels to provide VCR functions. Client buffering techniques can be applied to the periodic broadcast model, but interactive channels are not available. Even if interactive channels are available, it is not preferable because using interactive channels compromises the scalability of the NVOD service. As an alternative to interactive channels in the periodic broadcast model, VCR functions that cannot be covered by the client buffer can be accommodated by switching channels and receiving from multiple channels. Fei et al. proposed Active Buffer Management (ABM), a client buffer management scheme, to provide VCR functions in staggered PB[11]. This scheme focuses on raising the probability of servicing users' VCR requests with a fixed client buffer. However, when using existing client buffering schemes[2,5,6,7,15], consecutive VCR actions in the same direction(forward or backward) result in service disruption since the play point will ultimately move to the boundary of the buffer. At this time and in this direction, the VCR functions can no longer be provided. The idea of ABM is to keep the play point in the middle of the buffer so that there is a lower probability that VCR actions will move the play point beyond the buffer capability. In ABM, a buffer manager adjusts the contents of the buffer after VCR actions so that the relative position of the play point in the buffer remains central. The buffer manager is presumed to be able to receive data from three channels simultaneously. When the broadcast of each segment is finished, i.e.,$t_0 + k \cdot d$, the buffer manager decides which segments it will receive during the next d seconds, based on the position of the play point. However, although ABM increases the likelihood that VCR actions may be provided, it did not address the method of determining whether a request can be provided. Moreover, it receives the whole segment or nothing and the decision on reception schedule is invoked every d seconds. Thus, since it cannot adapt itself rapidly to a change in the user's VCR action pattern, the probability of VCR implementation may become low.

In this paper, we analyze the conditions necessary to guarantee VCR functions and then propose a reception schedule which satisfies these conditions, with minimal resource requirements. Since our proposed scheme receives video frames as a unit, unlike ABM, it can keep up rapidly with a changing VCR action pattern. The symbols that are used in the next stage of th presentation are shown in Table 1.

Table 1. Notations

S_i	ith segment
d	length of segment (sec.)
s	size of segment (KB)
K	number of segments
γ	play rate(fps)
b	channel bandwidth required for γ

3 VCR Functions in Periodic Broadcast

3.1 Staggered Broadcasting

Staggered broadcasting starts video broadcasts over the allocated channels at fixed time intervals. Assume that there are K channels dedicated to a video of length L. The K channels are labeled as $0, 1, 2, \ldots, K-1$. The video broadcast starts every $L/K(= d)$ seconds and each channel broadcasts the whole video

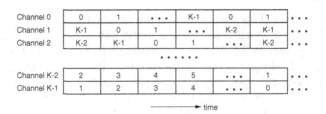

Channel 0	0	1	. . .	K-1	0	1	. . .
Channel 1	K-1	0	1	. . .	K-2	K-1	. . .
Channel 2	K-2	K-1	0	1	. . .	K-2	. . .
			. . . . . .				
Channel K-2	2	3	4	5	. . .	1	. . .
Channel K-1	1	2	3	4	. . .	0	. . .

time →

Fig. 1. Staggered Broadcasting

repeatedly as shown in Figure 1. If the broadcast of a video starts at channel 0 at the system setup time t_0, the broadcast starts over channel k at $t_0 + k \cdot d$ and is repeated. Therefore, the video is broadcast every d seconds over K channels and accordingly, the maximum service latency is d seconds. Here, the K video chunks of length d that make up the video are called *segments*. During a segment time(i.e., d seconds), all K segments are broadcast over different channels. And, we assume that broadcast of all the segments are synchronized at the level of frames. In other words, if the jth frame of a segment is broadcast at time t, the jth frames of the other segments are also broadcast at t.

3.2   VCR Functions

VCR functions include *play forward, play backward, fast forward, fast backward, slow forward, slow backward, jump forward, jump backward, pause,* and so on. We consider the following VCR functions in this paper:

1. Play Forward/Backward (PF/PB): Playback the video at a normal playback rate in either the forward or backward direction.
2. Fast Forward/Backward (FF/FB): Playback the video at n times the normal playback rate in either the forward or backward direction. We assume n is 3 for simplicity in this paper, but our work can be applied generally to FF/FB functions.
3. Slow Forward/Backward (SF/SB): Playback the video at a $1/m$ times the normal playback rate in either the forward or backward direction.
4. Pause (PA): Stop the playback for a period of time.
5. Jump Forward/Backward (JF/JB): Jump immediately to the destination frame.

The functions can be conveniently classified into *forward functions* and *backward functions*, and although Pause(PA) has no direction, it can be regarded as one. In addition, the functions were categorized as *continuous* and *discontinuous functions* according to continuity in a series of frames displayed as the result of each one, which does not involve temporal notion. JF and JB functions are discontinuous functions and the remainder are continuous. Although PA holds a frame on the screen for the duration paused, when subsequent playback is resumed, the next frames are displayed in regular order. Since any next frames are not skipped at resume. That is why we regard PA as a continuous function.

3.3   Conditions for Continuous VCR

There are physically only broadcasting streams or channels in PB model, but we can give users an illusion that they are being serviced by dedicated streams. These *virtual* streams of the users' view are possible by effective client-side buffering and prefetching, and they can provide VCR functions just as the dedicated streams of TVOD. We first derive the conditions for providing continuous VCR functions consistently and find theoretically the minimum buffer requirement satisfying the conditions. In Sect. 3.4, using these conditions, we propose a reception schedule that provides VCR functions with the minimum buffer requirement. Discontinuous functions are not considered in this subsection.

The video frame of a video currently accessed by a clients is known as the *play point*, and the frames already displayed are called "past" frames and those that have not been displayed yet are called "future" frames. The *forward* and *backward buffers* are defined as the buffers keeping the future and the past frames, respectively. Figure 2 illustrates the relation of video object, broadcast channel, and client buffer. $\Delta(k_0, k)$ is the *distance* between the play point k_o and a future

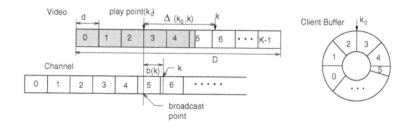

Fig. 2. Video, Segment, and Buffer

frame k at a normal play rate γ. For example, the distance between the first frame of S_0 and the first frame of S_2 is $2d$. Thus, the consumption time, $c(k)$, is the time remaining until frame k is consumed, and meets the condition

$$c(k) \geq \frac{\Delta(k_0, k)}{3}.$$

That is, $c(k)$ is greater than or equal to the time taken to consume all the frames between the frames k_o and k by FF or FB, whose play rates are three times the normal rate(i.e., 3γ). We thereby derive the condition for guaranteeing continuous functions as follows.

Theorem 1. *Let $\mathcal{B}$ be a set of frames contained by the buffer. Continuous VCR functions can be provided if the following condition is satisfied:*

$$\forall k \notin \mathcal{B}, \quad \frac{\Delta(k_0, k)}{3} \geq b(k), \tag{1}$$

where $b(k)$ is the next broadcasting time of a frame k.

PROOF   If, for all k, we can satisfy

$$b(k) \leq c(k) \quad \text{or} \quad k \in \mathcal{B},$$

it is evident that continuous VCR actions can be provided. Since $c(k) \geq \Delta(k_0, k)/3$, $\Delta(k_0, k)/3 \geq b(k)$. Finally, Eq. 1 is valid. □

$\mathcal{B}_f$ is the set of frames contained by the forward buffer and $\mathcal{B}_b$ the set of those contained by the backward buffer. Since $\mathcal{B} = \mathcal{B}_f \cup \mathcal{B}_b$, for all the future frames and all the past frames respectively, Eq. 1 must be satisfied to provide continuous VCR functions. That is, for all future frames not in the forward buffer, their distances must be greater than or equal to $3b(k)$, and the situation for past frames is identical. The minimum buffer requirement for guaranteeing the continuous functions can be determined using THEOREM 1.

Lemma 1. *The minimal client buffer space required for a client to provide continuous VCR functions consistently is 6s, where s is a segment size.*

PROOF   In order to satisfy Eq. 1, all the frames k such that $\Delta(k_0, k) < 3$ must be in the buffer or be broadcast before $c(k)$. In the worst case, $3d\gamma$ future frames and $3d\gamma$ past frames must be in the buffer. Therefore, since data size of $d\gamma$ frames is s, buffer space of at least $6s$ is required. □

3.4   Reception Schedule

It is impossible to meet Eq. 1 for d seconds after a client begins to receive the video data. Since each segment is broadcast at a bandwidth of b, d seconds are required to receive the whole segment. Hence, the FF actions of S_0 and S_1 may not be serviced for d seconds since the service start. In order to provide the FF function fully, the reception of S_0 must be finished within $d/3$ seconds after the service start and that of S_1 should be finished within $2d/3$ seconds. As this reception is impossible in staggered broadcasting, we propose a reception schedule scheme to guarantee all the continuous functions *after d seconds*, with a reception bandwidth requirement of $3b$.

Our presentation in this subsection focuses on the continuous forward(CF) function, since almost identical considerations apply to the case of the continuous backward(CB) function. Since all frames are transmitted every d seconds, the maximum of $b(k)$ in Eq. 1 is d. Thus, all future frames k such that $\Delta(k_0, k) \geq 3$ do not have to be contained by the forward buffer. Therefore, when play point k_0 is a frame of a segment S_i, the target segments we have to be concerned with for the future frames are S_i, S_{i+1}, S_{i+2}, and S_{i+3}, and similarly the target segments for the past frames are S_i, S_{i-1}, S_{i-2}, and S_{i-3}. K segments are transmitted synchronously over K channels(Fig. 1). Accordingly, the jth frames of all K segment are transmitted at the same time. Fig. 3 illustrates the target channels transmitting the target segments and the candidate frames for reception. In the figure, the play point k_0 is a frame of S_5, and the shaded area means the frames whose distances from k_0 are less than $3d$. Thus, the target segments are S_5, S_6,

S_7, and S_8, and the candidate frames are k_1, k_2, and k_3. Our reception schedule scheme puts into the buffer the frames not yet buffered among the candidate frames. When the client is running CF actions, the candidate frames can be in

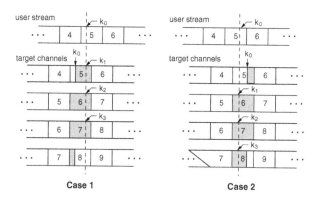

Fig. 3. Candidate Future Frames

two cases. Case 1 occurs when the frame index within segment of the play point is larger than those of the frames being currently broadcast, and Case 2 occurs in the other case(Fig. 3). Hence, the schedule receives data from at most three channels in both cases.

Since the client buffer needs to keep the frames with distances less than $3d$, the buffer requirement is $6s$(LEMMA 1). The frames k such that $\Delta(k_0, k) \leq 3d$ are called *essential frames*. If Eq. 1 meets, all essential frames k such that $b(k) > c(k)$ should be in the buffer. Hence, the number of the essential future frames in the buffer is less than or equal to $3d\gamma$. That is, data size of these future frames is less than or equal to $3s$. Therefore, if the size of the forward buffer,$|\mathcal{B}_f|$, is larger than or equal to $3s$, all essential future frames k are kept in the buffer. The case of the backward buffer $\mathcal{B}_b$ is identical. Since $|\mathcal{B}_b| = 6s - |\mathcal{B}_f|$, if $|\mathcal{B}_f| < 3s$, the candidate past frames do not have to be received because they all would be in the buffer, and if $\mathcal{B}_f \geq 3s$, the future candidate frames do not have to be received. Finally, the required reception bandwidth of our scheme is $3b$. Fig. 4 summarizes our reception algorithm. Once a new frame is put into buffer according to the algorithm, the frame with the longest distance from the play point is replaced. Therefore, since the client buffer is required to keep only essential frames with the essential frames, the buffer requirement is $6s$ from LEMMA 1.

EXAMPLE   Fig 5 illustrates how our scheme works with a scenario on user behavior. The figure shows reception schedule and change of the forward buffer size on the user behavior. When the service starts at t_0, the client begin to receive S_0, S_1,and S_2 and display S_0 simultaneously, and data is accumulated in the buffer at a rate of $\frac{2}{3}s$ per d seconds. At t_1, the forward buffer has S_1 and S_2. S_0 has been consumed and this is in the backward buffer. From t_1 to t_2 , the frames of S_3 and S_4 are the candidates, since if S_1 and S_2 are displayed by

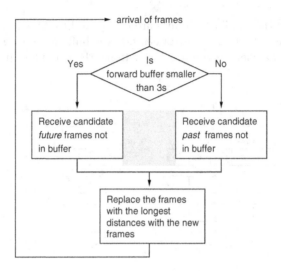

Fig. 4. Reception Schedule

a FF action, the frames of S_3 and S_4 are required before the next broadcast of them (i.e.,t_2). Hence, the reception scheme receives them from t_1 to t_2. At t_2, the buffer has three segments, S_2, S_3, and S_4, and the user performs a long FF action S_2, S_3, and S_4 to t_9. The client begins to receive S_5, S_6, and S_7 at t_2, t_3, and t_4, respectively. Then, S_5 are displayed by PF from t_5 to t_6, and simultaneously the client receives S_8. The forward buffer size does not exceed $3s$. □

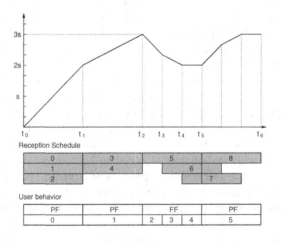

Fig. 5. Example

3.5   Discontinuous VCR Actions

Now we concern ourselves with the discontinuous functions such as JF and JB. Fig. 4 is the algorithm guaranteeing continuous functions without considering discontinuous functions. Discontinuous actions render the buffered content received according to the algorithm useless. Moreover, it is impossible to jump immediately to the requested destination due to buffer restrictions in client-side and service latency in the periodic broadcast. Nevertheless, it is necessary to provide continuous functions at some level of guarantee even after jump actions are performed. The client must be able to display the video by at least PF immediately after the jump. We aim at the same VCR provision as guaranteed when the service starts, except for continuous backward(CB) actions. CB actions do not have a meaning at service start, but they do in the case of jump actions. Thus, it need to be considered how to provide CB actions after a discontinuous action (e.g., their provision can be guaranteed after d seconds or after the nearest $d\gamma$ past frames are buffered). Since, however, the theoretical analysis is complicated and then more work is needed, we leave it to our future work. Instead, CB functions after jumps are provided by best effort according our scheme but not guaranteed in this paper.

As mentioned in Sect. 3.3, FF actions may not be serviced since Eq. 1 cannot be satisfied from service start until d seconds elapse. In order to provide PF functions consistently, the following condition must meet for all frame k such that $\Delta(k_0, k) \le d$:

$$\Delta(k_0, k) \ge b(k) \quad \text{or} \quad k \in \mathcal{B}. \tag{2}$$

This condition meets at the service start ($k_0 = 0$) in staggered broadcasting. Therefore, the condition also must meet after jump action. In addition, since all the frames of a video are transmitted every d seconds, the same VCR provision as guaranteed at the service start can be possible.

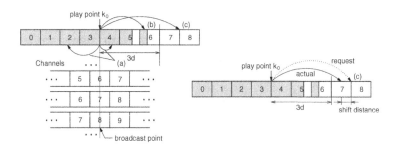

Fig. 6. Jump Actions and Destination Shift

Fig 6 illustrates how jump actions work for a snapshot of buffer state and play point. The shaded area means the frames kept in buffer and the snapshot is the state at t_4 in Fig. 5. The jump actions can be classified into three cases. (a) and (b) are the cases in which the destination points k_s are buffered, and (c) is the case in which the destination point is a non-essential frame not buffered.

In case (a), since all frames k such that $\Delta(k_s, k) \le d$ are kept in the buffer, (2) is satisfied and accordingly the jump to k_s is possible. On the other hand, in case (b) k_s is buffered but the condition is not satisfied, and in case (c) even k_s is not in the buffer. Thus, it is inevitable to jump to the frame nearest the requested destination point among the currently broadcasting frames in case (b) and (c). These are called *destination shift*. In summary, our scheme moves the play point to the requested frame k_s if, (2) is satisfied for future frames with distances less than d, and otherwise it moves the play point to the nearest frame k_t to k_s among frames being currently broadcasted. All the frames k such as $\Delta(k_s, k) \le d$ need not to be checked for the condition. If a frame k_t within the range is broadcast before $\Delta(k_s, k_t)$ seconds and all the frames k such that $k_s < k < k_t$ satisfy (2), the other frames within the range also satisfy it. Let us jth frames of each segment are being broadcast over K channels, when the user requests the destination frame k_s. Then, k_s would lie between jth frames of any two successive segments. Since a segment length is d seconds, the distance between the two frames is d seconds. Hence, the maximum shift length between the requested destination and the actual one is $d/2$ and the average is $d/4$.

4   Simulation

In this section, we demonstrate the viability of our reception schemes for VCR functions through simulations. The simulations are made for two scenarios on user behavior, at which the user does only continuous actions (OCA) and all actions (ALL), respectively. Table 2 shows the probabilities that the user requests each action under OCA and ALL. Since there is no data recognized on users' VCR action pattern, we chose the probabilities arbitrarily. However, users' action pattern dose not affect the feasibility of our scheme. The holding duration of a

Table 2. User Action Patterns

	CONT.							DISC.	
	PF	PB	FF	FB	SF	SB	PA	JF	JB
OCA	1.00							0.00	
	0.32	0.06	0.32	0.10	0.08	0.04	0.08	0.00	0.00
ALL	0.80							0.20	
	0.26	0.05	0.26	0.08	0.06	0.03	0.06	0.10	0.10

continuous action is exponentially distributed with a mean of 10 seconds, and the jump distance of a discontinuous action are also exponentially distributed with a mean of 60 seconds for the ALL case. The jump distance is the distance between the current play point and the destination point. The segment length d is 60 seconds, the number of channels K is 32, and play rate γ is 30 fps. However, K and γ do not make any effect on the simulation results, and are related only to the running time of the simulation.

Fig. 7 and Figure 8 show the variation of amount of buffered essential frames for OCA and ALL cases. We have not encountered any jitter under all the scenarios during simulation, since our schemes restrict some actions during the period when the actions are not guaranteed to be provided (e.g., FF actions are rejected for d seconds after the service starts). The results confirm that our reception schemes provide VCR functionality at the guarantee level which we presented in the previous sections. In addition, the results demonstrate require that the buffer requirement of the schemes is $6s$, which is the minimal buffer space required for providing VCR functions consistently. Figure 8 is the result for ALL case having 60 seconds as a mean jump distance. The larger the mean jump distance is, the more content buffered are corrupted by the jump and this is confirmed by the result. The vertical droppings of the line in the figure mean the corruption of buffered content.

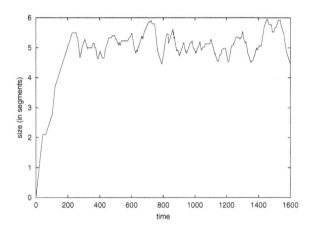

Fig. 7. Only Continuous Actions (OCA)

When a discontinuous action is requested, a destination shift may occur. Since the average shift distance is a important performance metric for the discontinuous actions, we observed the shift distances caused by jump actions during the simulations. Table 3 shows distance per shift, proportion of the actions causing no shift, and average shift distance, while varying mean distance between play point and the requested destination. The distance per shift is the average shift distance experienced by the actions having caused a shift, and the average shift distance is that of all jump actions. The distance per shift are about 15 seconds, respectively. Since d is 60 seconds, the result agrees with the analytic result that the average distance is $d/4$. As the mean jump distance is longer, the proportion of the actions without shift decreases and the average shift distance increases. That is because long jump actions are not probably serviced by the buffered data.

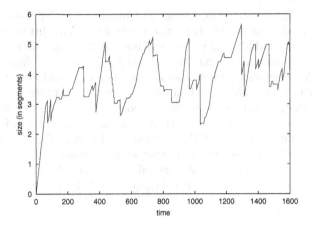

Fig. 8. ALL Actions (ALL, mean 60 sec.)

Table 3. Destination Shift

mean dist	per-shift dist.	no shift	avg. shift dist.
30	13.76	0.83	2.34
60	16.94	0.58	7.11
90	15.32	0.35	9.96
120	17.11	0.21	13.52
150	15.92	0.10	14.33
180	15.82	0.09	15.82

5   Discussion

Since the proposed scheme works at the frame-level, the computational overhead caused by the algorithms must be reasonable. Otherwise, hiccup or jitter will occur on the screen by the overhead. Our reception schedule algorithm(Figure 4) have little computational overhead, which is $O(1)$. The algorithm for discontinuous actions require $O(d \cdot \gamma)$ time complexity, which is not great, and this can be reduced by optimization. Even if the overhead is a burden on the client, a little delay is acceptable due to the characteristics of discontinuous functions.

We have assumed that each channel is synchronized at the frame level. However, our schemes can be applied to the case that the channel is less frequently synchronized (e.g., every γ frames) by buffering a chunk of frames as a unit. Also, although we assumed three-times FF and FB functions, our schemes are easily extended to n-times FF and FB functions by replacing 3 with n in the equations presented throughout this paper.

6 Conclusion

A near video-on-demand(NVOD) is a more scalable approach by batching multiple clients to a shared stream or broadcasting videos. The advent of digital video broadcasting systems, such as digital satellite, CATV, etc, makes periodic broadcasting more feasible. Staggered video broadcasting, one of periodic broadcasting technique, broadcasts multiple streams of the same video at staggered times, with one stream serving multiple clients. In order to provide subscribers with a high-quality VOD service, it is desirable to add VCR functionality such as fast forward and fast backward, but it is not easy to provide VCR functionality in NVOD, especially video broadcasting service where any dedicated or interaction channel is not available.

In this paper, we analyze the conditions necessary to provide VCR functions and then propose a reception schedule which satisfies these conditions, with minimal resource requirements. Since our proposed scheme receives video frames as a unit it can keep up rapidly with a changing VCR action pattern. Our scheme makes it possible for users to enjoy the freedom of VCR actions without increasing the overall network bandwidth requirement, and requests only a little more buffer space and three times the bandwidth from the clients' side.

References

1. IEEE Standard 802.6. Distributed Queue Dual Bus (DQDB) Metropolitan Area Network (MAN), December 1990.
2. Emmanuel L. Abram-Profeta and Kang G. Shin. Providing Unrestricted VCR Functions in Multicast Video-On-Demand Servers. In *Proc. of IEEE International Conference on Multimedia Computing and Systems*, pages 66–75, Austin, Texas, June 1998.
3. C.C. Aggarwal, J.L. Wolf, and P.S. Yu. A Permutation-based Pyramid Broadcasting Scheme for Video-on-Demand Systems. In *IEEE International Conference on Multimedia Computing and Systems(ICMCS'96)*, pages 118–126, Hiroshima, Japan, June 1996.
4. C.C. Aggarwal, J.L. Wolf, and P.S. Yu. On Optimal Batching Policies for Video-On-Demand Storage Servers. In *IEEE International Conference on Multimedia Computing and Systems(ICMCS'96)*, Hiroshima, Japan, June 1996.
5. Kevin C. Almeroth and Mostafa Ammar. A Scalable Interactive Video-On-Demand Service Using Multicast Communication. In *Proc. of International Conference of Computer Communication and Networks (ICCCN'94)*, San Francisco, California, September 1994.
6. Kevin C. Almeroth and Mostafa Ammar. On the Performance of a Multicast Delivery Video-On-Demand Service with Discontinuous VCR Actions. In *Proc. of International Conference on Communication (ICC'95*, Seattle, Washington, June 1995.
7. Kevin C. Almeroth and Mostafa Ammar. On the Use of Multicast Delivery to Provide a and Interactive Video-On-Demand Service. *IEEE Journal of Selected Areas in Communications*, 14(6):1110–1122, 1996.
8. J. Y. L. Boudec. The Asynchronous Transfer Mode: A Tutorial. *Computer Networks and ISDN Systems*, 24:279–309, 1992.

9. A. Dan, D. Sitaram, and P. Shahabuddin. Scheduling Policies for an On-demand Video Server with Batching. In *Proc. of ACM Multimedia*, pages 15–23, Oct 1994.
10. A. Dan, D. Sitaram, and P. Shahabuddin. Dynamic Batching Policies for an On-demand Video Server. *Multimedia Systems*, 4(3):112–121, June 1996.
11. Zongming Fei, Ibrahim Kamel, Sarit Mukherjee, and Mostafa H. Ammar. Providing Interactive Functions for Staggered Multicast Near Video-On-Demand Systems (Extended Abstract). In *Proc. of IEEE International Conference on Multimedia Computing and Systems(Poster Session)*, volume 2, pages 949–953, Florence, Italy, June 1999.
12. Lixin Gao, Jim Kurose, and Don Towsley. Efficient Schemes for Broadcasting Popular Videos. In *Proceedings of the 8th International Workshop on Network and Operating Systems Support for Digital Audio and Video (NOSSDAV '98)*, Cambridge, UK, July 1998.
13. K.A. Hua and S. Sheu. Skyscraper Broadcasting: A New Broadcasting Scheme for Metropolitan Video-on-Demand Systems. In *ACM SIGCOMM '97*, pages 89–100, Cannes, France, September 1997.
14. L. Juhn and L. Tseng. Harmonic Broadcasting for Video-on-Demand Service. *IEEE Transactions on Broadcasting*, 43(3):268–271, September 1997.
15. Wanjiun Liao and Victor O. Li. The Split and Merge Protocol for Interactive Video-On-Demand. *IEEE Multimedia*, 4(6):51–62, 1997.
16. D. J. Marchok, C. Rohrs, and M. R. Schafer. Multicasting in a Growable Packet (ATM) Switch. In *Proc. of IEEE INFOCOM*, pages 850–858, Bal Harbour, Florida, 1991.
17. J.-F. Pâris, S.W. Carter, and D.D.E Long. A Low Bandwidth Broadcasting Protocol for Video on Demand. In *IEEE International Conference on Computer Communications and Networks (ICCCN'98)*, pages 690–697, October 1998.
18. J.-F. Pâris, S.W. Carter, and D.D.E Long. Efficient Broadcasting Protocols for Video on Demand. In *International Symposium on Modeling, Analysis and Simulation of Computer and Telecommunication Systems (MASCOTS'98)*, pages 127–132, July 1998.
19. J.-F. Pâris, S.W. Carter, and D.D.E Long. A Hybrid Broadcasting Protocol for Video on Demand. In *Proc. of Multimedia Computing and Networking Conference (MMCN'99)*, pages 317–326, January 1999.
20. M. A. Rodrigues. Erasure Node: Performance Improvements for the IEEE 802.6 MAN. In *Proc. of IEEE INFOCOM*, pages 636–643, San Francisco, California, 1990.
21. S. Sheu, K.A. Hua, and T.H. Hu. Virtual Batching: A New Scheduling Technique for Video-On-Demand Servers. In *Proc. of the 5th DASFAA'97*, Melbourne, Australia, April 1997.
22. S. Viswanathan and T. Imielinski. Metropolitan Area Video-on-Demand Service Using Pyramid Broadcasting. *Multimedia Systems*, 4(4):197–208, August 1996.

A Fully Scalable and Distributed Architecture for Video-on-Demand

Fernando Cores, Ana Ripoll, and Emilio Luque

Computer Science Department - University Autonoma of Barcelona – Spain
Fernando.Cores@uab.es A.Ripoll@cc.uab.es E.Luque@cc.uab.es

Abstract. In spite of the attractiveness of Video-on-demand (VoD) services, their implantation to the present has not been as widespread as could have been desired due to centralized VoD systems have a limited streaming capacity and its grown is costly. One level proxy-based systems have been proposed to increase the system capacity but their scalability are still limited by the main network bandwidth. Our investigation are focussed on designing a flexible LVoD (large-scale Video-on-Demand) system capable of easy scaling with limited costs, which can adapt its size to the needs of the system. To achieve a scalable LVoD system, it is essential that the communications system bandwidth is able to grow in keeping with system growth (with a reasonable cost and limited loss of efficiency). To get these requirements we have proposed a hierarchical tree topology based on the use of independent local networks with proxies. To allow the system's grow, the functionality of the proxy has been modified in such a way that it works at the same time as cache for the most watched movies, and as a mirror for the remaining movies. The evaluation of these systems has been done using an analytical model. The results shows that this architecture guarantees unlimited and low-cost growth for LVoD systems, the VoD system capacity can easily be adapted to any number of users and the system is fault-tolerant.

1   Introduction

Video-on-demand (VoD) systems have been one of the most active areas of research in recent years due to the coming together of two factors: the growing interest from diverse sectors of industry (entertainment, education, information, cable companies, telecommunications, etc.) in developing such systems, and the great complexity that these systems have (integrating various types of information together with real-time requisites, very strict quality of service levels, a great number of users and a high volume of information).

In spite of the attractiveness of these services for the public in general, their implantation to the present has not been as widespread as could have been desired. The construction of large-scale video-on-demand (LVoD) is currently limited both by the capacity of the server as well as by the capacity for simultaneous transmissions that can be supported by a communication network (network bandwidth), limitations on the subsequent growth of these systems, the significant initial investment required and high maintenance costs, among others.

M.J. van Sinderen and L.J.M. Nieuwenhuis (Eds.): PROMS 2001, LNCS 2213, pp. 59-73, 2001.
© Springer-Verlag Berlin Heidelberg 2001

For the large-scale distribution of multimedia content in wide-area networks for commercial use, requirements are not fulfilled by any of the currently existing approaches. These systems would require arranging the servers that provide video retrieval and playback services in a distributed system in order for them to support a large number of concurrent streams. Furthermore, the construction of these systems would require substantial initial investment. This is due to the need to create larger systems than those originally required, given their zero scalability.

LVoD systems would be scalable, because of the need for their rapid expansion, caused by an increase in users or by the inclusion of new services (video conferences, Internet, etc.). Failure to contemplate scalability in the design of such systems may lead to system overload, which in turn could cause client service rejection, since the requirements of real-time streaming for video playing are not to be guaranteed.

In order to achieve scalable LVoD, it is essential that the communications system bandwidth is able to grow in keeping with system growth. It is also essential that this growth be produced at a reasonable cost and with limited loss of efficiency. The aim of our research is to obtain a LVoD system in which system size does not depend on currently-available technology, and that can adapt itself to requirements of system-user growth. In this paper, we focus on the following objective: achieving a flexible LVoD system capable of easy scaling, with limited costs.

The paper is organized in the following way: in section 2, we will first undertake an overview of the solutions proposed in the literature for increasing VoD system capacity. Following this, in sections 3 and 4, we will study the factors that limit scalability in the current systems, and will outline our proposal based on a hierarchical topology. In order to evaluate these systems, in section 5, we will propose an analytical model, and in section 6, will study the efficiency and scalability of the systems in question. Finally, in the last section, we will indicate the main conclusions to be drawn from our discussion, and we will suggest lines of future research deriving from this study.

2   Related Work

In past years, research into VoD systems has mainly been focussed on policies that attempt to improve the available bandwidth efficiency. These techniques basically aim at increasing the number of users that can be served with a limited bandwidth. Such approaches are grouped into two broad policy groups: broadcasting and multicasting techniques.

In broadcasting techniques, streams (minimum unit of video transmission) are sent to all clients, and they subsequently decide whether the information interests them. If they are not interested, they can simply ignore it. There are various broadcasting techniques, and these are differentiated principally in terms of the number of streams used in the broadcasting of a movie and the transmission frequency of each one of the pieces into which the video is divided. Some of the most widely-used broadcasting techniques are pyramid [11] and skyscraper broadcasting [6].

The main difference between broadcasting and multicasting techniques is the range of clients to whom the streams are directed. With multicasting techniques, information is sent to a reduced group of clients who have previously requested the data received, and as a result, there is never any bandwidth wastage. The most widely-known multicasting techniques are batching [1][2], piggybacking [3], patching [7][9] and merging [4][13].

All of these techniques aim to improve the bandwidth performance available within the system, but do not increase it. One of the solutions proposed for increasing the size of the VoD systems is the connection to users via independent networks [5]. In these systems, users are grouped in networks segments known as local networks, whose traffic is independent with respect to other segments, in such a way that the system bandwidth is able to be, at least in theory, the bandwidth accumulated by each one of the individual networks. Nevertheless, in order to increase the bandwidth in these systems, it is not enough simply to group users into independent networks, since, if all users have to access the same server and its network, this would create a bottleneck, and the system would therefore be saturated.

The key to the successful of these systems with independent networks and to obtaining better performance lies in the fact that certain requests can be served locally without the need to access the origin of the data through the main network. Various techniques are proposed in the literature to realize this objective. Some are based on placing VoD servers close to clients' networks so that these users are not required to access the server, and thereby creating a system of hierarchical servers [12]. This strategy involves considerable cost; as a result, certain proposals have opted for reducing the size of local servers in such a way that they do not store all the movies available within the system, but instead, only those with a higher access frequency. These servers are managed as main server caches and are called proxies, just as their Internet counterparts. There are a variety of policies for managing proxy content, depending on whether they store complete movie or only certain parts (prefix-proxy[8][14]).

The general topology of a system based on proxies (see Fig. 1) consists of a main server, which is connected, through the main network, to a group of independent networks with their proxy.

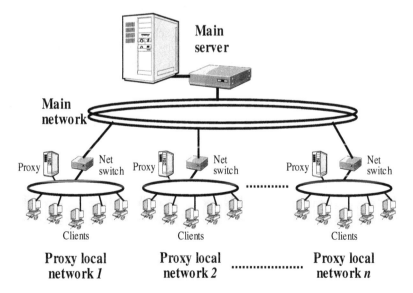

Fig. 1. One-level proxy VoD system.

Another alternative proposed for increasing the size of VoD systems is the distribution of request management throughout all the system components, allowing the clients themselves to serve other users, through their local buffer (Chaining[10]).

3   Scalability in VoD Systems

Of the main components of a VoD system (server and transmission network), server bandwidth is always greatest, given that bus technology offers a better cost/performance ratio and better scalability. This scalability can be achieved through the inclusion of new disks, using cluster methodology or using various independent servers connected to the same service network. Even with this, however, the establishment of VoD servers capable of handling thousands of simultaneous streams is both complex and costly, due to the high performance level required.

On the other hand, network bandwidth is smaller (due to its associated costs), becoming the true bottleneck when the system grows, and considerably limiting the system's final size. The reason for its poor scalability is that network bandwidth is limited by currently-available technology and it can not grown. The system network bandwidth available only can be increased either by the inclusion of independent servers with their own service networks (implying high costs due to the need for a new server, and a poor sharing of streams between clients) or by the inclusion of additional networks to the system server (implying that growth is limited by installation type, that a more complex server is necessary and that there will be a poor stream sharing). In short, the final size and growth of VoD systems depend, ultimately, on the capacity (bandwidth) of the connection network with the end client.

As we have already seen, the solution proposed by the literature to the problem of increasing service capacity in VoD systems is the use of a central server that is connected, via the main network, to a group of independent networks with their proxy. The effectiveness of these proxies is based on the pattern of user requests for movies following a Zipf(0) distribution [1], few movies have a high percentage of total requests, and therefore, even with a small cache, a high percentage of requests can be attended (e.g. with a cache of 20% of movies available, values in the region of 50% success can be attained). This percentage of success is not sufficiently high to avoid server congestion if there is an excessive increase in the number of local networks. The problem with these systems is that requests that cannot be served locally end up in the main server, which becomes, once again, both a bottleneck and a growth-limiting factor. In spite of these systems obtain greater system's effective bandwidth in comparison to centralized systems without proxies, they do not successfully solve either the problem of the system's limited size or that of scalability. Since, as clients number grow (with the consequent increase in local networks), there comes a point at which the network and main server cannot cope with the traffic generated by proxy cache misses, and its growth is halted. Consequently, there is the renewed need for entire system replication techniques, or for a re-dimensioning of the server and main network in order to increase system capacity.

In order to attain a scalable communication system, it is essential to solve the (physical) limitations of centralized systems (a single network or single server), as these will always be constrained by currently-available technology. For this reason, we will focus on distributed systems in order to facilitate future system growth. The distributed topology proposed is described in the following section.

4   Our Approach: A Hierarchical Proxy VoD System

Our proposal consists of an expansion of the proxy technique, currently restricted to a single level, using a tree topology that provides the system with unlimited scaling capacity as well as greater flexibility when deciding on its size and its form of growth.

The structure of this topology, shown in figure 2, consists of a series of levels, in accordance with the number of local networks and the order of the tree (binary, tertiary, etc.). All the topology nodes have the same components: a network, a proxy and its clients.

The main network, to which both the VoD server as well as the first level hierarchy is connected, is located on the main level. The first level hierarchy is made up of a series of local networks (depending on the tree order) that form the following tree level (level 1). Subsequent networks are successively hung from each one of the previous local level networks until reaching the final level. It must be emphasized that this topology requires neither that the levels be complete (although it is recommendable to fill a given level before starting on the next, in order for the system to be balanced), nor that all the tree levels have the same number of connected networks (the same order). Furthermore, if the main network has also clients connected, we then have a homogeneous system.

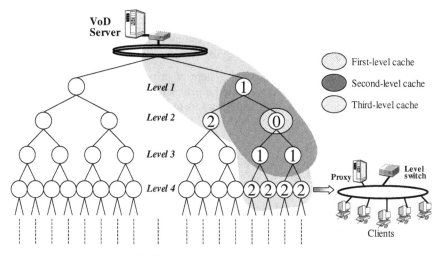

Fig. 2. Hierarchical proxy VoD system.

This hierarchical system has the advantage that, when one level's proxy misses the number of proxies that can be accessed increases too. That is, this topology allows the proxies group, formed by all those local networks situated at the same distance from the node in which the request has been made, to define a cache level in the topology hierarchy. The size of each cache level will be defined as the sum of the individual capacity for each one of the proxies on this level. Also, figure 2 illustrates the different hierarchical levels of cache in the system.

On an initial analysis, a hierarchical tree topology has very desirable qualities from the perspectives of scalability and versatility; since the addition of a new local network only implies the inclusion of a switch to separate the traffic in the two network segments, without modifying any other component in the system. This topology also provides great versatility as the system can initially be composed of any number of networks, and can grow both in length (by adding new levels) and also in width (increasing the order of some tree nodes).

Nevertheless, the simple inclusion of a hierarchical system with proxies does not, in itself, obtain improvements in the system's scalability or efficiency: since, as all the proxies are replicating the same movies, if a proxy cannot serve a request from its client, then it is also very probable that none of the other proxies will be able to serve this request, and the solution will then require accessing the main server. We therefore need a new proxy organization and functionality that would allow us to increase the hit probability as the request climbs the various levels on the tree.

Consequently, our proposal lies in dividing the storage space available in proxies into two parts: one of these will continue functioning as a proxy, storing the most requested movies; the other proxy space will be used for making a distributed mirror of the main server's information. This new scheme is aimed at achieving:

1. To reduce the average distance of those requests that have failed in their local proxy, since, when distance is increased, mirror size also grows and the hit probability is greater.
2. To reduce server saturation, since all the requests generated in nodes situated beyond a determined server distance cannot reach the server, and therefore its workload is less.
3. To increase system fault tolerance, as the failure of a tree node does not prevent the rest of the system from continuing its work.

In order to evaluate both the classical system of proxies as well as our proposal based on the co-operation between cache and mirror schemes within the proxy, we are going to define an analytical model that allows us to compare the network efficiency and requisites offered by both approaches.

5   Analytical Model

In order to validate the proposed architecture we have to demonstrate two important points: first, that this architecture can scale without causing network saturation (the main problem in scalability), and second, that the effectiveness lost by the scalability is not excessive. To do this we have developed an analytical model to measure the efficiency of the previously-mentioned proxy-based systems. In this model, we calculate the system's effective bandwidth that indicate the number of simultaneous streams that can be served simultaneously. In order to estimate the system's growth capacity, we also evaluate the growth of traffic generated by the system itself. These measurements will provide us with an idea of the system's limitation with respect to the number of users that it can admit, and its grade of scalability.

In order to realize this analysis, we assume a unicast policy, i.e., each user is assigned their own dedicated stream. This assumption is valid since our study is directed at evaluating the capacity of the system with respect to the independent streams that it is capable of managing. These results will be independent of whether bandwidth management policies can later be used (broadcasting, multicasting, etc.) in order to increase the efficiency and number of final clients for the system.

In addition, we assume a system with the following characteristics: a bandwidth for each local network of B_c Mbps, a proxy size that is sufficient to store Cp movies of the Vs available within the system, and a server and main network bandwidth of B_p Mbps.

5.1 One Level Proxy System

As we have already commented, these systems are made up of a series of local networks, all of which are directly connected through the network to the main server.

Generically, the effective bandwidth of a proxy-based system (B_e) is evaluated as the maximum bandwidth available within the system (B_m) less the additional bandwidth (B_{fp}) required by proxy misses, given that these misses imply using the main network in order to attend them from the main server.

$$B_e = B_m - B_{fp} \tag{1}$$

This maximum bandwidth available within the system is obtained as the sum of the bandwidth of all the networks forming part of the SVoD, according to the following expression:

$$B_m = B_p + B_c \cdot n \tag{2}$$

where B_p is the bandwidth of the main network, B_c is the bandwidth of the local networks and n is the number of local networks.

In order to obtain the additional bandwidth (B_{fp}) required by proxy misses, we need to calculate the probability of these misses. If we assume that the proxies store the most watched Cp movies in their cache, and that the movie access pattern follows a Zipf(0) distribution with a skew factor of z, we can then calculate proxy-miss probability (p_{fp}) in accordance with the following formula:

$$p_{fp} = 1 - \sum_{m=1}^{Cp} \frac{1}{m^z \cdot \sum_{i=1}^{Vs} 1 / i^z} \tag{3}$$

In this way, we can calculate additional bandwidth due to proxy miss as the probability of miss in each proxy (p_{fp}), multiplied by the traffic generated in all the system's local networks ($B_c * n$), that is:

$$B_{fp} = B_c \cdot n \cdot p_{fp} \tag{4}$$

This parameter indicates a bandwidth that the main network would be required to have in order for the system to be able to manage the n local networks.

Substituting expressions (2) and (4) within (1), effective bandwidth is then:

$$B_e = B_p + B_c \cdot n - B_c \cdot n \cdot p_{fp} = B_p + B_c \cdot n \cdot (1 - p_{fp}) \tag{5}$$

Using expressions (5) and (4), figure 3 illustrates a scalability analysis for one level proxy-based system, using effective bandwidth and the load received by the main network in accordance with the system's number of local networks. This study has been carried out for systems with different proxy sizes. The figure illustrates results using proxies with a capacity for storing 20%, 30% and 40% of the system's movies.

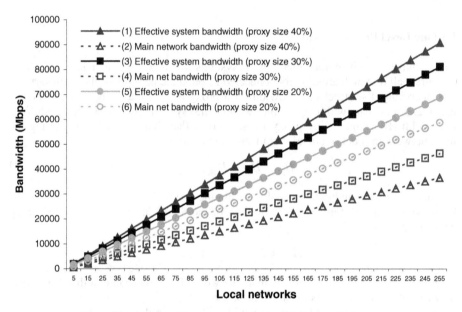

Fig. 3. Scalability of one level proxy based LVoD systems.

We can extract the following conclusions from the results shown in figure 3:
1. Proxy-based systems considerably increase the system's effective bandwidth (series 1, 3 and 5) and therefore the number of users that it can serve.
2. This system capacity increase is obtained at the expense of increasing the bandwidth requirements of the main network and main server. Thus, in series 2, 4 and 6, we can see that the width required by the main network increases linearly with the number of local networks within the system. Consequently, as the main network has a limited bandwidth (that cannot grow), the system has a limited capacity for growth.
3. Proxy cache size needs to have the capacity to store a high percentage of the movies available on the system. This is because, when a proxy is used with the capacity for 20% of the movies (series 5 and 6), the greater part of effective bandwidth obtained (68,000 Mbps for a system with 254 local networks) comes from the main network's bandwidth (58,000 Mbps), and therefore, for small proxy sizes, it is more economically viable to connect clients directly to the main network than to use local networks with proxies. This completely centralized system would have an effective bandwidth of 58,000 Mbps, with a saving in costs for all the local networks.

Nevertheless, when proxy capacity is sufficiently large (sizes of 30% and 40%), the success in proxy cache increases, reducing access to the server network. For example, as we can see in figure 3, using a proxy with a size of 40% with 254 local networks (series 1 and 2), an effective bandwidth of 90,000 Mbps are obtained, which require nothing less than a main network with a 36,000 Mbps bandwidth.

5.2 Hierarchical Proxy-Based System

Having seen the effectiveness of using one level proxy-based systems, we now consider in what ways we can extend this analysis in order to evaluate systems based on a hierarchical topology of proxies.

As a means of facilitating this study, we assume a complete tree topology (all levels are full), with L levels in which the order (o) identifies the number of local networks connected within each one of the tree nodes.

If we analyze expression (1) in the previous section, the only parameter that would be affected with the topology modification is additional bandwidth required, to serve client requests that have missed their local proxy. In this topology, when a request is not able to be met by the proxy of one given level, it accesses the following level, and so on, successively, increasing the bandwidth required. This cost (B_{fp}) will be determined by the number of levels (distance) that the request has cross before reaching the server or proxy that attends it, as we can see in figure 4.

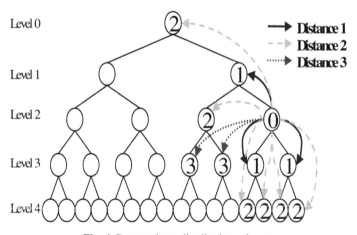

Fig. 4. Proxy misses distribution scheme.

5.2.1 Proxy with Caching

As an initial approximation, in order to evaluate the total proxy-miss cost (B_{fp}) we could assume that cache misses can be obtained by adding the misses produced in every level. That is, the additional cost generated from a node of a given level can be calculated as the percentage of its networks' traffic (B_c), which has failed in its proxy and which is being attended by proxies situated at distance 1 (B_c*p_{fp}), plus the percentage of traffic that is not served from the distance 1 proxies and that is attended by proxies at distance 2 ($B_c*p_{fp}*p_{fp}$), and so on, successively, until reaching level 0, in which the main server is found; this server will attend the request in the final instance. This cost, generated by a node of a given level, have to be multiplied by the number of nodes in this level in order to obtain the total bandwidth required by the level.

$$B_{fp} = B_c \cdot \sum_{v=1}^{L} o^v \sum_{d=1}^{v} p_{fp}^d \tag{6}$$

Nevertheless, this expression is not realistic as it assumes that the hit probability in higher-level proxies is the same as that for the proxy in its local network. Furthermore, as the proxies always attempt to store the most watched movies, a high level of information redundancy is generated, having negative repercussions on the proxy hit probability. This is because, if a request has already missed a proxy, it will very probably miss again with the remaining proxies, as they all replicate the same movies. It is therefore most likely that the hit probability in those proxies, situated at a distance greater than 1, from where the request has generated is practically zero.

A more realistic form of calculating additional cost in this hierarchical system is to assume that those requests that cannot be attended to by their local proxy have to be attended, instead, from the main server and - as a result - a cost proportional to distance (v), which separates them from the main server, will have to be considered. Taking this into account, total proxy-miss cost can be evaluated as:

$$B_{fp} \approx B_c \cdot \sum_{v=1}^{L} o^v \cdot p_{fp} \cdot v \tag{7}$$

This formula indicates that this hierarchical structure for proxies does not make sense, as it does not increase the probability of proxy success, and the distance that has to be covered by the requests, if the proxy fails, is greater, with the consequent increase in the penalization of the system's effective bandwidth.

We now move on to study the viability of this topology through the inclusion of a mirror in the proxies aimed at increasing the probability of their success.

5.2.2 Proxy with Caching and Mirroring

With this new approach that we propose for proxies, their storage space is not modified, but rather is distributed between two different schemes: a percentage that continues managing the space as a cache for storing the most watched movies, and the rest that is used as a mirror of those movies less frequently accessed.

With this system, the probability of success from the initial node is greater, as the group of proxies situated at the same distance x from the local network in which the request is made can be seen as a single storage space formed by the group of mirrors from each of the proxies. In figure 4, we saw how a node situated at level 2, which misses its local proxy, can access 3 proxies situated at distance 1; if these are unable to attend the request, then it will have to access the 6 proxies situated at distance 2, and so on successively, until its request is attended by a given proxy, or it finally reaches its main server.

In order to facilitate this analysis, let us assume that the distribution of movies in each one of the mirrors is realized in an equal manner, and that this form of probability for success in the mirrors is constant and independent of its position in the hierarchy. From this supposition, the probable failure of a request made at level v and accessing all the proxies situated at a distance less than or equal to d is:

$$p_{fm}(v,d) = 1 - \left(p_{ap} + p_{fp} \cdot \frac{M_p \cdot Nd(v,d)}{V_s - C_p} \right) \tag{8}$$

in which:

p_{ap} Is the probability of proxy cache hit $(1-p_{fp})$.
$Nd(v,d)$ Number of local networks at a distance less than or equal d from level v.
Mp Is the proxy space reserved for the mirror movies.

This expression indicates that the probability of success at distance 0 (local proxy in which the request was made) is the accumulated probability that the request can be met from cache or from the proxy mirror, whilst, for greater distances, only the probability of success for proxy mirrors situated at the same distance is considered.

In this way, the required bandwidth for proxy misses (cache+mirror) would be evaluated as:

$$B_{fp} = B_c \cdot \sum_{v=1}^{L} o^v \cdot \sum_{d=0}^{v} p_{fm}(v,d) \tag{9}$$

Substituting this expression in the expression (1), we obtain the following effective bandwidth:

$$B_e = B_m - B_c \cdot \sum_{v=1}^{L} o^v \cdot \sum_{d=0}^{v} p_{fm}(v,d) \tag{10}$$

On the other hand, we can evaluate the traffic (requests) received by the main server, which characterizes overload in the main network as:

$$S_p = B_c \cdot \sum_{v=0}^{L} \frac{o^v \cdot p_{fm}(v,v)}{r_s(v)} \tag{11}$$

This expression implies that, as the distance grows between the networks in which the requests were generated and the server, the number of proxies that can attend them also grows, thereby reducing the volume of traffic that arrives at the main network. The parameter r_s (request to server) identifies the traffic percentage that is attended by the main server. If the traffic generated by proxy misses is distributed equally between neighboring mirrors situated at the same distances then r_s can be evaluated as:

$$r_s(v) = Nd(v,v) \tag{12}$$

But, the request cannot always be distributed equally between proxies and the main server, due to proxies having only a portion of the movies and not being able to serve as many requests as the main server. In order to avoid this assumption we propose another distribution based on hit probability, as we show in the following expression:

$$r_s(v) = 1 + \frac{p_{fm}(v,v) - p_{fm}(v,v+1)}{p_{fm}(v,v)} \tag{13}$$

Summarizing the proposed scheme, based on proxies with caching and mirroring, we can say that it behaves as a VoD distributed architecture, as it manages to decentralize both the traffic from the communications system (through the hierarchical system) as well as that of the server itself (through the mirrors and caches).

6   Evaluation of the Proposed Architecture

In this section, we will use the previously-defined analytical model in order to evaluate the scalability and performance of the proposed topology.

As we have commented, in order to demonstrate that our topology is scalable, we need to ensure that system growth does not modify the requirements (bandwidth) of the existing elements, or, if it grows, that this growth is limited. To do this, we have to make sure that none of the bandwidths in any of the system components grows when the system expands. In hierarchical systems, as the element that can receive greatest load is that situated at the highest level of the hierarchy (the server and the main network in our case), then we only need to prove that the main network and the server do not become saturated as the system grows.

We assume that the system used has the following characteristics: the bandwidth of the main and local networks is 500 Mbps, it has 100 different movies and an access pattern modeled through a Zipf(0) distribution, with a skew factor of 0.729 (the asymmetry factor that is most used in the literature for modeling VoD systems [1]). Figure 5 illustrates the effective bandwidth (B_e) according to the expression (10) and the main network load (S_p) defined by expression (11), for LVoD systems based on topologies with binary trees, and using proxies with a capacity for 30% and 40% of the movies.

As can be observed, as the number of connected local networks grows, main network load not only grows but also initially diminishes, only to stabilize itself later (at around 280 Mbps with proxies of a 40% size and at 380 Mbps with a 30% size, series 3 and 4 respectively), independently of the number of levels that are added. Therefore, having assumed in the analytical model a homogenized behavior for all networks (this means that clients are also connected to the main network), the previously-obtained results can be directly extrapolated to the other levels, and can therefore guarantee the scalability of all the system networks.

Moreover, the performance obtained for this system, understood as its effective bandwidth (series 1 and 2), grow linearly as the number of local networks increases. If we assume that, in the classical system of one level proxy, the system's main network always has sufficient capacity to attend to all proxy misses, and that therefore the bandwidth of this network grows on the system's expansion, we can compare the performance obtained by our architecture with those obtained through a system of one level proxy (Fig. 3).

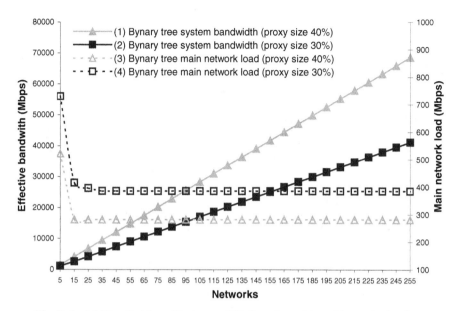

Fig. 5. Scalability of a hierarchical proxy LVoD system with caching and mirroring.

From such a comparison, we can conclude that a decrease in the effective bandwidth of a hierarchical system with respect to the same system, but with a proxy level, depends on the size of the proxies in question. That is, this loss of performance can be quantified at 49% (81000 Mbps in the figure 3 as against 41000 Mbps in figure 5) for a system with 254 local networks and a 30% proxy. Nevertheless, if we increase proxy size to 40% of the system's movies, then the difference in performance hardly reaches 23% (90000 Mbps as against 69000 Mbps). This reduction in performance is due to the fact that when sufficiently large proxies are used, misses do not extend beyond those proxies situated at distance 1 (exactly as occurs in one-level proxy system), improving performance.

On the other hand, performance in this hierarchical proxy system can also be affected by the distribution of proxy storage space between caching and mirroring schemes. In order to study the influence of this parameter, in the figure 6 we show the performance obtained by the system whilst the Cp parameter has been varied in expression (8), which measures the proxy-hit probability. The results have been obtained using a system formed by 254 local networks (7 levels) and with a proxy capacity to store 30% and 40% of the movies. The figure illustrates the effective bandwidth as well as maximum, mean and minimum bandwidth (main network) for system networks.

As we can see, when we use a lower capacity proxy (30%, fig 6a), the best result is obtained using a mirror with 73% of the available space, leaving the cache with the

27% remaining. On using a larger proxy (40%, fig 6b), the percentages vary, the best performance being obtained when proxy space is distributed equally between the two schemes.

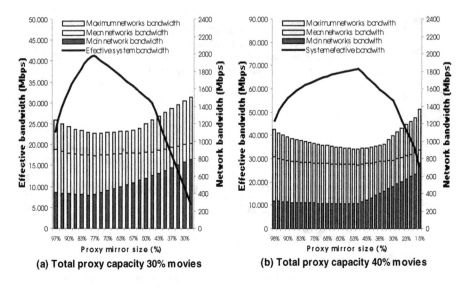

(a) Total proxy capacity 30% movies

(b) Total proxy capacity 40% movies

Fig. 6. Cache and mirror size with a binary tree topology.

7   Conclusions

We have proposed a hierarchical tree topology based on the use of independent local networks. These networks use a local proxy in order to meet requests without the need to access the main server. In case of proxy miss, the server is not accessed directly, but instead, the system attempts to server the request from closer local networks within the topology. In order to increase system scalability, the functionality of the proxy has been modified in such a way that it works at the same time as cache for the most watched movies, and as a mirror for the remaining movies.

This architecture guarantees unlimited and low-cost growth for the VoD system. Additionally, the capacity of the system can be easily adapted to any number of users, and therefore does not require a initial over-dimensioning in order to facilitate subsequent growth. This increase in system capacity may facilitate the inclusion of new services (video conference, access to high quality multimedia Internet contents, etc.) in order to increase system profitability.

The use of a distributed architecture results in a system that is fault-tolerant. And the use of independent networks and distributed mirrors in the proxies to replicate the system's movies allows for the fact that, although any of the networks, proxies or even the main server might fail, service can partially be continued from the local network proxies. Furthermore, by distributing the request service between proxies, the size of the service required (and its cost) is smaller that of a partially or totally centralized system.

Although the bandwidth required by the tree topology is greater, this does not necessarily imply greater cost. One-level proxy systems require a main network with a bandwidth that is considerably greater than that of a hierarchical system. Assuming that the cost of a network does not grow in a linearly with the bandwidth, but rather, that its growth is more likely to be exponential, we can then predict that the cost of the tree topology will be lower.

On the other hand, the architecture proposed (in keeping with most distributed systems) needs to sacrifice part of its efficiency in order to withstand fault tolerance and scalability. Nevertheless, as we have confirmed, this reduction in features decreases with the increase in proxy storage capacity.

Our future research will focus on increasing hierarchical topology performance through an increase in proxy-hit probability and by adapting classical bandwidth management policies (broadcasting, multicasting) to our architecture.

References

1. A. Dan, D. Sitaram, and P. Shahabuddin, "Dynamic batching policies for an on-demand video server," Multimedia Systems 4, pp. 112--121, June 1996.
2. A. Dan, D. Sitaram, and P. Shahabuddin, "Scheduling Policies for an On-Demand Video Server with Batching", *Proc. 2nd ACM Int'l. Multimedia Conference (ACM MULTIMEDIA '94), San Francisco, CA, Oct. 1994, pp. 15-23.*
3. C. Aggarwal, J. Wolf, and P. S. Yu, "On optimal piggybacking merging policies for video-on-demand systems," Performance Evaluation Review, vol. 24, pp. 200--209, May 1996.
4. D. L. Eager, M. K. Vernon, and J. Zahorjan, "Minimizing Bandwidth Requirements for On-Demand Data Delivery", Proc. MIS'99, Indian Wells, CA, Oct. 1999.
5. F. A. Tobagi, "Distance learning with digital video," IEEE Multimedia Magazine, pp. 90-94, Spring 1995.
6. K. A. Hua and S. Sheu, "Skyscraper Broadcasting: a new broadcasting scheme for metropolitan video-on-demand systems," in SIGCOMM 97, pp. 89--100, ACM, (Cannes, France), Sept. 1997.
7. Hua, Ying Cai and Simon Sheu, Patching : A Multicast Tecnique for true Video-on-Demand Services, ACM Multimedia'98, pages 191-200.
8. Luigi Rizzo and Lorenzo Vicisano. "Replacement policies for a proxy cache." Technical Report RN/98/13, UCL-CS, 1998.
9. S. Sen, L. Gao, J. Rexford, and D. Towsley, "Optimal Patching Schemes for Efficient Multimedia Streaming", Proc. 9 th Int'l Workshop on Network and Operating Systems Support for Digital Audio and Video (NOSSDAV'99), Basking Ridge, NJ, June 1999.
10. S. Sheu, K. A. Hua, and W. Tavanapong "Chaining: A Generalized Batching Technique for Video-On-Demand Systems", In Proc. IEEE Int'l Conf. On Multimedia Computing and Systems (ICMCS)'97, Ottawa, Ontario, Canada, June 3-6, 1997, pp. 110-117.
11. S. Viswanathan and T. Imielinski, "Metropolitan area video-on-demand service using pyramid broadcasting," Multimedia Systems 4, pp. 197--208, Aug. 1996.
12. S.-H. G. Chan and F. Tobagi, "Caching schemes for distributed video services", in Proceedings of the 1999 IEEE International Conference on Communications (ICC'99), (Vancouver, Canada), June 1999.
13. S.W. Lau, J.C.S. Lui and L. Golubchik, Merging Video Streams in a Multimedia Storage Server: Complexity and Heuristics, Multimedia Systems, 6(1), 1998, 29-42.
14. Subhabrata Sen, Jennifer Rexford, and Don Towsley. "Proxy prefix caching for multimedia streams." In Proceedings of the IEEE Infocom, 1999.

A Mechanism for Multicast Multimedia Data with Adaptive QoS Characteristics

Christos Bouras[1, 2] and A. Gkamas[1, 2]

[1]Computer Engineering and Informatics Dep., Univ. of Patras, GR-26500 Patras, Greece
[2]Computer Technology Institute, Riga Feraiou 61, GR-26221 Patras, Greece
{bouras, gkamas}@cti.gr

Abstract. In this paper, we describe a mechanism for adaptive transmission of multimedia data, which is based on real time protocols. The proposed mechanism can be used for multicast multimedia data over heterogeneous networks, like the Internet, and has the capability to adapt the transmission of the multimedia data to network changes. In addition, the adaptive multicast transmission mechanism uses an inter-receiver fairness function in order to treat the group of receivers with fairness in a heterogeneous environment. The proposed mechanism uses a "friendly" to the network users congestion control policy to control the transmission of the data. We evaluate the adaptive multicast transmission mechanism through a number of simulations in order to examine its fairness to the group of receivers and its behavior against TCP and UDP data streams.

1 Introduction

The multicast transmission of real time multimedia data is an important component of many current and future emerging Internet applications, like videoconference, distance learning and video-on-demand. The heterogeneous nature of the Internet makes the multicast transmission of real time multimedia data a challenge. Different receivers of the same multicast multimedia data may have different processing capabilities, different loss tolerance and different bandwidth available in the paths leading to them. Should the sender application let the receiver with the least capacity dictate the adaptation? Is it fair the sender application ignores such a receiver? General speaking the sender application must treat the group of receivers with fairness.

Today, the underlying infrastructure of the Internet does not sufficiently support Quality of Service (QoS) guarantees. The new technologies, which are used for the implementation of networks, like the Asynchronous Transfer Mode (ATM) provide capabilities to support QoS in one network domain but it is not easy to implement QoS among various network domains, in order to provide end-to-end QoS to the user. As a result, in the future users may have the capability to request specific end-to-end QoS even over the Internet, but this is not feasible today. In addition, many researchers stand that the cost for providing end-to-end QoS is too big, and it is better to invest on careful network design and careful network monitoring, in order to identify and upgrade the congested network links [6].

M.J. van Sinderen and L.J.M. Nieuwenhuis (Eds.): PROMS 2001, LNCS 2213, pp. 74-88, 2001.
© Springer-Verlag Berlin Heidelberg 2001

The proposed mechanism uses RTP/RTCP (Real time Transmission Protocol / Real time Control Transmission Protocol) [15] for the transmission of the multimedia data. The RTP protocol seems to be the de facto standard for the transmission of multimedia data over the Internet and is used by mbone tools (vit, vat, etc) and ITU H.323 applications. In addition RTCP offers capabilities for monitoring the transmission quality of multimedia data. We use RTCP for the implementation of the network monitoring capabilities of the proposed mechanism.

In this paper, we concentrate on the implementation of a mechanism for monitoring the network condition and estimating the appropriate transmission rate for multicast multimedia data in one multicast stream, in order to satisfy most the heterogeneous group of receivers. The most prominent feature of the proposed adaptive multicast transmission mechanism is that the proposed mechanism provides the most satisfaction to the group of receivers, with the current network condition, and at the same time is trying to have "friendly" behavior to other network applications. In addition, the network monitoring capabilities, of the proposed mechanism, is based on a combination of parameters in order to determine the network conditions. Moreover, all the required modules for the implementation of the adaptive transmission mechanism are located on the server side only. This means, that any application, which is compatible with the transmission of multimedia data through RTP sessions (for example mbone tools) can access our service and benefit from its adaptive transmission characteristics.

The multicast transmission of multimedia data over the Internet has to accommodate receivers with heterogeneous data reception capabilities. To accommodate heterogeneity, the sender application may transmit one multicast stream and determine the transmission rate that satisfy most the receivers ([3], [1], [16], [9], [13]), may transmit at multiple multicast streams with different transmission rates and allocate receivers at each stream ([8], [5]) or may use layered encoding and transmit each layer to a different multicast stream ([11], [4], [20]). An interesting survey of techniques for multicast multimedia data over the Internet is presented in paper [10]. It is important for adaptive real time applications to have "friendly" behavior to the dominant transport protocols of today's Internet [7]. Paper [14] presents an end-to-end rate-based congestion control mechanism for the transmission of real time data in the Internet, which follows the macroscopic behavior of TCP.

The subject of adaptive multicast of multimedia data over networks with the use of one multicast stream has engaged researchers all over the world. During the adaptive multicast transmission of multimedia data in a single multicast stream, the sender application must select the transmission rate that satisfies most the receivers with the current network conditions. Three approaches can be found in the literature for the implementation of the adaptation protocol in a single stream multicast mechanism: equation based [13], network feedback based ([3], [1], [16], [9]) or based on a combination of the above two approaches [17]. I. Busse et al. in [3] select the appropriate transmission rate based on the percentage of the receivers that are congested and the percentage of the receivers that are loaded. D. Sisalem in [16] proposes the Loss Based Adjustment (LBA) mechanism for selecting the appropriate transmission rate. The LBA mechanism is using the number of receivers (among other parameters) in order to select the appropriate transmission rate. D. Sisalem et al. in [17] extend the LBA mechanism in order to use an equation based adaptation mechanism, except of the network feedback based adaptation mechanism. H. Smith et al. in [18] propose the Target Bandwidth Rate Control (TBRC) mechanism. The

TBRC mechanism is using the dependency of the packets during the multicast transmission (among other parameters) in order to maximize the usable bandwidth for the receivers. T. Jiang et al. in [9] introduce the Receiver Fairness (RF) and the Inter-Receiver Fairness (IRF) functions. The sender application is using the RF and IRF functions in order to determine the rate that satisfy most the group of receivers.

In this paper we present a mechanism for adaptive multicast of multimedia data over networks with the use of one multicast stream based on network feedback. The proposed mechanism is an extension of our work presented in [2]. Paper [2] presents an unicast congestion control mechanism for adaptive multimedia applications. The rest of this paper is organized as follows: In section 2, we give a brief overview of the adaptive multicast transmission mechanism. Section 3 presents the algorithms on which the operation of adaptive multicast transmission mechanism is based. Detailed description of our simulation results is presented in section 4. Finally, section 5 concludes the paper and discusses some of our future work.

2   Overview of Adaptive Multicast Transmission Mechanism

This section gives an overview of the adaptive multicast transmission mechanism operation. We assume that we have a sender application, which transmits multimedia data to a group of n receivers with the use of multicast in one stream. The sender application is using RTP/RTCP protocols for the transmission of the multimedia data. Receivers receive the multimedia data and inform the sender application for the quality of the transmission with the use of RTCP receiver reports. The sender application collects the RTCP receiver reports, analyses them and determines the transmission rate r that satisfy most the group of receivers with the current network conditions.

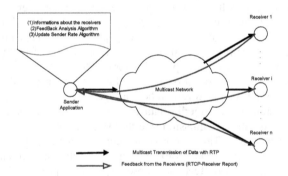

Fig. 1. Architecture of adaptive multicast transmission mechanism

The sender application keeps information about each receiver i, and each time receives one RTCP receiver report from receiver i, estimates the receiver i's preferred transmission rate r_i (which represent the transmission rate that this receiver will prefer if it was the only one receiver in the multicast transmission of the multimedia data). The estimation of receiver i's preferred transmission rate r_i is done with the use of feedback analysis algorithm, which is described in section 3.1. The feedback analysis algorithm is an extension of our work, which is presented in [2].

The sender application uses the IRF and RF_i functions which are presented in [9], in order to determine the transmission rate that satisfy most the group of receivers. RF_i function for the receiver i is defined in [9] as follows:

$$RF_i(r) = \frac{\min(r_i, r)}{\max(r_i, r)} \quad (1)$$

Where r_i is the transmission rate that the receiver i prefers (r_i represents the transmission rate that this receive will prefer, if it was the only one receiver in the multicast transmission of the multimedia data) and r is the transmission rate that the sender application is planning to use. From the equation (1) it is obvious that the RF_i function has values in [0.0, 1.0], and the receiver i is satisfied when the $RF_i \approx 1.0$ and complete satisfied when $RF_i = 1.0$ (when $r_i = r$). The receiver i is not satisfied when the $RF_i \ll 1.0$. Receiver i can encounter dissatisfaction either of packet loss (when $r_i < r$) or of unutilized bandwidth (when $r_i > r$). IRF function for a group of n receivers is defined in [9] as follows:

$$IRF(r) = \sum_{i=1}^{n} a_i * RF_i(r) \quad (2)$$

subject to $\sum_{i=1}^{n} a_i = 1$ and $0 \leq a_i \leq 1.0, i = 1,...,n$.

Where r is the transmission rate that the sender application is planning to use and a_i is the weight of the receiver i to the computation of the IRF value. From the equation (2), it is obvious that for greater values of IRF function the group of receivers is more satisfied and for lesser values of IRF function the group of receivers is less satisfied.

The sender application in repeated time spaces estimates the transmission rate r for the multicast transmission of the multimedia data. The sender application is using as satisfaction measurement the IRF function defined in equation (2) and is usually treating all receivers as equal, which means that the weight a_i for all the receivers $i, i = 1...n$ in IRF function is $a_i = \frac{1}{n}$ [1]. If the sender application wants to treat unequally the group of receivers, can assign priority to some receivers with the use of unequal a_i values. The sender application estimates the transmission rate r for the multimedia data with the use of update sender rate algorithm, which is described in section 3.2. Figure 1 shows the architecture of the proposed adaptive multicast transmission mechanism.

---

[1] The number n of the receivers can easily be computed by the RTCP protocol

3   Algorithms of Adaptive Multicast Transmission Mechanism

This section gives a detailed description of the algorithms on which the operation of adaptive multicast transmission mechanism is based. We present two algorithms: (1) The feedback analysis algorithm which is used for the estimation of receiver i's r_i preferred transmission rate and (2) the update sender rate algorithm which is used for the estimation of sender transmission rate r.

3.1   Feedback Analysis Algorithm - Estimation of Receiver i's r_i Preferred Transmission Rate

Feedback analysis algorithm analyses the feedback information that the receiver i sends to the sender application (with the use of RTCP receiver reports), concerning the transmission quality of the multimedia data. Every time the sender application receives a RTCP receiver report from the receiver i, runs the feedback analysis algorithm in order to estimate the preferred transmission rate r_i, which will satisfy the receiver i. The receiver i's preferred transmission rate r_i represent the transmission rate that this receiver will prefer if it was the only one receiver in the multicast transmission of the multimedia data.

Feedback analysis algorithm is using the values of packet loss rate and the delay jitter from the RTCP receiver report and passes them through the appropriate filters. The use of filters is essential in order to avoid a solely phenomenon to affect the behavior of the feedback analysis algorithm and lead to wrong estimations of the receiver i's preferred transmission rate r_i. More particularly the value of the packet loss rate passes the following filter:

$$LR^i{}_{new} = a * LR^i{}_{old} + (1-a) * LR^i{}_{net} \qquad (3)$$

Where: $LR^i{}_{new}$: The new filtered value of packet loss rate for the receiver i. $LR^i{}_{old}$: The previous filtered value of packet loss rate for the receiver i (When the multicast transmission of the data starts $LR^i{}_{old} = 0$). $LR^i{}_{net}$: The value of the packet loss rate from the RTCP receiver report that the receiver i sent. a: This parameter specifies how aggressive the feedback analysis algorithm will be to the values of the packet loss rate, which receives from the RTCP receiver report. For the parameter a stands $0 \le a \le 1$. The value of the delay jitter passes the following filter:

$$J^i{}_{new} = \beta * J^i{}_{old} + (1-\beta) * J^i{}_{net} \qquad (4)$$

Where: $J^i{}_{new}$: The new filtered value of delay jitter for the receiver i. $J^i{}_{old}$: The previous filtered value of delay jitter for the receiver i (When the transmission of the data starts $J^i{}_{old} = 0$). $J^i{}_{net}$: The value of the delay jitter from the RTCP receiver report that the receiver i sent. β: This parameter specifies how aggressive the feedback analysis module will be to the values of the delay jitter, which receives from the RTCP receiver report. For the parameter β stands $0 \le \beta \le 1$.

We can designate the operation of the feedback analysis algorithm with the appropriate selection of α and β parameters values. The feedback analysis algorithm characterizes the network on the following conditions, based on the filtered values of packet loss rate and delay jitter: (1) Condition congestion: When the network is in congestion condition, the packet loss rate is high and the transmission quality of the data is low. The receiver i encounters dissatisfaction due to packet losses. In this case the receiver i's preferred transmission rate r_i is less than the current transmission rate.

(2) Condition load: When the network is in load condition the transmission quality is good. The packet loss rate is in affordable value, which does not cause problems to the presentation of the multimedia data. The current transmission rate satisfies the receiver i. In this case the receiver i's preferred transmission rate r_i is near to the current transmission rate. (3) Condition unload: When the network is in unload condition either packet losses does not exist or the packet loss rate is very small. The receiver i encounters dissatisfaction due to unutilised bandwidth. In this case receiver i's the preferred transmission rate r_i is more than the current transmission rate.

The changes among the network conditions for the receiver i are based on the filtered values of the packet loss rate and delay jitter concerning this receiver. More particularly, for the packet loss rate we define two values LR_c (congestion packet loss rate) and LR_u (unload packet loss rate), which control the changes among the network conditions based on the following procedure:

$$if\ (LR^i{}_{new} \geq LR_c) \rightarrow congestion$$
$$if\ (LR_u < LR^i{}_{new} < LR_c) \rightarrow load \tag{5}$$

$$if\ (LR^i{}_{new} \leq LR_u) \rightarrow unload$$

The analysis of the filtered delay jitter by the feedback analysis algorithm is based on the fact that abrupt increase of delay jitter may denote that the queues of the routers on the transmission path to receiver i had been overloaded and this may cause congestion to the network during the next moments. Feedback analysis algorithm apprehends the abrupt increase of delay jitter as a precursor of network congestion and set the network condition for receiver i to congestion. More particularly the feedback analysis algorithm uses the following procedure for the analysis of filtered delay jitter:

$$if\ (J^i{}_{new} > \gamma * J^i{}_{old}) \rightarrow congestion \tag{6}$$

Where γ is a parameter, which specifies how aggressive the feedback analysis algorithm will be to the increase of delay jitter. In other words γ specifies quantitatively the expression "abrupt increase of delay jitter".

In order to estimate the new value of the receiver i's preferred transmission rate r_i, we use the following procedure:

$$if\ (network = unload) \rightarrow r_{i-new} = r_{i-old} + R_{increase}$$
$$if\ (network = load) \rightarrow r_{i-new} = r_{i-old} \tag{7}$$

$$if\ (network = congestion) \rightarrow r_{i-new} = r_{i-old} * (1 - LR^i_{new})$$

$$r_{i-old} = r_{i-new}$$

Where: r_{i-new} : The new value of the receiver i's preferred transmission rate r_i. r_{i-old} : The old value of the receiver i's preferred transmission rate r_i. $R_{increase}$: The factor with which the sender application increases the transmission rate in the case of available bandwidth.

When the network condition of receiver i is unload, we increase the preferred transmission rate r_i by adding a factor $R_{increase}$, in order to decrease the dissatisfaction of receiver i due to unutilized bandwidth. When the network condition of receiver i is congested, the preferred transmission rate r_i is reduced by multiplying with the factor $1 - LR^i_{new}$ (which means that we set the receiver i's preferred transmission rate r_i to be the maximum transmission rate that will not cause packet losses to the receiver i), in order to decrease the dissatisfaction of receiver i due to packet losses. When the network condition of receiver i is load we do not change the receiver i's preferred transmission rate r_i, because the receiver i is satisfied with the current transmission rate. In addition the preferred transmission rate r_i of the receiver i cannot be greater than a value r max and cannot smaller than a value r min. The values of r max and r min depends on the network and application type.

The operation and the behavior of the feedback analysis algorithm are influenced by the parameters, which are used ($\alpha, \beta, \gamma, LR_c, LR_u, R_{increase}$). The choice of the above parameters depends on the network and the kind of the dominant traffic in it. The appropriate parameters for each network can be defined through a series of experiments and simulations. From our simulations, we found some values that tune the behavior of the feedback analysis algorithm: $\alpha = 0.75$, $\beta = 0.8$, $\gamma = 2$, $LR_c = 0.055$, $LR_u = 0.01$ and $R_{increase} = 50.000bps$. More information about the tuning of the above parameters can be found in [2].

3.2   Update Sender Rate Algorithm - Estimation of Sender Transmission Rate r

The sender application in repeated time spaces estimates the transmission rate r for multicast the multimedia data with the use of update sender rate algorithm. The estimation of the sender application transmission rate r is aiming to increase the satisfaction of the group of receivers based on the satisfaction measurement that the function IRF of equation (2) provides. When the sender application estimates the new transmission rate r tries to provide to the group of receivers the better satisfaction that the current network conditions can provide.

The update sender rate algorithm is using an Additive Increase Multiplicative Decrease (AIMD) mechanism in order to estimate the new transmission rate r. This algorithm is similar to the algorithm that the TCP rate control uses [19]. We chose an algorithm similar to TCP's rate control algorithm for fairness reasons to the allocation of network resources (like bandwidth), especially during network congestion periods.

When the sender application is estimating the new transmission rate r, it has three opportunities: (1) To increase the transmission rate by adding a factor, $R_{increase}$ (r_{incr}). (2) To keep the previous transmission rate (r_{stay}). (3) To decrease the transmission rate by multiplying with a factor less that 1, $R_{decrease}$ (r_{dcr}).

The update sender rate algorithm is selecting as new transmission rate r, the transmission rate r from { r_{incr} , r_{stay} , r_{dcr} } which provides the most satisfaction to the group of receivers, which means the transmission rate r from { r_{incr} , r_{stay} , r_{dcr} } that has the greater *IRF* value. In addition the update sender rate algorithm is updating the old value of the preferred transmission rates of all the receivers in order the feedback analysis algorithm to be aware of the current transmission rate. Here is the summary of the update sender rate algorithm operation:

$$r_{incr} = r_{old} + R_{increase}$$
$$r_{stay} = r_{old}$$
$$r_{dcr} = r_{old} * R_{decrease}$$
$$r_{new} = MaxIFR_{r=r_{incr},r_{stay},r_{dcr}}[IFR(r)]$$
$$receiver - i_{i=1..n} : r_{i-old} = r_{new}$$

$$r_{old} = r_{new}$$

(8)

Where r_{new} is the new transmission rate of the sender application, and r_{old} is the previous transmission rate of the sender application. In addition the transmission rate r_{new} cannot be greater than a value r max and cannot smaller than a value r min. The values of r max and r min depends on the network and application type.

The update sender rate algorithm does not take directly into account the current network condition, during the estimation of new transmission rate r_{new} for the sender application. The current network conditions are taken directly into account by the feedback analysis algorithm, during the estimation of receivers' preferred transmission rates r_i. Because the values of the receivers' preferred transmission rates r_i are involved to the calculation of $IFR(r)$ the update sender rate algorithm takes indirectly into account the current network conditions. The simulation that we made (Section 4) shows that the approach of update sender rate algorithm to take in account the satisfaction of the receivers directly and to take in account the current network condition indirectly work well.

With the above described procedure the transmission rate of the sender application is always set to the value that satisfy most the group of receivers with the current network conditions. In our simulations we use the following values for the parameters of the update sender rate algorithm: r max $= 2.000.000bps$, r min $= 200.000bps$, $R_{increase} = 50.000bps$ and $R_{decrease} = 0.75$.

4   Simulations

In this section, we present a number of simulations that we made in order to analyze the behavior of the adaptive multicast transmission mechanism. Primary aims of the simulations were the study of adaptive multicast transmission mechanism fairness regarding the group of receivers and mechanism's behavior regarding the dominant traffic model of today's Internet (TCP and UDP traffic). We implemented our mechanism and run simulations in the LBNL network simulator ns-2 ([12]). We run three simulations: (1) Multicast transmission of adaptive multimedia in heterogeneous receivers. (2) Multicast transmission of adaptive multimedia in heterogeneous receivers and UDP traffic at the same time. (3) Multicast transmission of adaptive multimedia in heterogeneous receivers and TCP traffic at the same time. During all the simulations we used the following values for the parameters of our algorithms:
$\alpha = 0.75$, $\beta = 0.8$, $\gamma = 2$, $LR_c = 0.055$, $LR_u = 0.01$, $r\max = 2.000.000bps$,

$r\min = 200.000bps$, $R_{increase} = 50.000bps$, $R_{decrease} = 0.75$ and $a_i = \dfrac{1}{n}$, $i, i = 1...n$ where

n is the number of the receivers. During our simulations we had 20 receivers.

4.1   Simulation One: Multicast Transmission of Adaptive Multimedia in Heterogeneous Receivers

In this simulation we investigate the behavior of the adaptive multicast transmission mechanism and its capability to treat with fairness a heterogeneous group of receivers. Figure 2 shows the topology of this simulation. The bandwidth of each link is given to the simulation topology and varies from 0.5 Mbps to 2.0 Mbps. All the links in the simulation topology have delay 10 ms and they use the drop-tail[2] (FIFO) policy to their queue. In addition, all the links in the simulation topology are full duplex. During this simulation, we have one sender application (S) that multicast multimedia data to a group of 20 receivers (R1 to R20) with the use of the adaptive multicast transmission mechanism. Receivers R1 to R10 are connected to router n2 and receivers R11 to R20 are connected to router n3. The receivers transmit RTCP receivers reports with the use of the RTCP adaptive feedback mechanism and the sender application runs the update sender rate algorithm every 1 second. We run this simulation for 100 seconds and the sender application starts transmitting data with transmission rate of 1.5 Mbps.

Figure 3 shows the sender application transmission rate and the values of IRF function. When the sender application starts transmitting data with transmission rate 1.5 Mbps all the receivers, except R1, R2, R3, R11 and R12, encounter dissatisfaction due to packet losses because their available bandwidth is less than 1.5 Mbps. The sender application starts reducing the transmission rate in order to treat with fairness all the receivers. The sender application reduces its transmission rate near to 0.6 Mbps (5th second). In this point, the dissatisfaction that the "fast" receivers (for example R1 or R9) encounter due to unutilized bandwidth is more that the dissatisfaction that the "slow" (for example R4 or R12) receivers encounter due to

---

[2] Drop-tail is the most common queue policy to Internet routers.

packets losses. The sender application starts increasing the transmission rate in order to treat with fairness all the receivers. At 15th second the transmission rate of the sender application is stabilized near to 1.0 Mbps and the sender application keeps this transmission rate until the end of the simulation. At 15th second the sender application has found the transmission rate that satisfy most the group of receivers with the current network conditions. In addition from 15th second to 100th second the value of *IRF* function is stable because the sender application does not change its transmission rate.

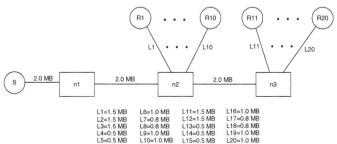

L1=1.5 MB	L6=1.0 MB	L11=1.5 MB	L16=1.0 MB
L2=1.5 MB	L7=0.8 MB	L12=1.5 MB	L17=0.8 MB
L3=1.5 MB	L8=0.8 MB	L13=0.5 MB	L18=0.8 MB
L4=0.5 MB	L9=1.0 MB	L14=0.5 MB	L19=1.0 MB
L5=0.5 MB	L10=1.0 MB	L15=0.5 MB	L20=1.0 MB

Fig. 2. Topology of simulation one

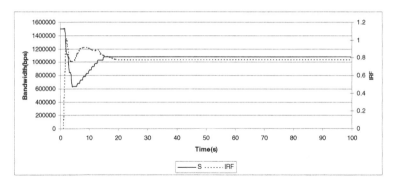

Fig. 3. Sender application bandwidth and IRF function values of simulation one

The adaptive multicast transmission mechanism behaves well: after some time the sender application finds the transmission rate that satisfy most the group of receivers and keeps that transmission rate while the network conditions are not changed. In addition the value of transmission rate (~ 1.0 Mbps) that satisfy most the group of receivers is the expected due to the fact that the most of the receivers prefer transmission rate of 1.0 Mbps.

4.2   Simulation Two: Multicast Transmission of Adaptive Multimedia in Heterogeneous Receivers and UDP Traffic at the Same Time

In this simulation, we transmit at the same time multimedia data with the use of the adaptive multicast transmission mechanism and UDP traffic. During this simulation, we investigate the behavior of the adaptive multicast transmission mechanism during network congestion produced by a greedy UDP traffic. Figure 4 shows the topology of this simulation. The topology of this simulation is the same with the topology of simulation one, except for that we have added two nodes A and B connected to router n1 and router n3 respectively. We have again one sender application (S) that multicast multimedia data to a group of 20 receivers (R1 to R20) with the use of the adaptive multicast transmission mechanism. Receivers R1 to R10 are connected to router n2 and receivers R11 to R20 are connected to router n3. In order to produce UDP traffic, we attach to node A, a CBR (Constant Bit Rate) traffic generator (CBR-Source), which transmits data to a CBR-Receiver attached to node B. The CBR-Source produces UDP traffic with constant transmission rate of 1.5 Mbps. The receivers transmit RTCP receivers reports with the use of the RTCP adaptive feedback mechanism and the sender application runs the update sender rate algorithm every 1 second. We run this simulation for 100 seconds and the sender application starts transmitting data with transmission rate of 1.5 Mbps. The CBR-Source starts the transmission of the data at 30th second, and stops the transmission of the data at 70th second.

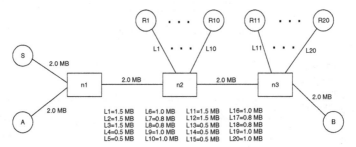

Fig. 4. Topology of Simulations two

In this simulation the sender application except of treat with fairness the group of receivers, it must share the bandwidth of the congested links between the router n1, n2 and between router n2, n3 with the CBR-Source, when the CBR-Source transmits data. Figure 5 shows the sender application transmission rate, the CBR-Receiver bandwidth and the values of *IRF* function. The sender application finds the transmission rate that satisfies most the group of receivers (15th second) after some instability in the transmission rate. When the transmission of UDP traffic starts (at 30th second), congestion occurs to links between the router n1, n2 and between router n2, n3. The receivers prefer smaller transmission rates due to congestion condition, and the sender application reduces its transmission rate near to 0.5Mbps and keeps this transmission rate for the next 40 seconds, during which the transmission of UDP traffic takes place. When the transmission of UDP traffic stops (70th second), the sender application gradually reserves again the available bandwidth. The value of *IRF* function is stable when the transmission rate of the sender application is stable, and floats between 0.77 and 0.97 when the transmission of UDP traffic takes place. The *IRF* function has higher values, when the transmission of the UDP traffic takes place, because all the receivers encounter packet losses due to congested links between the router n1, n2 and between router n2, n3 and all the receivers are satisfied with the small transmission rate that the sender application selects.

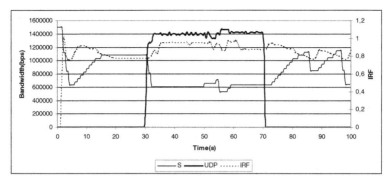

Fig. 5. Sender application bandwidth, UDP-Receiver bandwidth and IRF function values of simulation two

It is obvious from Figure 5 that the proposed mechanism has "friendly" behavior to UDP traffic and good behavior during network congestion condition. When the transmission of UDP traffic starts the sender application reduces its transmission rate and when the transmission of UDP traffic stops the sender application reserves again the available bandwidth.

4.3   Simulation Three: Multicast Transmission of Adaptive Multimedia in Heterogeneous Receivers and TCP Traffic at the Same Time

In this simulation, we transmit at the same time multimedia data with the use of the adaptive multicast transmission mechanism and TCP traffic. During this simulation, we investigate the behavior of adaptive multicast transmission mechanism against TCP traffic. Figure 6 shows the topology of this simulation. The topology of this simulation is the same with the topology of simulation two except for the capacity of some links has changed. We have again one sender application (S) that multicast multimedia data to a group of 20 receivers (R1 to R20) with the use of the adaptive multicast transmission mechanism. Receivers R1 to R10 are connected to router n2 and receivers R11 to R20 are connected to router n3. In order to produce TCP traffic, we connect to node A and B, a FTP server and a FTP client respectively. The FTP server transmits a file to FTP client using "4.3BSD Tahoe TCP" protocol [19]. The receivers transmit RTCP receivers reports with the use of the RTCP adaptive feedback mechanism and the sender application runs the update sender rate algorithm every 1 second. We run this simulation for 100 seconds and the sender application starts transmitting data with transmission rate of 1.5 Mbps. The transmission of the file from the FTP server to FTP client, starts at 30th second and stops at 70th second.

In this simulation, the sender application except of treat with fairness the group of receivers it must share the bandwidth of the congested links between the router n1, n2 and between router n2, n3 with the TCP traffic when the FTP transmission of the file take place. Figure 7 shows the sender application transmission rate, the TCP source bandwidth and the values of *IRF* function. The sender application finds the transmission rate that satisfies most the group of receivers (15th second) after some instability in the transmission rate. When the transmission of TCP source starts (at 30th second), congestion occurs to links between the router n1, n2 and between router n2, n3. The receivers prefer smaller transmission rates due to congestion condition, and the sender application releases bandwidth in order the TCP traffic to use it. In contrast with the previous simulation, the sender application does not keep steady its transmission rate during the 30th and the 70th seconds, when the transmission of TCP traffic takes place. When the transmission of the TCP traffic takes place, the sender application realizes some bandwidth (about 0.3 Mbps) for a while and reserves it again. When the transmission of TCP traffic stops (70th second) the sender application gradually reserves again the available bandwidth. The value of *IRF* function is stable when the transmission rate of the sender application is stable and floats between 0.79 and 0.90 when the transmission of TCP traffic takes place, because the transmission of TCP traffic produce instability to the adaptation mechanism and the sender application changes continually its transmission rate.

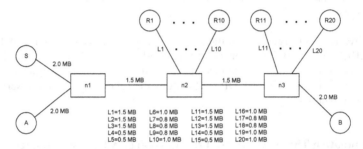

Fig. 6. Topology of Simulations three

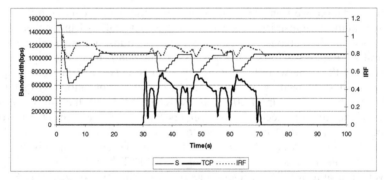

Fig. 7. Sender application bandwidth, TCP source bandwidth and IRF function values of simulation three

It is obvious from Figure 7 that the behavior our mechanism to TCP traffic is not so "friendly" as the behavior to UDP traffic. The sender application would have ideal behavior if it reduces its transmission rate and keeps it steady while the transmission of TCP traffic takes place. Nevertheless, the TCP traffic has transmission rate of more than 0.5 Mbps many times and maximum transmission rate of 0.8Mbps during the simulation, which is good performance for TCP transmission. In addition, the sender application many times realizes bandwidth and provides it to TCP source and in one case (32nd second) the sender application realizes 0.3 Mbps of its bandwidth.

5   Conclusion - Future Work

In this paper, we present a mechanism for multicast transmission of adaptive multimedia data in a heterogeneous group of receivers. We are concentrating to the design of a mechanism for monitoring the network condition and estimating the appropriate rate for the transmission of the multimedia data in order to treat with fairness the receivers. In addition, we investigate the behavior of the proposed mechanism against the dominant transport protocols of today's Internet (TCP and UDP). The proposed mechanism uses RTP/RTCP protocols for the transmission of multimedia data. Through a number of simulations, we draw the following conclusions: (1) The proposed mechanism treats with fairness the group of receivers. (2) The proposed mechanism has "friendly" behavior both to UDP and TCP traffic streams.

Our future work includes the improvement of the proposed mechanism's behavior against TCP traffic. In addition we will investigate the behavior of the proposed mechanism during the multicast transmission in very large group of receivers. The multicast transmission in very large group of receivers encounters the feedback implosion problem ([1]). Furthermore, we will investigate the scalability of proposed mechanism and how the proposed mechanism will deal with the feedback implosion problem. Moreover, we plan to extend the proposed mechanism with the use of multicast in multiple streams in order to treat with more fairness a heterogeneous group of receivers.

References

1. Bolot, J. C., Turletti, T., Wakeman, I. Scalable feedback control for multicast video distribution in the internet. In Proceedings of SIGCOMM 1994, pages 139--146, London, England, August 1994. ACM SIGCOMM.
2. Bouras, Ch., Gkamas, A., Streaming Multimedia Data With Adaptive QoS Characteristics, Protocols for Multimedia Systems 2000, Cracow, Poland, October 22-25, 2000, pp 129-139.
3. Busse, I., Deffner, B., Schulzrinne, H. Dynamic QoS control of multimedia applications based on RTP, Computer Communications, Jan. 1996.
4. Chang Y.C., Messerschmitt D., Adaptive layered video coding for multi-time scale bandwidth fluctuations, submitted to IEEE Journal on Selected Areas in Communications.
5. Cheung, S. Y., Ammar, M., Xue, L. On the Use of Destination Set Grouping to Improve Fariness in Multicast Video Distribution, In proceedings of INFOCOM 96, March 1996, San Fransisco. Georgia Tech, College of Computing, Technical Report GIT-CC-95-25 July 1995.
6. Diot, C. On QoS & Traffic Engineering and SLS-related Work by Sprint, Workshop on Internet Design for SLS Delivery, Tulip Inn Tropen, Amsterdam, The Netherlands, 25 - 26 January 2001.
7. Floyd, S. Fall, K. Promoting the Use of End-to-End Congestion Control in the Internet, Submitted to IEEE/ACM Transactions on Networking, 1998.
8. Jiang, T., Zegura, E. W., Ammar, M. Inter-receiver fair multicast communication over the internet. In Proceedings of the 9th International Workshopon Network and Operating Systems Support for Digital Audio and Video (NOSSDAV) , pages 103--114, June 1999.
9. Jiang, T., W., Ammar, Zegura, E. M. Inter-Receiver Fairness: A Novel Performance Measure for Multicast ABR Sessions. SIGMETRICS 1998: 202-211

10. Li, X., Ammar, M. H., Paul, S. Video Multicast over the Internet IEEE Network Magazine, April 1999
11. McCanne, S., Jacobson, V. Receiver-driven layered multicast. 1996 ACM Sigcomm Conference, pages 117--130, August 1996.
12. McCanne, S., Floyd, S.The UCB/LBNL network simulator, software online. http://www.isi.edu/nsnam/ns/
13. Pandhye, J., Kurose, J., Towsley, D., Koodli, R. A model based TCP-friendly rate control protocol, Proc. International Workshop on Network and Operating System Support for Digital Audio and Video (NOSSDAV), Basking Ridge, NJ, June 1999.
14. Rejaie, R., Handley, M., Estrin, D. RAP: An end-to-end rate-based congestion control mechanism for real time streams in the Internet, Proc. IEEE Infocom, March 1999.
15. Shculzrinne, H., Casner, Frederick, Jacobson, "RTP: A Transport Protocol for Real-Time Applications", RFC 1889, IETF, January 1996.
16. Sisalem, D. Fairness of adaptive multimedia applications. ICC '98. 1998 IEEE International Conference on Communications. Conference Record. Affiliated with SUPERCOMM'98 IEEE, 1998. p.891-5 vol.2. 3 vol. xxxvii+1838 pp
17. Sisalem, D., Wolisz, A. LDA+ TCP-Friendly Adaptation: A Measurement and Comparison Study, in the 10th International Workshop on Network and Operating Systems Support for Digital Audio and Video (NOSSDAV'2000), June 25-28, 2000, Chapel Hill, NC, USA.
18. Smith, H., Mutka, M., Rover, D. A Feedback based Rate Control Algorithm for Multicast Transmitted Video Conferencing, Accepted for publication in the Journal of High Speed Networks.
19. Stevens, W., TCP Slow Start, Congestion Avoidance, Fast Retransmit and Fast Recovery Algorithms, RFC 2001, January 1997
20. Vickers, B. J., Albuquerque, C. V. N., Suda, T. Adaptive Multicast of Multi-Layered Video: Rate-Based and CreditBased Approaches, Proc. of IEEE Infocom , March 1998

Bandwidth Measurements of ALM Trees for Content Distribution

Rui J. Lopes*, Laurent Mathy, and David Hutchison

Lancaster University, Computing Department
{lopes, laurent, dh}@comp.lancs.ac.uk

Abstract. The use of Application Level Multicast (ALM) is extremely promising for content distribution. For these applications appropriate cost functions for deciding between different ALM tree configurations are required, and for these cost functions bandwidth measurement mechanisms are most likely to be important. Existing end-to-end measurement techniques cannot address several ALM and network topology scenarios. Enhancing existing techniques with cooperation mechanisms allows them to cope with the specificity of ALM, namely with transport link sharing. Simulation results indicate that these techniques can produce estimates with reasonable accuracy.

1 Motivations

Application Level Multicast (ALM), also known as host-based distribution, is a technique that may be used to provide multicast distribution services in situations where no support is provided by the network for multicast. This situation occurs, for instance, when the network infrastructure does not support the IP-multicast routing protocols. Another advantage resulting from implementing multicast at the application layer for content distribution is that it allows individual control and flexibility for each connection (e.g., content filtering [14] or transcoding [1]) while keeping multicast bandwidth efficiency [13].

A key aspect in ALM is the strategy adopted for building its spanning tree. In the proposed method, for each new ALM node that joins the tree a cost function is recursively computed for all possible "local topologies". The ALM tree is then shaped to the least costly configuration. Due to the nature of ALM the measurement mechanisms involved in cost estimation should not depend neither from knowledge of the transport network nor from cooperation of its nodes. These cost functions are likely to be application dependent and possibly based on different metrics. For content distribution applications cost functions based on network bandwidth measurements are highly likely.

Well known end-to-end bandwidth measurement techniques exist, both for unicast and network layer multicast scenarios. However, these techniques cannot address scenarios where ALM tree branches share network links. The bandwidth

---

* Rui J. Lopes is the recipient of a PhD grant (PRAXIS XXI) from the Portuguese Science and Technology Ministry (MCT)

M.J. van Sinderen and L.J.M. Nieuwenhuis (Eds.): PROMS 2001, LNCS 2213, pp. 89–102, 2001.

measurement techniques proposed in this paper overcome these limitations using cooperation mechanisms between different ALM measurement processes/agents.

In Section 2 the generic ALM architecture and the specific aspects of its application to content distribution are presented. Particular attention is devoted to link bandwidth share by different ALM tree branches, namely the need for end-to-end measurement mechanisms that take this into account. In the following section existing end-to-end measurement techniques are described and is justified why these cannot cope with the bandwidth related specificities of ALM. In Section 4.2 these mechanisms are tested using simulation. The results obtained indicate that these techniques can provide estimates with reasonable accuracy. This paper concludes by discussing implementation aspects of the proposed techniques and pointing relevant related research issues for future study.

2   ALM Architecture

2.1   Generic ALM Architecture

With ALM, an overlay structure is dynamically built by, and between, interested applications. Also, because the purpose of this overlay structure is multicast content distribution, it is natural to build it as a spanning tree. Each end system that participates in the multicast group is then responsible for forwarding received data to all other ALM entities connected to it in the tree. The advantage of performing data forwarding at the application level is that each end system may be programmed to either passively retransmit every single piece of data it receives or actively filter data according to some specific logic (for instance, upstream traffic may be aggregated to avoid the source implosion problem, while downstream traffic may be filtered to adapt to the link congestion or the actual computing power of downstream receivers).

Building an overlay tree among hosts presents a significant challenge. To be deployable in practice, the process of building the tree should not rely on any network support that is not already ubiquitous. Furthermore, to ensure fast and easy deployment, the method should avoid having to rely on "its own infrastructure" (e.g. servers, "application-level" routing protocols, etc.), since the acceptance and deployment of such infrastructure could hamper the deployment of the protocol relying on it. Consequently, one of our major requirements was to design a tree building control protocol that operate between end-systems exclusively, and considers the network as a "black-box". End-systems can only gain "knowledge" about the network through host-to-host measurement samples.

From a scalability point of view, it is also unrealistic to design a method where pre-requisite knowledge of the full group membership is needed before the spanning tree can be computed. This is especially true in the context of multicast sessions with dynamic group membership. For robustness and efficiency, as well as scalability, it is also preferable to avoid making use of a centralised algorithm.

Our goal was therefore to design a distributed method which builds a spanning tree among the hosts of a multicast session without requiring any particular interactions with network routers nor any knowledge of the network topology, and which does so with only partial knowledge of the group membership.

The distributed method we have designed [12] is based on a simple "recursive" algorithm that takes into account, at each iteration, a parent node (P), its existing children (C_i – whose number is limited by the parent) and a "new comer" node (N) joining the subtree rooted P. Briefly, P evaluates all possible "local topologies" involving these nodes. These topologies are

- the topology where N is accepted as a child of P
- the topologies resulting from "redirecting" N to join any of the subtrees rooted at the C_is
- any of the topologies resulting from accepting N as a child and "sending" any of the C_is to join the subtree rooted at any other C_i or N.

The best topology is then selected according to a cost function whose input is a full matrix of host-to-host measurement samples taken between all the above mentioned "local" entities.

2.2   ALM for Content Distribution

Bandwidth measurements. Existing applications of our ALM method have used cost functions based on hop-count or delay metrics. Although, in the context of content distribution it is highly desirable that the cost functions used for ALM tree configuration are based on bandwidth measurements. Examples of these are cost functions that do not allow any branch in the ALM tree to have a bottleneck bandwidth or available bandwidth smaller than a certain threshold, or cost functions which lead to an ALM tree configuration that minimizes the consumption of available bandwidth.

Regardless of the particular application and respective cost functions, the bottleneck bandwidth is a fundamental end-to-end quantity given that is reflects the *absolute maximum* data rate that an application can expect to achieve. This quantity is also a starting point in many techniques for estimating the available bandwidth, which is the bottleneck bandwith minus the bandwidth currently being used by other applications. The end-to-end measurement techniques described in the core of this paper, Section 4, address this estimation problem in the context of application layer multicast.

Link sharing between ALM branches. In the context of ALM, there are two relevant aspects that require different bottleneck bandwidth estimation techniques.

The first aspect concerns each ALM tree path when considered individually. In this case, the bottleneck estimation techniques described in Section 3 are adequate. The subject of this measurements is the unicast connection in the transport network that is establish between each parent and child in the ALM tree. A second aspect concerns the "interference" effects that may occur between flows from different ALM tree branches, namely due to link sharing in the transport network. Figure 1 represents three different examples of ALM tree and transport network topologies where link sharing occurs.

In the case illustrated in Figure 1a the two sibling nodes C_0 and C_1 share the same links in the transport network between nodes S and N. In this case, where there is a common source, the occurrence of link sharing can be foretold from the ALM tree structure. Assuming that $C_{S\to N}$, $C_{N\to C_0}$ and $C_{N\to C_1}$ represent respectively the bottleneck bandwidth between nodes S-N, N-C_0 and N-C_1 the bottleneck bandwidth that is associated to branches S-C_0 and S-C_1 is defined by $C_{S\to C_0} = min\left(\frac{C_{S\to N}}{2}, C_{N\to C_0}\right)$ and $C_{S\to C_1} = min\left(\frac{C_{S\to N}}{2}, C_{N\to C_1}\right)$. The term $\frac{C_{S\to N}}{2}$ in both equations reflects the sharing of links in between nodes S and N.

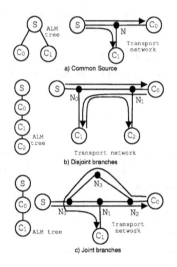

Fig. 1. Link sharing

In the case illustrated in Figure 1b the two different ALM tree branches S-C_0 and C_1-C_2 share the same links in the transport network between nodes N_0 and N_1. In this case the presence of sharing cannot be foretold from the ALM tree structure, and there are no common ALM nodes between these branches (i.e., they are disjoint). Assuming that $C_{S\to N_0}$, $C_{N_0\to C_1}$, $C_{N_0\to N_1}$, $C_{N_1\to C_2}$, and $C_{N_1\to C_0}$ represent respectively the bottleneck bandwidth between nodes S-N_0, N_0-C_1, N_0-N_1, N_1-C_2 and N_1-C_0, the bottleneck bandwidth associated to branches S-C_0 and C_1-C_2 is defined by:

$$C_{S\to C_0} = min\left(C_{S\to N_0}, \frac{C_{N_0\to N_1}}{2}, C_{N_1\to C_0}\right),$$

$$C_{C_1\to C_2} = min\left(C_{C_1\to N_0}, \frac{C_{N_0\to N_1}}{2}, C_{N_1\to C_2}\right).$$

In the case illustrated in Figure 1c the two different ALM tree branches S-C_0 and C_1-C_2 share the same links in the transport network between nodes N_0 and N_1. In this case the presence of sharing cannot be foretold from the ALM tree structure and the middle ALM node is common to the two branches (i.e., they are joint). It can be proven that link sharing in this case can only occur if routing in the underlying transport network is asymmetric. For this case, the bottleneck bandwidth associated to branches S-C_0 and C_0-C_1 is defined by:

$$C_{S\to C_0} = min\left(C_{S\to N_0}, \frac{C_{N_0\to N_1}}{2}, C_{N_1\to N_2}, C_{N_2\to C_0}\right) \text{ and },$$

$$C_{C_0\to C_1} = min\left(C_{C_0\to N_2}, C_{N_2\to N_3}, C_{N_3\to N_0}, \frac{C_{N_0\to N_1}}{2}, C_{N_1\to C_1}\right).$$

The end-to-end measurement techniques proposed in the core of this paper, Section 4, aim at estimating these quantities for the link sharing scenarios illustrated above. These techniques are designed in order to cope with the particular aspects of ALM and result from modifications introduced in well known end-to-end measurement techniques (described briefly in Section 3).

3   End-to-End Measurements

There are mainly two approaches for tackling the problem of estimating bandwidth constrains from network links. The first approach relies on knowledge about the transport network, namely its topology, capacity and traffic at each link. These techniques assume cooperation in the estimation process from nodes in the transport network. A second approach relies solely on end-to-end measurements. This latter approach has been adopted for ALM in the context of content distribution. The rationale for this steams mainly from the nature of ALM. On one hand, on the fact that the several components of the protocol make no assumption on the nature of the underlying transport protocols nor rely on the cooperation of the transport network nodes. On the other hand on the fact that the ALM protocol is implemented at the applications layer and hosted at nodes on the network edge terminals (i.e., the ALM nodes) where the bandwidth measurement protocol components can be easily integrated.

End-to-end measurement techniques based on the packet pair principle have been used, both in the context of unicast and network layer multicast, for the estimation of two important network path characteristics: bottleneck bandwidth and available bandwidth. In this paper several improvements to these techniques are presented for measurements required in application layer multicast. These improvements focus on measuring shared bottleneck bandwidth.

3.1   End-to-End Unicast Measurements

The packet pair principle (PP) has been used for end-to-end bandwidth estimatives, namely for purposes of traffic control [2]. The packet pair principle is based on the fact that the time interval at the bottleneck link between two probe packets, sent back to back, is kept in higher capacity links (see Figure 2). That is, if L and C are respectively the probe size and the bottleneck link capacity then the interarrival time, d, at the receiver between the two probes is $d = \frac{L}{C}$.

The major problems with the estimates' accuracy result from the presence of background traffic [6]. The two possible effects of background traffic are overestimates due to queuing, or underestimates due to inter-

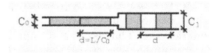

Fig. 2. Packet pair principle

leaving. In order to mitigate these effects the use of batches of probes and the use of different probe sizes has been proposed [4][9].

Inadequacy of unicast end-to-end measurements for ALM. Using this technique the effects of eventual link sharing cannot be fully observed or estimated. This is due to the lack of cooperation between individual estimation processes. When estimating the bottleneck bandwidth in two ALM tree branches that share one or more links, either the probes associated with these processes do not mix at the shared link(s); or if they do, it is hard to distinguish the effects of this link sharing from background traffic.

3.2   End-to-End Multicast Measurements

Similar techniques have been used in the context of network layer multicast. These aim generally at characterising the internal network behaviour (network tomography) [11], namely on estimating its loss [3], delay [7] characteristics and multicast tree configuration [10]. The estimation of bottleneck bandwidth is addressed in [10] but not taking into account the effects of link sharing.

These techniques are usually based on computing the correlation between loss and delay measurements performed at the multicast tree leaf nodes.

Inadequacy of multicast end-to-end measurements for ALM. Given the fact that ALM relies on unicast connections between each of the ALM tree nodes, techniques that assume the use of network layer multicast are not adequate. More relevant in the ALM context are variations of these techniques that use unicast probes [8][5]. The main characteristic of these techniques is that they use packet stripes (i.e., packet probes with different destinations are interleaved). The limitations presented by these techniques for ALM result from the fact that they do not consider other type of link sharing than from having a common packet source.

4   End-to-End Measurements for ALM

4.1   Packet Probe Interleaving

This section addresses the estimation of the bottleneck bandwidth on each branch of the ALM tree while taking into account that different branches may share one or more transport links. Namely, the techniques presented aim at estimating the quantities expressed in the equations of Section 2.2.

These techniques are based on the packet pair principle. Through the inclusion of cooperation between the measuring processes associated with different ALM tree branches it is possible to take into account relevant link shares that these branches may have. These cooperation mechanisms are based on probe interleaving. That is, in a stream of probes involved in cooperating estimates, packet probes from/to different sources/destinations are interleaved. The appropriate source/destination choice for each packet in the interleaved packet probe stream guarantees that the measurement obtained at each destination is influenced (in a controlled way) by relevant link sharing with other destinations.

For each of the link sharing examples presented in Section 2.2, a cooperation mechanisms is described as well as its implementation using packet probe interleaving. The use of these mechanisms in several link share scenarios and the corresponding estimates obtained trough simulation are presented in Section 4.2.

Common source link sharing. In the scenario of link sharing between two siblings in the ALM tree, illustrated in Figures 1a and 3, the cooperation mechanisms involved in the bottleneck bandwidth estimation must capture the "interference" effects between flows $S \rightarrow C_0$ and $S \rightarrow C_1$.

The pattern for the probe packet stream that implements this cooperation mechanism results from interleaving probe packets with C_0 and C_1 as destination (see Figure 3).

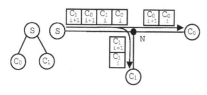

Fig. 3. PP interleaving for common ALM source scenario

Due to this packet interleaving pattern each receiver knows that each probe pair received was interleaved by exactly another packet while traveling trough the shared links. Therefore, if $\frac{C_{S \to N}}{2} < C_{N \to C_0}$ the bottleneck bandwidth estimative obtained at receiver C_0 is $C_{C_0} = \frac{C_{S \to N}}{2}$, thus capturing the flow interference effects from link sharing. The same reasoning applies to the estimatives obtained at receiver C_1.

Disjoint branch link sharing. In the scenario of link sharing between two disjoint branches in the ALM tree, as illustrated in Figures 1b and 4, the cooperation mechanisms involved in the bottleneck bandwidth estimation must capture the "interference" effects between flows $S \to C_0$ and $C_1 \to C_2$.

The pattern for the probe packet stream that implements this cooperation mechanism results from interleaving probe packets with C_0 and C_1 as destination from both S and C_1 (see Figure 4). Due to the fact that there are two packet probe sources (S and C_1), each receiver (C_0 and C_2) cannot know the ex-

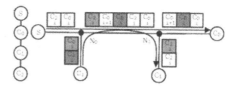

Fig. 4. PP interleaving for disjoint ALM branches scenario

act number of packets that have interleaved between two consecutive packets received.

The possibility of having different interleaving patterns results in several modes on the estimates that each receiver produces. That is, when considering two consecutive probe packets they could have been interleaved by zero, one or two probe packets with the other receiver as destination, thus leading to estimates where the term associated with path $N_0 \to N_1$ is respectively $C_{N_0 \to N_1}, \frac{C_{N_0 \to N_1}}{2}$ and $\frac{C_{N_0 \to N_1}}{3}$, instead of $\frac{C_{N_0 \to N_1}}{2}$.

This degree of uncertainty can be mitigated due to knowledge of the packet probe pattern produced by each sender. Using this knowledge there are a set of rules that can be used to estimate the number of probe packets that interleaved between two consecutive received probe packets. Examples are:

1. In the links between nodes N_0 and N_1, consecutive probe packets with destination $C_0(C_2)$ from source $S(C_1)$ are interleaved by:
   - exactly one probe packet from $S(C_1)$ with destination $C_2(C_0)$, and
   - zero or more probe packets from $C_1(S)$ with destination $C_2(C_0)$.

2. In the links between nodes N_0 and N_1, two consecutive probe packets with destination $C_0(C_2)$ from source S and C_1 (C_1 and S) are interleaved by:
   - zero or one probe packets from S with destination $C_2(C_0)$, and
   - zero or one probe packets from C_1 with destination $C_2(C_0)$.

Heuristics based on these rules are used in Section 4.2 to select appropriate estimate modes.

Joint branch link sharing. In the scenario of link sharing between two joint branches in the ALM tree, as illustrated in Figures 1c and 5, the cooperation mechanisms involved in the bottleneck bandwidth estimation must capture the "interference" effects between flows $S \rightarrow C_0$ and $C_0 \rightarrow C_1$.

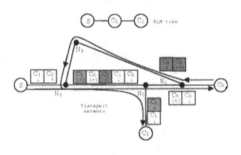

The pattern for the probe packet stream that implements this cooperation mechanism results from interleaving probe packets with C_0 and C_1 as destination from sender S and probes packets from source C_0 with C_1 as destination (see Figure 5). Due to the fact that there are two packet probe sources (S and C_0) the receiver C_1 cannot know the exact number of packets that interleaved between two consecutive

Fig. 5. PP interleaving for joint ALM branches scenario

received packets. Given the similarities with the previous scenario similar rules can be established for this scenario.

4.2   Simulation Results

Simulation configuration. The techniques described in the previous subsection where tested for different scenarios trough simulation using the ns-2 network simulator. The main objects in the simulation are the probe sender and receiver agents, the transport network links and nodes, and background traffic sources. Each transport network node has attached 10 background traffic sources (B_0 to B_9). These are Pareto sources with the traffic shape factor set to 1.9, producing an aggregate background traffic with rate values between 50% and 80% of the links capacity.

Due to the effects of background traffic on the time interval measured between the arrival of consecutive probes the bottleneck bandwidth estimates cannot be based on a single measurement but from a set of packet pairs. These values are grouped into intervals (statistical modes) and the number of measurements inside each interval counted (by a similar process used in [9]). In the case where there is a single probe source the bottleneck bandwidth estimative is obtained from the strongest mode (i.e., the interval comprising the higher number of measurements). In the case of probe flows from more than one source there are several sender/receiver probe mixing patterns (see Section 4.1). Therefore, the estimation method in this case is based on reasoning upon the bandwidth values of the strongest modes using a set of heuristics derived from the probe pattern generated by each sender. These heuristics try to fit the obtained mode values to feasible probe mixing patterns and from this detect if link sharing has occurred or not. From this result and from the bandwidth values of selected modes a final bottleneck bandwidth estimate is computed.

In the following of this section for each of the possible sharing scenarios described in Section 2.2 a simulation configuration and the corresponding estimatives obtained at each receiver are presented. The parameters for each scenario are the bandwidth values (in Kbps) for each link in the transport network. In the graphs presented the x and y axis represent respectively bandwidth values (in bps) and number of measurements inside a bandwidth interval. For the scenarios where there is more than one probe source the different lines correspond to different probe patterns at the receiver (see Figure 6).

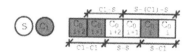

Fig. 6. Probe pattern at C0

Common ALM source link sharing. The simulation configuration for testing the bottleneck estimation in the case of link sharing between ALM tree siblings is represented in Figure 7.

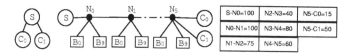

S-N0=100	N2-N3=40	N5-C0=15
NO-N1=100	N3-N4=80	N5-C1=50
N1-N2=75	N4-N5=60	

Fig. 7. Simulation scenario for common ALM source

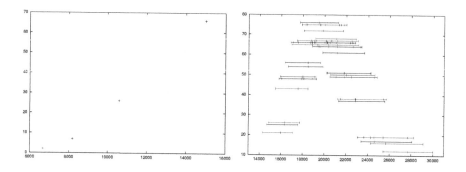

Fig. 8. Simulation results for common ALM source scenario

ALM node S acts as a probe packet source and ALM nodes C_0 and C_1 act as destinations. Given the above parameters the bottleneck bandwidth value for path $S \rightarrow C_0$ and $S \rightarrow C_1$ is respectively $C_{S \rightarrow C_0} = min\left(\frac{40}{2}, 15\right)$ and $C_{S \rightarrow C_1} = min\left(\frac{40}{2}, 50\right)$. That is, the bottleneck for branch $S-C_0$ is not located at a shared link ($N_5 \rightarrow C_0$), whilst for branch $S-C_1$ its bottleneck is due to one of the shared links ($N_2 \rightarrow N_3$). Figure 8 represents the bottleneck bandwidth estimatives obtained at receivers C_0 and C_1. It can be observed that both estimatives have the higher relative frequency modes located within the vicinity of the expected bottleneck bandwidth values (15 and 20Kbps). In the case of branch $S-C_1$ the estimative obtained captures the occurrence of link sharing.

Disjoint ALM branch link sharing. The simulation configuration for testing the bottleneck estimation in the case of link sharing between disjoint ALM tree branches is represented in Figure 9.

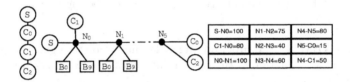

Fig. 9. Simulation scenario for disjoint ALM branches (with sharing)

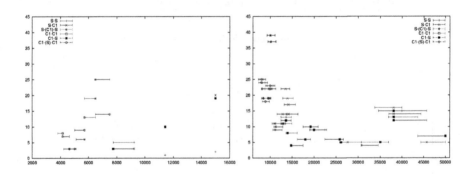

Fig. 10. Simulation results for isjoint ALM branches (with sharing)

In this configuration ALM nodes S and C_1 act as a probe packet sources and ALM nodes C_0 and C_2 act as probe packet destinations. Given the above parameters the bottleneck bandwidth value for paths $S \rightarrow C_0$ and $C_1 \rightarrow C_2$ is respectively $C_{S \rightarrow C_0} = min\left(100, \frac{40}{2}, 15\right)$ and $C_{C_1 \rightarrow C_2} = min\left(100, \frac{40}{2}, 50\right)$, the latter being due to link sharing.

Figure 10 represents the bottleneck bandwidth estimatives obtained at receivers C_0 and C_2. In Figure 10a the strongest modes are located in the vicinity
of bandwidth values 7.5 and 15 Kbps corresponding to two different probe mixing patterns. The fact that there are only two modes indicates that either the
packets from one stream are not interfered by the other probe stream or that
this interference occurs at links that do not constitute a bottleneck. Therefore,
the estimated value for the bottleneck bandwidth for ALM branch $S - C_0$ is
15 Kbps and is not due to any link sharing. In Figure 10b the strongest modes
are found in the vicinity of values 10, 8, 13.3, 40 and 20 Kbps. The bandwidth
values for these modes are only compatible with the hypotesis of occurrence of
link sharing, and the obtained values corresponding to mixing patterns where 3,
4, 2, 0 and 1 probe packets interleave between two probe packets for which the
arrival interval has been measured. More, the bandwitdth value of the shared
link is 40Kbps which corresponds to a 20Kbps value for ALM branch $S - C_2$.

A second simulation scenario, without any link sharing was designed for
testing the branch measurements technique. This is represented in Figure 11.
Given this parameters the bottleneck bandwidth value for paths $S \rightarrow C_0$ and
$C_1 \rightarrow C_2$ is respectively $C_{S \rightarrow C_0} = 15$ and $C_{C_1 \rightarrow C_2} = 40$.

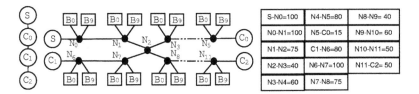

Fig. 11. Simulation scenario for disjoint ALM branches (without sharing)

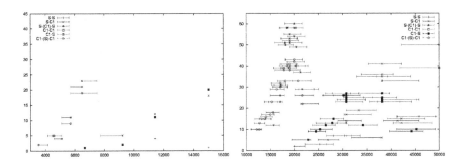

Fig. 12. Simulation results for disjoint ALM branches (without sharing)

The measurements obtained at C_0 for branch $S - C_0$ are similar to the previous scenario (see Figures 12a and 10a), therefore leading to the same results. In Figure 12b it can be observed that the strongest modes correspond to bandwidth values around 20, 40 and 30 Kbps. The only compatible hypothesis with these results considers the existence of two modes[1] , therefore there is no link sharing and the bottleneck bandwidth value for ALM branch $C_1 - C_2$ is 40Kbps.

Joint ALM branch link sharing. The simulation configuration for testing the bottleneck estimation in the case of link sharing between joint ALM tree branches is represented in Figure 13. ALM nodes S and C_0 act as probe packet sources and ALM nodes C_0 and C_1 act as probe packet receivers.

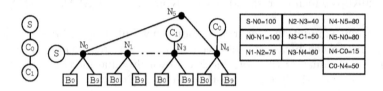

Fig. 13. Simulation results for joint ALM branches

The strongest modes in Figure 14a are found in the vicinity of values 15, 10 and 7.5 Kbps. The only consistent hypotesis for these modes is that the bottleneck bandwidth value for ALM branch $S - C_0$ is 15Kbps, and does not result from any link sharing. In Figure 14b it can be observed that the strongest modes correspond to bandwidth values around 20 and 40Kbps. These values are only compatible with the hypothesis of two modes resulting from sharing a 40Kbps link, therefore the bottleneck bandwidth value for ALM branch $S - C_1$ is 20Kbps .

5   Implementation Issues

Complexity and accuracy. When considering the practical implementation of the techniques described in this paper the issues of accuracy and complexity are paramount. Given that the estimatives are computed using the statistical relative frequencies of each detected mode it is expected that its accuracy will increase with the number of samples. This increase in the number of probe packets has a negative impact on the network traffic and on the required time to obtain the estimates. The latter aspect is quite relevant due to its impact on the latency involved in the ALM *join* process. Use of caching and ALM node clustering can be used to reduce the set of measurements required.

Use of measurements caching is justified by the incremental nature of the ALM tree building process, that is, new ALM nodes *join* the tree and therefore

---

[1] The value 30Kbps results from queuing at link $N_{10} \rightarrow N_{11}$.

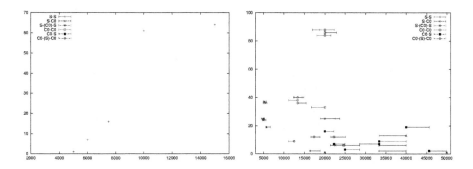

Fig. 14. Simulation results for joint ALM branches

can make use of previous measurements. It is also expected that the bottleneck change rate will be small when compared with typical session durations. Another key aspect of the ALM architecture is the clustering of nodes based on their IP addresses. This can be used to derive heuristics that will reduce the required set of measurements, namely by skipping measurements that investigate the occurrence of link sharing between ALM tree branches in different clusters.

Session measurements. During a content distribution session the measurement techniques presented can be used in what is usually referred to as passive probing. In passive probing, instead of deliberately injecting probe packets in the network, measurements are obtained using the content traffic packets therefore introducing only a very small amount of overhead in the network. This overhead corresponds to timing information and unique identifiers that packet headers must convey for the inter packet arrival measurement process. If RTP and RTCP are used for content streaming this overhead is still further reduced due to the use of appropriate protocol packet fields.

6   Conclusions and Further Work

In this paper several aspects of using ALM for content distribution were discussed. One of these aspects that was particularly emphasised is the need for appropriate cost functions and metrics for deciding between different content distribution overlay trees. Bottleneck bandwidth is one of these fundamental metrics. Differences between ALM and both unicast and network layer multicast lead to the redefinition of this quantity, namely in the presence of link sharing between ALM tree branches. Due to this redefinition existing end-to-end measurement techniques were proven to be inadequate for ALM. The inclusion of cooperation, via probe interleaving, between measurement processes overcomes these limitations. Results obtained from simulation showed that the proposed techniques can estimate the bottleneck bandwidth in the presence of link sharing with an acceptable accuracy.

For a practical implementation, several issues require further study. Among these is the establishment of cost functions for relevant content distribution scenarios, namely taking into account other metrics (e.g., delay, available bandwidth). Other relevant topics of study involve performance and cost evaluations of the proposed techniques in respect to both network (e.g., traffic overhead and connection setup time) and ALM node resources (e.g., CPU and memory).

The authors would like to thank their colleagues Dr. Andrew Scott, Ed Hartley and Stefan Schmid for their valuable comments on this paper.

References

1. Elan Amir, Steven McCanne, and Randy Katz. An active service framework and its application to real-time multimedia transcoding. In *Proc. of the ACM SIG-COMM'98*, Vancouver, BC, Canada, September 1998.
2. J-C. Bolot. End-to-end packet delay and loss behavior in the Internet. *Journal of High-Speed Networks*, 2(3):305–323, December 1993.
3. R. Caceres, N.G. Duffield, J. Horowitz, and D. Towsley. Multicast-based inference of network-internal loss characteristics. *IEEE Trans. on Information Theory*, 45:2462–2480, 1999.
4. R. Carter and M. Crovella. Measuring bottleneck link speed in packet-switched networks. *Performance Evaluation*, 27(8):297–318, October 1996.
5. M.J. Coates and R. Nowak. Network loss inference using unicast end-to-end measurement. In *Proc. of ITC Conference on IP Traffic, Modelling and Management*, Monterey, CA, USA, September 2000.
6. Constantinos Dovrolis, Parameswaran Ramanathan, and David Moore. What do packet dispersion techniques measure? In *Proc. of the IEEE INFOCOM'01*, Anchorage, AK, USA, April 2001.
7. N.G. Duffield and F. Lo Presti. Multicast inference of packet delay variance at interior network links. In *Proc. IEEE INFOCOM'00*, Tel Aviv, Israel, March 2000.
8. Net:LossInferenceE2E:CoNo00 N.G. Duffield, F. Lo Presti, V. Paxson, and D. Towsley. Inferring link loss using striped unicast probes. In Proc. of the IEEE INFOCOM'01, Anchorage, AK, USA, April 2001.
9. Vern Paxson. *Measurements and Analysis of End-to-End Internet Dynamics*. PhD thesis, University of California, Berkeley, April 1997.
10. Sylvia Ratnasamy and Steven McCanne. Inference of multicast routing trees and bottleneck bandwidths using end-to-end measurement. In *Proc. of the IEEE INFOCOM'99*, NewYork, NY, USA, March 1999.
11. Y. Tsang, M.J. Coates, and R. Nowak. Passive network tomography using em algorithms. In *Proc. IEEE International Conference on Acoustics, Speech, and Signal Processing*, May 2001.
12. Rolland Vida, Luis Costa, Serge Fdida, Roberto Canonico, Laurent Mathy, and David Hutchison. Specification of a multicast monomedia protocol. Deliverable 2.1.1, Project IST-1999-10 504 GCAP, January 2001.
13. Dapeng Wu, Yiwei Thomas Hon, Wenwu Zhu, Ya-Qin Zhang, and Jon M. Peha. Streaming video over the internet: Approaches and directions. *IEEE Trans. on Circuits and Systems for Video Technology*, 11(1), February 2001.
14. Nicholas J. Yeadon, Francisco Garcia, David Hutchison, and Doug Shepherd. Filters: QoS support mechanisms for multipeer communications. *IEEE Journal of Selected Areas in Communications*, 14(7):1245–1262, 1996.

GCAP: A New Multimedia Multicast Architecture for QoS

Michel Diaz[1*], Roberto Canonico[2], Luis Costa[3], Serge Fdida[3], David Hutchison[4],
Laurent Mathy[4], Andreas Meissner[5], Stephane Owezarski[1], Rolland Vida[3],
and Lars Wolf[5,6]

[1] LAAS-CNRS, 7 Avenue du Colonel Roche, 31077 Toulouse cedex 4, France
{diaz, sowe}@laas.fr
[2] Università di Napoli Federico II, Dip. di Informatica, Via Claudio 21, 80125 Napoli, Italy
roberto.canonico@unina.it
[3] LIP6 - University of Pierre et Marie Curie, 4, place Jussieu, 75252, Paris Cedex 05, France
{Luis.Costa, Serge.Fdida, Rolland.Vida}@lip6.fr
[4] Lancaster University, Computing Department, Lancaster LA1 4YR, UK
{dh, laurent}@comp.lancs.ac.uk
[5] Fraunhofer IPSI, Dolivostrasse 15, 64293 Darmstadt, Germany
Andreas.Meissner@ipsi.fraunhofer.de
[6] Technical University of Karlsruhe, Zirkel 2, 76128 Karlsruhe, Germany
Lars.Wolf@uni-karlsruhe.de

Abstract. Despite its obvious suitability for distributed multimedia applications, multicasting has not yet found widespread application. Having analyzed shortcomings of today's approaches, we devise in the *GCAP project* a new end-to-end transport architecture for multimedia multicasting that supports partial order and partial reliability. In this paper, we argue that, at the network layer, *single-source multicasting* (PIM-SSM) should be chosen. Consequently, our *Monomedia Multicast* protocol provides, along with reliability and QoS monitoring functionality, an ALM based multicast solution referred to as TBCP *(Tree Building Control Protocol),* to be used as back channel for SSM, e.g. for retransmission requests. On top of the Monomedia protocol, our *Multimedia Multicast* protocol handles multimedia *sessions* composed of multiple monomedia connections: The FPTP *(Fully Programmable Transport Protocol)* allows applications to specify, through its API, the (global) synchronization and (individual) reliability requirements within a multimedia session. Our group management approach is focused on *group integrity*.

1 Introduction

Distributed *multimedia* applications typically require Quality of Service (QoS) support from networks and systems due to their handling of time-critical media such as audio and video. Additionally, in many of such applications, several participants are involved, which makes the use of *multicast* transmission methods attractive in order to save network bandwidth. Unfortunately, due to the management complexity of current multicast protocols, they have not found as widespread a use as expected. The goal of our work within the framework of the *GCAP project* [8] is to address

---

* Corresponding author. Further authors are listed in alphabetical order.

M.J. van Sinderen and L.J.M. Nieuwenhuis (Eds.): PROMS 2001, LNCS 2213, pp. 103-115, 2001.
© Springer-Verlag Berlin Heidelberg 2001

these shortcomings and to provide for QoS support for applications [6], to simplify the development of applications, and to make usable and manageable multicast support available by introducing a *simplified multicast model*.

To address the requirements of multimedia multicast applications, we provide mechanisms to handle and coordinate a set of receivers and a set of time-critical multimedia objects exchanged between many communicating entities. Communication protocols at the transport and higher layers are necessary, e.g. for the transmission of data between the communicating end systems, but also for higher-level coordination functions like group management and integrity (for instance, to ensure that all mandatory group members of a videoconference are available and, hence, group integrity requirements are fulfilled). In today's approaches, such a design and implementation effort is part of the development at the application layer – placing this burden again and again on every application developer and wasting development time, as opposed to an approach where such functionality is provided once and can be reused. Hence, GCAP follows a general approach and proposes the design of new protocols within a new *transport architecture*. Furthermore, it aims to rapidly deploy and to optimize such innovative architectures using an *active network* based approach.

To support multicast, multimedia transport services and protocols for group communication, GCAP adds new functions to the present Internet architecture. There are two ways for realizing this in the IP protocol stack:

1) to design a whole new end-to-end transport protocol to extend the classical UDP/TCP, and to use it as the new end-to-end transport protocol;
2) to introduce, on top of UDP and TCP, a new layer (referred to as the *GCAP transport layer*), to be located between the traditional transport layer and the application layer, to handle the new functions proposed for GCAP.

For ease of implementation and distribution, we have opted to use the latter.

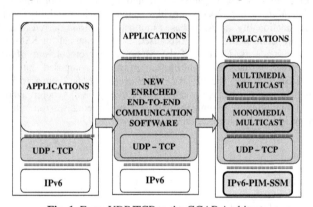

Fig. 1. From UDP/TCP to the GCAP Architecture

The basis of our architecture is the PIM-SSM IPv6 layer where a flow of data is sent from one source to a set of receivers. This set of flows in the networks is called a multicast *channel*. Of course, based on IP, the channel handles datagrammes, without reliability. The second step of GCAP is to provide in a generic way the *reliability* required by different applications. For this reason, the new GCAP transport layer, dedicated to support multimedia multicast applications, has been designed. It consists of two sub-layers, *monomedia multicast* and *multimedia multicast*, able to provide users with a complete set of reliability services. In the first sub-layer, this reliability is designed as a *monomedia connection*, and in the second as a *multimedia connection*, i.e. a set of monomedia connections, where synchronisation and losses are related to provide a general *partially reliable* service. This set of monomedia connections is also called a *multimedia session*. The resulting global architecture is shown in figure 1.

The outline of this paper is as follows. Single source multicasting is discussed in section 2. Monomedia and multimedia aspects of our work are detailed in sections 3 and 4, respectively. Finally, section 5 concludes this paper.

2   Multicast Network Support

This section explains the multicast network support choice made in the GCAP project. The first part briefly reviews the current IP Multicast architecture to understand why its deployment in the Internet was slowed down. The second part presents the source-specific multicast service model which was chosen as the network support in the GCAP architecture.

2.1   The Current IP Multicast Architecture

The current IP Multicast architecture is composed of a service model that defines a group as an open conversation from m sources to n receivers, an addressing scheme based on IP class-D addresses, and routing protocols. Any host can send to a multicast group and any host can join the group and receive data. A multicast group is identified by a class-D IP address which is not related to any topological information, as opposed to the hierarchical unicast addressing model. Therefore, multicast address allocation is complicated and multicast forwarding state is difficult to aggregate.

At this time, there is no scalable solution to inter-domain multicast routing in the Internet. The currently adopted architecture is based on the IGMP/PIM-SM/MBGP/MSDP protocols. Hosts report their interest in specific multicast groups to their local router through the IGMP protocol (*Internet Group Management Protocol*) [5]. Intra-domain routing is done by PIM-SM (*Protocol Independent Multicast – Sparse Mode*) [7]. PIM-SM domains are connected using the MBGP (*Multiprotocol Extensions for Border Gateway Protocol - 4*) [2] and MSDP (*Multicast Source Discovery Protocol*) [13] protocols.

The PIM-SM protocol is adapted to sparsely populated groups for which flood-and-prune techniques are inadequate. PIM-SM builds unidirectional shared trees that are rooted on a special router, called *rendezvous point* (RP). Inside a PIM-SM domain each multicast group is mapped to one RP. A multicast source encapsulates the data in unicast and sends it to the RP. The RP then multicasts the data on the shared tree.

If the sending rate of the source exceeds a previously fixed threshold, PIM-SM builds a source tree for this specific source. Current implementations set the used threshold to one packet. As soon as the first packet is received, the protocol changes the shared tree for the source based one. The RP and the shared tree are therefore used only for source discovery.

The use of PIM-SM in the inter-domain level has two main problems: designing a scalable mechanism for mapping multicast groups to RPs and the fact that ISPs do not desire to host the RPs for other ISPs' multicast groups. Besides, since PIM-SM relies on the unicast routing protocol to construct multicast trees, join messages may reach non-multicast routers, complicating PIM's operation. The short-term solution to these problems is to use MBGP and MSDP. MBGP allows multiple routes to be announced for different protocols. In this way, routers may construct one routing table with unicast-capable routes and another with multicast-capable routes. MSDP provides a solution to the ISP interdependence problem. RPs within one domain are interconnected and connected to RPs in other domains using MSDP to form a loose mesh. When a source in a specific domain starts sending, the RP in this domain sends a MSDP *Source Active* message to RPs in other domains. Members located in other domains send source-specific join messages following the MBGP routes in the inter-domain level. This solution does not scale because RPs exchange information about all active sources located at all domains.

The complexity of the IP Multicast architecture slowed down the multicast service deployment, to the benefit of application level solutions or distributed caching architectures. A different approach to this problem is to simplify the architecture. This is the main idea of the Source-Specific Multicast (SSM) service model.

2.2   The Source-Specific Multicast Service

The SSM model [10] restricts the multicast distribution to *1 to m* introducing the multicast channel abstraction. A distribution tree is constructed for each channel. A channel is identified by a (S,G) pair, where S is the unicast address of the source and G is a class-D multicast address. Only S is able to send data to channel (S,G), channels (S1,G) and (S2,G) being different by definition. Address collision problems are avoided as the unicast address of the source is unique. Multicast address allocation becomes a problem local to the source. The multicast address G does not need to be globally unique anymore.

In IPv4 an exclusive address range, 232/8, has been allocated by IANA for SSM channels, enabling the coexistence of source specific service with the traditional IP Multicast (any-source multicast) service. In IPv6, the range FF2::/11 through FF3x::/11 is defined for SSM services [9].

Multicast channel subscription in IPv4 is done using the IGMPv3 [5] protocol. Version 3 of IGMP adds support for "source filtering", that is, the ability for a host to report interest in receiving packets *only* from specific source addresses, or from *all but* specific source addresses, sent to a particular multicast address. This information may be used by multicast routing protocols to avoid delivering multicast packets from specific sources to networks where there are no interested receivers. IGMPv3 provides a superset of the functionality needed by SSM, namely, to report the interest on a (S,G) pair.

In IPv6, IGMP was renamed as MLD (*Multicast Listener Discovery*) and included in ICMP (*Internet Control Message Protocol*). Version 2 of MLD [17] implements the same functionality as IGMPv3, in particular, the ability to report source filters for each multicast address listened to.

The other component of the SSM model is the PIM-SSM [3] routing protocol that constructs the multicast distribution tree. PIM-SSM is a modified version of PIM-SM that implements the source-specific service on the reserved SSM address range. PIM-SSM is able to construct source-specific trees with no need to previously construct a shared tree (as PIM-SM does). PIM-SSM has therefore no need for RPs and all the mechanisms for RP election and group mapping. On the other hand, PIM-SSM supposes that receivers know the channel identifier, i.e., the address of the source and the class-D multicast address. The way channel identifiers are discovered is not defined by the SSM service, but it could be done by mechanisms such as e-mail, web announcements, the *sdr* tool, etc.

When a receiver wants to join a multicast channel, it sends an IGMPv3 (IPv4) or MLDv2 (IPv6) request to its designated router, specifying the (S,G) address pair. If the address G is in the exclusive address range, the designated router sends a *join(S,G)* message towards the source in order to be added to the distribution tree of channel (S,G). If instead the address G is outside the SSM address range, the router behaves according to the PIM-SM specification, sending a *join(*,G)* request towards the RP.

3   Monomedia Multicasting

In this section, we address the *monomedia multicast sub-layer* in GCAP, whose role is to provide meaningful end-to-end services, on top of the PIM-SSM model. However, at this level of the architecture, the focus is on the control of individual communications, rather than on their integration and interpretation as part of a multimedia session. Hence, this monomedia multicast transport sub-layer is mainly concerned with mechanisms for the control and monitoring of data sent over a PIM-SSM channel. The services provided by this layer enhance the PIM-SSM service with several forms of reliability and monitoring.

As already mentioned, one of the main characteristics of the SSM model is that only the SSM channel source is allowed to send on the channel. This property has an important implication for higher level protocols and applications: no multicast "back-channel" is available for receivers to multicast feedback to the group. This lack of multicast facility to send control/feedback information, together with the restriction of a single, well-known sender, breaks several transport and application level protocols.

It is worth noting that, although a class of protocol mechanisms relying on statistical methods and based solely on direct feedback to the source have been proposed in the literature [4] [14], these mechanisms only perform efficiently for large multicast groups (exceeding 10^4 participants) and are therefore not applicable with the vast majority of interactive applications considered in GCAP. We have thus opted for an approach using transport-level distribution structures for control purposes.

3.1   The Tree Building Control Protocol

By transport-level distribution structure, we mean that the GCAP monomedia multicast sub-layer builds, and maintains, its own "communication overlay", encompassing all relevant transport entities, using readily available unicast communications. This transport-level distribution structure is built as a spanning tree connecting the source and the receivers of the associated PIM-SSM channel.

Since the solution of sending all control information to the SSM channel source and then letting the channel source "reflect" this information back onto the SSM channel can clearly not be scalable, a different solution based on application level multicasting has been devised in GCAP. This approach requires the building of a bi-directional spanning tree by means of an application level tree building protocol, called TBCP. This *Tree Building Control Protocol* [18] is a new tree building protocol designed at Lancaster University. TBCP can build a loop-free spanning tree connecting TBCP entities that may run either in end systems or in programmable *edge devices*. Such a spanning tree is built by means of a distributed algorithm that does not require interaction with multicast routers or any knowledge of network topology.

TBCP has been designed according to the *Application Level Multicast* (ALM) model, also known as application-based distribution. ALM is a new technique used to provide multicast distribution services in situations where no support is provided by the network for multicast. This situation occurs, for instance, when the network infrastructure does not support the IP-multicast routing protocols. As we already mentioned in the previous section, another case in which the ALM approach may be helpful is when the network only supports an SSM multicast service, and the user wants to deploy end-to-end communication protocols that require the availability of a full duplex multicast distribution tree.

When the ALM technique is used to implement multicast communication, each end system that participates in the multicast group is also responsible for forwarding received data to all other ALM entities connected to it in the tree. The advantage of performing data forwarding at the application level is that each end system may be programmed to either passively retransmit every single piece of data it receives or actively filter this information according to some protocol-specific logic (for instance, upstream traffic may be aggregated to avoid the source implosion problem, while downstream traffic may be filtered to adapt to the link congestion or the actual computing power of downstream receivers). The tree built by TBCP is used in GCAP to deliver control data among the members of a multicast session. By using a TBCP tree connecting transport-layer entities (which may run either in end-systems or in the active edge devices discussed later), it is possible to implement the control protocols that require a multicast distribution of messages originated by SSM receivers.

In the process of building the TBCP tree, TBCP entities interact through a sort of signalling protocol which uses point-to-point TCP connections to exchange protocol messages. To join a tree, a TBCP entity needs to establish a TCP connection with the root TBCP entity, and begin a join procedure (whose details are outside the scope of this paper). Hence, a TBCP tree may be identified by the pair (S,SP), where S is the IP address of the node on which the root entity is running, and SP is the TCP port number used by the root entity to listen to new connection requests.

Once a TBCP tree has been built, it can be used to deliver control data among all the nodes that have joined the tree. For a TBCP tree to be used by several protocol entities, a set of *data channels* is associated to a TBCP tree. Each data channel is uniquely identified by a 16-bit identifier, called *ChannelID*. Figure 2 shows a TBCP tree with three active data channels.

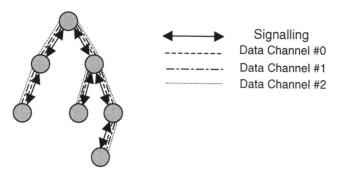

⟵⟶	Signalling
----------	Data Channel #0
—·—·—·—·	Data Channel #1
··················	Data Channel #2

Fig. 2. A TBCP Tree with three active Data Channels

Finally, it should be noted that the term *data channel* used by TBCP must not be confused with the term *SSM channel*. Incidentally, the way information is delivered on a specific TBCP Data Channel depends on how the forwarding entity for that channel is programmed. For a given tree, in fact, some data channels may be used as broadcast channels (i.e. a datagram sent by any node is forwarded to all the other tree nodes), while other channels may implement an SSM behaviour (i.e. only the tree root is authorised to inject packets into the tree). More complex usage of a data channel may be requested by other protocols if some form of message aggregation is required.

3.2   Reliability

Reliability in the Monomedia Multicast service sub-layer is realized by reliable multicast protocols running on top of the TBCP tree. Such protocols will be designed as a "mapping" of well known reliable multicast protocols (e.g. RMTP, PGM, etc.) onto the GCAP architecture, i.e. these well known reliable multicast protocols will be modified to fit GCAP communication constraints.

Three reliable multicast services will be supported:
- *Fully unreliable service.* This service provides best-effort datagram delivery where no provision is made to enable subsequent attempts to recover lost data.
- *Unreliable with selective recovery requests service.* This service provides best-effort datagram delivery but makes necessary provisions in order to enable the recovery of lost data for a specified recovery period of time. It should be noted that this service is "reactive" in the sense that the recovery period as well as the recovery requests are specified by the service user.
- *Fully reliable service.* This service provides a loss free transfer facility.

3.3   Monitoring

The *QoS monitoring* on a monomedia multicast connection will be based on an adaptation of the RTP/RTCP protocol. Here the situation is different than with the other protocols considered so far: with RTCP, low frequency feedback has to be distributed to all the participants (including the source) of the communication.

Because this feedback is kept to a small percentage of the overall data traffic, and each participant should see the feedback messages "as is", the overhead of distributing such feedback over the TBCP tree seems excessive: RTCP follows a model where sending the feedback, in unicast, to the SSM source, and having the source "reflect" it to the group on the SSM tree, is well suited.

Another useful service the Monomedia Multicast sub-layer provides is basic group *integrity condition checking*, defining minimal operating conditions on the monomedia multicast connections, such as the minimum number of participants or mandatory participants. These integrity mechanisms are well suited to run on top of the TBCP tree and form a basis for the more comprehensive integrity framework discussed in section 4.2.

3.4   Edge Devices

One of the most important properties of multicast is scalability. As a consequence, following the classical approach and ensuring compatibility with the TBCP monomedia sub-layer, our multicast architecture has been designed as a tree, where a node has to handle the reliability of its children nodes. The first implementation we are developing only has the sender, one intermediate tree level and the receivers. For simplicity and also because this is quite in agreement with real networks, the intermediate level is located at the entrance of the edge LANs where the users are, hence it appears in a specific router called an *edge device*, as it represents the connection of the edge of the LAN with the core network.

4   Multimedia Multicasting

In this section, we discuss how GCAP supports the requirements of multimedia applications. To address these requirements, GCAP is targeting a new transport layer where the relations between the different components of multimedia communications are defined at an extended end-to-end interface, i.e. a general *multimedia multicast API*. This allows the specification of powerful QoS parameters and of global multimedia synchronization requirements. In addition to these transport layer issues, we discuss how *channel* and *session integrity* is defined and maintained in GCAP.

4.1   Partial Order and Partial Reliability Transport

The multimedia multicast sub-layer, based on the monomedia multicast sub-layer, has to handle a set of multimedia *sessions*, each session consisting of multiple monomedia *connections*, which requires to specify the needed relations and interdependencies between these connections. Moreover, in several communication scenarios for group communication, it is also important and needed to maintain the integrity of the multimedia information over the lifetime of the session.

As a general concept, GCAP uses a partially reliable and partially ordered model to define a session. More precisely, the reliability and synchronization requirements characterize this session. First, for *partial reliability* support, the model is based on the consideration that a fully reliable communication increases the communication delay which may be worse than tolerating some multimedia losses, because losing video frames can be acceptable in given applications. Second, for *partial order* support, the model is based on the consideration that a fully ordered communication does not represent general multimedia objects, where the different sub-objects are defined in parallel and in sequence, and are then synchronized between themselves. Using such a well-defined specification, for instance using Time Stream Petri nets, an application can specify which packets must be received to maintain a given QoS. The model is used to represent the partial order, i.e. the synchronization, and the partial reliability, i.e. the number of requested receptions, of the media sub-object of a multimedia presentation. We point out that:

1) TCP only provides a fully ordered and a fully reliable service, while UDP provides only an unordered and unreliable service, but
2) multimedia data streams require both:
   - partial reliability (for example, it is not troublesome if some images of a 25 images/s video stream are lost), and
   - partial order (multimedia objects as serial and/or parallel compositions of multimedia data).

As a solution, a partial order connection protocol has been proposed [1] [15]. Its extension in GCAP has led to a new transport protocol, *FPTP (Fully Programmable Transport Protocol)*[†]. It delivers data units sent on several connections, following a given partial order. UDP and TCP can be seen as two specific cases of FPTP, and the partial order is any order between the total order (as TCP) and no order (as UDP).

Regarding partial reliability, when an acceptable loss of a message is detected:

1) the missing object can instantaneously be declared lost (leading to earliest indication of losses), and
2) the data received (in general the one that leads to the detection of the loss) can be delivered immediately to the application (leading to earliest delivery).

Of course, if the loss cannot be accepted in terms of requested reliability, recovery and retransmission will occur.

This required partial reliability, defined on top of the partial order model, results in earliest loss indications and deliveries; it is deduced from the application requirements [16]. Partial reliability is managed by *groups of media*, where the receiving entity can directly handle the set of all streams, and so it is possible to declare losses on all streams of the same multimedia connection. Handling the losses is of course derived from the synchronization model of the multimedia object.

With regard to partial order, what must be clearly understood is that the multimedia sub-layer handles together, as a group of connections, the synchronization of the different media. The basic Petri net model defines the partial order as the synchronization between the different objects of the multimedia presentation. An

---

[†] The detailed FPTP API will be provided and made available for comments and improvements near the end of the project, in November 2001, in a separate and dedicated public report to be found at [8]. Another public report will give the detailed GCAP measurements obtained by using the European infrastructure, i.e. the national research networks *Renater, Rederis, G-WiN, Super-Janet, ACOnet*, and their European interconnection *TEN155*.

example is given in figure 3. The higher part represents the partial order and the partial reliability of a simple application, i.e. a 16 unit period of a continuous object.

We now discuss in more detail the multipoint architecture. As the FPTP is a protocol based on the monomedia multicast infrastructure, it has to be based on the underlying spanning tree. The first prototype of the GCAP multimedia multicast sub-layer provides its services, integrating the concepts of partial order and partial reliability, on top of a fully *unreliable* monomedia multicast service.

During a session, the source sends data using PIM-SSM on the several monomedia data flows that have been created. This data is received by the end user. If a QoS violation is detected, the receiver asks the source to send the missing data via the monomedia TBCP channel interface. On the contrary, data fulfilling partial reliability is transmitted to the application by respecting the multimedia partial order synchronization specification and model. If some losses are detected, and if the QoS is violated, retransmission is requested.

It is important to understand in multicast that, for a set of users, each user can have his own definition of partial reliability. Of course, all of them use the same synchronization model as applicable to the multimedia presentation.

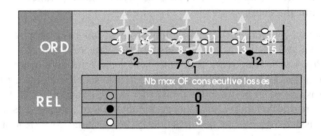

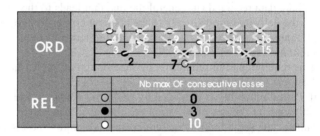

Fig. 3. Synchronisation and Partial Reliability for two Users

Figure 3 gives an example that shows two users requiring two different (partial) *reliability* values, i.e. giving two different sets of numbers of *acceptable losses* in the connection. The upper part of the figure is related to user 1 and the bottom part to user 2. It can be seen that the *synchronization* between the different media is the same for both users, as the multimedia object being sent by the sender is the same for both.

The difference between the two users appears in terms of acceptable losses. Here this means, for instance, that user 1 accepts, for the upper two of the four flows, (up to) three losses in the synchronization period given in the figure, while user 2 accepts (up to) ten losses in the same two flows during the same period. Moreover, the partial reliability, and thus the quality, is higher for the third medium of user 1 (one for user

1 and three for user 2, for the third flow) while it is equal for the fourth flow (zero for both). Of course, there is a direct relationship between the number of acceptable losses and the available throughput. A user having a high speed link, like user 1, can, for example, request 20 images per second, while another user using a slow link is able to request only one image per second, i.e. a quality ten times lower than that of user 1.

The behavior of the receiving entity of the protocol is then simply as follows: ACKs are generated as long as acceptable losses occur; and if too many messages are lost, i.e. when the number of the actual losses becomes higher than the number of acceptable losses, then error recovery starts.

Note that the interest of the approach is twofold:

- First, the definition and the specification of the partial reliability is local and so easy to define, as the user should know the capability of his network; and
- Second, the handling of the error acceptance and of the error recovery is also local, i.e. it can easily be different for each of the users of the multicast.

These two properties allow the system to be optimized from the user point of view, with the user having the poorest connection being able to request and handle the poorest quality without degrading the quality of the other participants of the multicast.

Finally, because the FPTP protocol has to have a recursive behavior for scalability, we decided to deploy it between the edge devices located at the entry of the LANs.

4.2 Channel and Session Integrity

While our FPTP is tailored to specific multimedia multicast *data transmission* requirements, a second multimedia multicast aspect addressed by GCAP is *multicast group integrity* (not to be confused with the *integrity of the multimedia information* discussed in the previous section). This concept, as first proposed in [11], refers to *conditions* imposed on groups with regard to membership set, member roles, topology, and group organization. Associated *action policies* state how to re-establish integrity in case it has been found violated. In GCAP's multimedia multicasting context, we apply an adapted version of the framework in [12] to *SSM channels* and multimedia *sessions*.

Two entities are involved in integrity control: A central *session manager* M, also responsible for each *channel's* integrity, and a *controller module* at each user U, who obtains permission from M for any operation relevant to session or channel integrity management. We refer to *users*, identified by a user ID, instead of *hosts*; a current mapping is kept by M. A user U who wants to join one or more SSM channels first requests permission from M for his intended operations, and, if granted, performs MLDv2 and TBCP join operations by way of his controller. Any subsequent member status changes, such as leaves, also require permission by M. Only privileged users, as identified according to a *user directory*, may modify integrity conditions and action policies, or establish or delete SSM channels within the session. All channel members are, implicitly, session members, too.

M maintains, per *channel*, a list of members with their roles, as well as a set of integrity conditions against which requests are checked (such as mandatory members and non-admissible users, or the minimum and maximum number of members permitted) and action policies (such as what to do if a mandatory member has died), complemented by *session* integrity conditions and action policies. For sessions, we allow *topological* restrictions by explicitly allowing or denying members in certain domains. Voting among channel or session members is supported by M as a means of reaching a group management decision, e.g. on a join request by a new user. Users may at any time obtain from M a set of applicable integrity conditions in order to avoid useless requests, such as attempting to join only the video channel while session integrity conditions mandate to join both the audio *and* the video channel.

5   Conclusion

In this paper, we have described the new approach to multimedia multicasting we are developing in the GCAP project. On top of PIM-SSM at the network layer, our monomedia multicast protocol provides a multicast feedback channel by way of a TBCP control tree. The special requirements of multimedia applications, namely partial order and partial reliability, are supported in our new FPTP that, by offering a powerful multimedia multicast API to applications, overcomes the limitations of current application layer multicasting approaches. Furthermore, group integrity was discussed in our multimedia multicasting context.

Having successfully tested TBCP at the monomedia layer as a building block, we are now preparing two major experiments involving the GCAP multimedia protocol: a media server experiment with time-sensitive data, and, involving the entire GCAP protocol suite, a multi-party multicast video conference experiment stretching across the national research networks of our countries.

We believe that GCAP is setting the stage for multimedia multicast research. However, a set of work has still to be done to obtain optimised software for handling multimedia and multicast, including models, simulations, congestion control, and to adapt it to real multi-network environments including fiber, wireless and satellite networks.

Acknowledgements. The GCAP work [8] has been supported by the European Union within the Information Societies Technology (IST) Framework as Project IST-1999-10504. Contributors are: Centre National de la Recherche Scientifique LAAS (France), Telebit Communication (Denmark), 6WIND (France), Fraunhofer Institute for Integrated Publication and Information Systems - FhG IPSI (Germany) (formerly GMD – Forschungszentrum Informationstechnik), Université Pierre & Marie Curie – Laboratoire LIP6 (France), University of Lancaster (UK), Universidad Carlos III de Madrid (Spain), Alcatel Space Industries (France), Telekom Austria (Austria), Technical University of Karlsruhe (Germany), and Ecole Nationale Supérieure Ingenieurs En Constructions Aéronautiques (France). The writing of this paper was coordinated by Andreas Meissner of Fraunhofer IPSI.

References

1.   P. D. Amer, C. Chassot, T. Connolly, P. Conrad, M. Diaz: Partial order transport service for multimedia and other applications. IEEE/ACM Transactions on Networking, October 1994, Vol. 2, No. 5

2.   T. Bates, R. Chandra, D. Katz, Y. Rekhter: Multiprotocol Extensions for BGP-4, RFC 2283, February 1998
3.   S. Bhattacharyya et al.: A framework for Source-Specific IP Multicast Deployment. Internet Draft - <draft-bhattach-pim-ssm-00.txt>, July 2000
4.   J-C. Bolot, T. Turletti, I. Wakeman: Scalable Feedback Control for Multicast Video Distribution in the Internet. In ACM SIGCOMM'94, pp. 58-67, London, UK, Sept. 1994
5.   B. Cain, S. Deering, B. Fenner, I. Kouvelas, A. Thyagarajan: Internet Group Management Protocol, Version 3. Internet Draft - <draft-ietf-idmr-igmp-v3-07.txt>, March 2001
6.   A. Campbell, G. Coulson, D. Hutchinson: A Quality of Service Architecture. ACM Computer Communications Review, April 1994
7.   B. Fenner, M. Handley, H. Holbrook, I. Kouvelas: Protocol Independent Multicast - Sparse Mode (PIM-SM): Protocol Specification (Revised). Internet Draft - <draft-ietf-pim-sm-v2-new-02.txt>, March 2001
8.   GCAP Project IST-1999-10504: Global Communication Architecture and Protocols for new QoS services over IPv6 networks. Website: http://www.laas.fr/GCAP
9.   B. Haberman, D. Thaler: Unicast-Prefix-based IPv6 Multicast Addresses. Internet Draft - <draft-ietf-ipngwg-uni-based-mcast-01.txt>, January 2001
10.   H. Holbrook and B: Cain. Source Specific Multicast for IP. Internet Draft - <draft-holbrook-ssm-arch-02.txt>, March 2001
11.   L. Mathy, G. Leduc, O. Bonaventure, A. Danthine: A Group Communication Framework. Broadband Islands '94 Connecting with the End-User, W. Bauerfeld, O. Spaniol, F. Williams, eds., Elsevier North-Holland, 1994, pp. 167-178
12.   A. Meissner, L. Wolf, R. Steinmetz: A novel Group Integrity Concept for Multimedia Multicasting. Proc. 8th International Workshop on Interactive Distributed Multimedia Systems (IDMS 2001), Lancaster, UK, September 2001
13.   D. Meyer (ed.): Multicast Source Discovery Protocol (MSDP). Internet Draft - <draft-ietf-msdp-spec-08.txt>, April 2001
14.   J. Nonnenmacher, E. Biersack, D. Towsley: Parity-based loss Recovery for Reliable Multicast Transmission. IEEE/ACM Transaction on Networking, Vol. 6, No.4, pp 349-361, August 1998
15.   P. Owezarski, M. Diaz, C. Chassot: A time efficient architecture for multimedia applications. IEEE Journal on Selected Areas in Communications, Vol. 16, No. 3, pp. 383-396, April 1998
16.   P. Owezarski, M. Diaz: New architecture for enforcing multimedia synchronization in videoconferencing applications. Telecommunication System, Vol. 11, No. 1-2, pp. 161-185, 1999
17.   R. Vida, L. Costa, R. Zara, S. Fdida, S. Deering, B. Fenner, I. Kouvelas, B. Haberman: Multicast Listener Discovery Version 2 (MLDv2) for IPv6. Internet Draft - <draft-vida-mld-v2-00.txt>, February 2001
18.   R. Vida, L. Costa, S. Fdida, R. Canonico, L. Mathy, D. Hutchison: Specification of a Multicast Monomedia Protocol. GCAP Project Deliverable D2.1.1, January 2001, available at http://www.laas.fr/GCAP/public/publications.html

Protection of Fairness for Multimedia Traffic Streams in a Non-cooperative Wireless LAN Setting

Jerzy Konorski

Faculty of Electronics, Telecommunications and Informatics
Technical University of Gdansk
ul. Narutowicza 11/12, 80-952 Gdansk, Poland
jekon@pg.gda.pl

Abstract. A single-channel, single-hop wireless LAN (WLAN) providing communication for a set of stations is considered in an ad-hoc configuration, using a distributed MAC protocol synchronised to a common slotted time axis. A framework for a non-cooperative setting is outlined featuring a number of non-cooperative stations intent on stealing the channel bandwidth for their multimedia traffic streams. The packet scheduling policy and station strategies being logically separate in such a setting, it is argued that protection of fairness for cooperative stations should rely on suitable redefinition of the scheduling policy so as to invoke a non-cooperative game between the competing stations with a possibly fair and efficient Nash equilibrium. An example of such a policy, called EB/ECD-Δ, is given and evaluated via simulation against a reference policy resembling the elimination-yield procedure of HIPERLAN/1.

1 Introduction

We consider a single-channel, single-hop wireless LAN (WLAN) providing interconnection for a set of stations in an ad-hoc configuration. Stations with packets ready to transmit contend for access to the shared radio channel using a distributed MAC protocol, implying that there is no central management in any form except that packet transmissions as well as the stations' actions dictated by the MAC protocol are assumed to be synchronised to a common slotted time axis. If multimedia services are supported, a typical traffic situation is for a number of stations to generate long trains of packets with minimum-bandwidth-type requirements that compete for the channel bandwidth in an interleaved fashion. This calls for fairness enforcement and bandwidth guarantees on the part of the MAC protocol. In response, various bandwidth allocation techniques have been devised; they are surveyed e.g. in [3]. We note, however, that in an ad-hoc configuration, most of the bandwidth allocation techniques may appear hard to apply at MAC level. Among the relevant reasons are station mobility (meaning that a station's actions are not always possible to enforce or prevent), and "volatility" (e.g., the set of stations is potentially highly variable and virtually impossible to trace down; stations' id's tend to exist on a temporary basis only or in any case be unavailable at MAC level). Faced with these difficulties, one should primarily rely on pure contention MAC whose inherent symmetry at least makes for fair if not efficient use of the channel bandwidth. In this paper we point out,

M.J. van Sinderen and L.J.M. Nieuwenhuis (Eds.): PROMS 2001, LNCS 2213, pp. 116-129, 2001.
© Springer-Verlag Berlin Heidelberg 2001

and try to find a remedy for, a possibility that even that inherent symmetry can be broken in the presence of non-cooperative stations.

To characterise non-cooperative behaviour in the MAC context, recall that a generic MAC protocol cycle consists of a scheduling phase followed by a transmission phase; in the former (known as the *scheduling penalty* and possibly further divided into sub-phases), stations take elective actions to produce one or more winners who subsequently transmit their packets. It is important to distinguish two MAC components: a common *scheduling policy* provides framework for taking elective actions and defines winning actions so as to ensure fair and efficient bandwidth use, whereas *station strategies* dictate stations what elective actions to take in successive cycles. Scheduling policies can be categorised orthogonally considering: time span (single- or multiple-cycle, depending on whether winning actions are defined based on the outcome of the latest cycle or a number of preceding cycles), mechanisms used (e.g., contention- or reservation-based – the latter typically attempt to schedule multiple packets per cycle), and per-slot channel feedback required (e.g., binary or ternary – in the latter, empty, busy or colliding slots are distinguished). Here we focus on single-cycle, contention-based, ternary-feedback scheduling policies.

In a *cooperative MAC setting*, the goals of the scheduling policy are global in nature and common to all stations; both station strategies and the scheduling policy are oriented toward these goals and so constitute a monolithic MAC protocol. In the near future, the very same features of the ad-hoc configuration that make bandwidth allocation difficult are likely to challenge this setting; on top of them, stations become increasingly "bandwidth-greedy" due to the growing portion of multimedia traffic, and at the same time increasingly self-programmable, possibly of irregular origin and thus not guaranteed to follow standard station strategies. Over time, some vendors may start offering 'bogus' MAC chips – required technology is now within reach of small- and medium-size manufacturers. Thus in the envisioned *non-cooperative MAC setting*, station strategies and the scheduling policy are logically separate; besides cooperative (c-) stations that use a standard contention strategy and adhere to the scheduling policy, there are a number of non-cooperative (nc-) stations that use various self-optimising strategies to increase their bandwidth share at the cost of c-stations i.e., commit bandwidth stealing; yet to conceal their nature and maintain proper synchronisation they too adhere to the scheduling policy. To protect c-stations with long packet trains to transmit, a change of the contention rules is proposed.

In subsequent sections, a framework for a non-cooperative MAC setting is outlined taking into account that nc-stations can forge winning actions in many ways. The underlying issues of verifiability and non-deniability are discussed and shown to give rise to a reasonable framework for a nc-station strategy and a *non-cooperative scheduling policy* i.e., one that, instead of putting in more administration, provides disincentives to steal bandwidth on a self-regulatory basis. An example of such a policy is given and evaluated.

Traces of the non-cooperative paradigm are present throughout computer networks literature, cf. competitive routing [8], Fair Share queuing [12], incentive compatible flow control [11], auction-like resource allocation [9], and power control in wireless networks [4]. A preliminary discussion of some of the notions introduced further as well as early proposals of non-cooperative scheduling policies can be found in [7].

2 Reference Scheduling Policy

Contention-based binary-feedback scheduling policies typically employ collision avoidance as in IEEE 802.11 DCF [5] or in the yield phase of ETSI HIPERLAN/1's elimination-yield (EY) [1]. Ternary feedback allows for collision detection; our reference policy is called *Elimination Burst with Extraneous Collision Detection* (EB/ECD) and works similarly as the elimination phase of EY: at the start of a protocol cycle, stations contend for access by transmitting elimination bursts of random lengths (drawn from $1..E$ slots) and the longest bursts win. Instead of engaging in a yield phase, the winner stations tentatively start their packet transmissions and after the first slot suspend transmission awaiting reaction from other stations (Fig. 1). On sensing a single packet transmission, a listening station issues a reaction (a one-slot burst), while refraining from reaction if a collision of packets is sensed. Any one station's reaction is enough to resume the suspended packet transmission (positive ACK semantics), whereas the lack of reaction prompts the winner stations to back off, thereby starting a new protocol cycle.

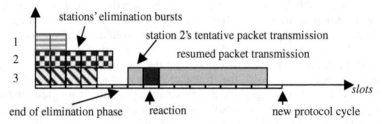

Fig. 1. EB/ECD protocol cycle

The absence of a yield phase simplifies the stations' actions and has little effect upon the bandwidth utilisation compared to EY, as confirmed by the following probabilistic argument. Let N be the number of stations generating multimedia streams, L – the packet length in slots, and S – the average scheduling penalty per protocol cycle; denote by P the probability of a successful packet transmission in a protocol cycle. Then the average bandwidth utilisation equals

$$B = \begin{cases} \dfrac{P}{1+S/L}, & \text{for EY} \\ \dfrac{1}{1+S/(P\cdot L)}, & \text{for EB/ECD} \end{cases} \tag{1}$$

To calculate P and S, let p_l denote the probability of burst length l, and $\Phi(r,k)$ the probability that in a protocol cycle exactly k stations transmit bursts whose length is maximum and equal to r. Assuming that the N stations always have packets ready to transmit (which typifies our competing multimedia streams environment) and that the yield deferments in EY are drawn from a uniform pdf over $0..Y-1$, we have

$$\Phi(r,k) = \binom{N}{k} p_r^k f_r^{N-k}, \tag{2}$$

$$S = \begin{cases} 1 + \sum\limits_{r=1}^{E}\sum\limits_{k=1}^{N} \Phi(r,k)\left[r + \sum\limits_{l=0}^{Y-1}\left(1-\frac{l}{Y}\right)^{k}\right], & \text{for EY} \\[4mm] 3 + \sum\limits_{r=1}^{E}(1 - f_r^{N}), & \text{for EB/ECD,} \end{cases} \tag{3}$$

$$P = \begin{cases} \sum\limits_{r=1}^{E}\sum\limits_{k=1}^{N} \Phi(r,k)\cdot\frac{k}{Y}\sum\limits_{l=0}^{Y-1}\left(1-\frac{l+1}{Y}\right)^{k-1}, & \text{for EY} \\[4mm] \sum\limits_{r=1}^{E}\Phi(r,1), & \text{for EB/ECD,} \end{cases} \tag{4}$$

where $f_r = \sum_{l=1}^{r-1}p_l$. In Fig. 2, B is plotted against E for EB/ECD and EY with optimum Y, assuming a truncated geometric pdf over $1..E$ with parameter 0.5, 1 or 2. Except for the latter parameter value, EB/ECD turns out to perform similarly as EY. Unfortunately, under EB/ECD and EY alike, straightforward bandwidth stealing strategies consist in transmitting "longer-than-random" elimination bursts. To prevent frequent collisions with other nc-stations using similar strategies, an nc-station might draw its elimination burst lengths from a pdf biased toward E.

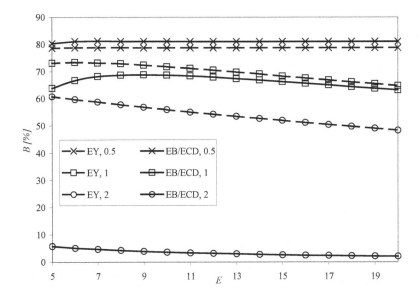

Fig. 2. Bandwidth utilisation under EY and EB/ECD; $N=10$, $L=50$, $Y=8$ for EY, truncated geometric pdf with parameter indicated

3 Framework for a Non-cooperative MAC Setting

Having ruled out purely malicious strategies of nc-stations (e.g., simply jamming other stations' packets), one still has to prevent more rational brute-force strategies consisting in forgery of winning actions. For the considered class of policies, two types of forgery can be envisaged: 1) taking illegitimate actions, 2) deliberate misinterpretation, in particular denial of sensing, of other stations' actions. To understand type 1 forgery, consider a station that suspends the transmission of an elimination burst to sense the channel for one slot and if any other bursts are still in progress, resumes its own (in EY, a station might even join in yield phase without having transmitted any elimination burst). Type 2 forgery occurs e.g., when a station starts its tentative packet transmission pretending not to have sensed the longer elimination bursts; alternatively, a packet transmission can be resumed on the claim that a reaction to the tentative first slot was sensed. Refraining from reaction after a single tentative packet transmission also falls into this category, with a listening station claiming that channel errors corrupted the packet into a perceived collision. Forgery of types 1 and 2 raise, respectively, the problems of *verifiability* and *non-deniability*.

3.1   Verifiability

A *verifier* is a conceptual administrative device, stand-alone or built in some c-station, used as a deterrent but not necessarily actually deployed. It should be able to detect type 1 forgery and impose predefined sanctions upon nc-stations. Verifiability can be categorised based on the verifier's detection capabilities e.g., *small-aperture* detection capability would permit to lock upon a particular station and track down its actions. In this case, further distinction pertains to the maximum lock time-span with station's identity perceived as unchanged; it is reasonable not to assume lock time-spans longer than one protocol cycle. Further we confine our interest to *small-aperture-verifiable* non-cooperative scheduling policies i.e., ones that define winning actions so that type 1 forgery is detectable by a small-aperture verifier. In such policies, stations' actions always involve transmission of some physical signals.

3.2   Non-deniability

Consider that elimination bursts and reactions are just jam sequences rather than meaningful bit patterns. For EB/ECD to prevent type 2 forgery, a sufficient assumption is then that a station cannot deny sensing carrier on the channel nor can it claim to have sensed carrier when none was transmitted. The former part is harder to verify in the presence of various fading phenomena; however, with the semantics used by EB/ECD denial of sensing carrier does not seem to lead to rational non-cooperative behaviour. (Note that reverse reaction semantics would enable an nc-station to prevent other station's packet transmission by reacting upon a single tentative packet transmission as if upon a collision thereof, blaming corruption.) Refraining from reaction by an nc-station on sensing a single tentative packet transmission, also blaming corruption, could be a rational strategy, but quite ineffective in the presence of at least one c-station's reaction. Even if all currently sensing stations were to be nc-stations, some of them too would have incentives to react if they recognised themselves as recipients of the packet (e.g., based on an address field contained in the tentative packet transmission).

4 Framework for an Nc-station Strategy

Under verifiability and non-deniability, and given that maintaining proper synchronisation is in an nc-station's own interest, the only strategy it is inclined to use consists in transmitting "longer-than-random" elimination bursts in successive protocol cycles. Denote by B_c and B_{nc} the bandwidth share obtained by a c- and an nc-station, respectively, and let B_{c0} correspond to the cooperative MAC setting. An nc-station strategy can be soundly assumed to be: *isolated* (not relying on collusion with other nc-stations), *insistent* (not reverting to cooperative behaviour unless forced to by a verifier), and *rational* (aiming to self-optimise B_{nc} and not just to diminish other stations' bandwidth shares at the price of self-damage). The latter property implies, among others, that inactive stations (those without packets to transmit) transmit no elimination burst in the current protocol cycle. As the simulation study in Sec. 7 shows, rationality may in some circumstances motivate reverting to cooperative behaviour (upon detection that $B_{nc} < B_c$ or $B_{nc} < B_{c0}$); we exclude this option for the sake of clarity. A further reasonable requirement is that bandwidth stealing be *statistically inconspicuous*; even though individual bursts in each protocol cycle are obscured by longer ones, the cycle-wise trajectory of winning actions is observable and might serve for statistical detection of stations consistently transmitting "longer-than-random" elimination bursts.

5 Framework for a Non-cooperative Scheduling Policy

To cope with non-cooperative behaviour, we seek a verifiable non-deniable EB/ECD-like scheduling policy that is both fair and efficient. These two requirements combined amount to ensuring that B_c is not much less than B_{c0} and that B_{c0} is not much less than $B_{c0|EB/ECD}$. In this section we propose a framework for a scheduling policy; to comply with the ad-hoc philosophy, neither the number nor identities of stations shall enter this framework. Recall that a station having a packet to transmit selects its action (i.e., elimination burst length) from $1..E$. Let f_l be the number of stations whose selected action in the present protocol cycle is l, expressed with the granularity permitted by ternary channel feedback i.e., f_l takes values from F={'0', '1', '>1'}. A vector $\mathbf{f}=(f_1 \ldots f_E) \in \mathrm{F}^E$ describes the channel feedback in a protocol cycle; it may be only partly observable, depending on the scheduling policy definition and implementation. A scheduling policy can be stated as a function $\omega\colon \mathrm{F}^E \to 0..E$, where

$\omega(\mathbf{f}) \in 1..E$ is a winning action and by convention $\omega(\mathbf{f})=0$ indicates a no-winner situation. Denote $\Theta(\mathbf{f})=\{l \in 1..E: f_l \neq '0'\}$; then in EB/ECD, $\omega(\mathbf{f})=\max\Theta(\mathbf{f})$ if $\Theta(\mathbf{f})$ is nonempty and $f_{\max\Theta(\mathbf{f})}='1'$, and 0 otherwise. We require, plausibly, that ω be

- *feedback compatible* i.e., each station should be able to determine $\omega(\mathbf{f})$ given the observed $\mathbf{f}$ (as a counterexample, consider a modification of EB/ECD whereby the longest elimination burst wins only if it is not much longer than the second-longest),
- *irreducible* i.e., it should map F^E onto $1..E$ lest some actions be dismissed a priori as non-winning, thereby reducing the actual action space (as a counterexample, consider a policy whereby the longest elimination burst wins only if it is sufficiently long),
- *decisive* i.e., $f_{\omega(\mathbf{f})}='1'$ lest station identities or some form of yield phase be involved, and
- *nontrivial* i.e., for any $l \in 1..E$ there should exist an $\mathbf{f} \in F^E$ with $f_l \neq '0'$ s.t. $\omega(\mathbf{f}) \neq l$ and $\omega(\mathbf{f})>0$; thus there are no "fail-safe" actions known a priori to either win or at least render other actions non-winning – otherwise, persistently repeating such an action in successive protocol cycles would let an nc-station trivially "play for time" (EB/ECD is a counterexample, action E being "fail-safe").

In EB/ECD, a c-station calculates (and an nc-station also self-optimises) its bandwidth share based on own actions and observed channel feedback in successive protocol cycles, $l^{(i)}$ and $\mathbf{f}^{(i)}$, as

$$B_x = \lim_{I \to \infty} \frac{L \cdot \sum_{i \in 1..I} \mathbf{1}[\omega(\mathbf{f}^{(i)}) = l^{(i)}]}{\sum_{i \in 1..I}(L \cdot \mathbf{1}[\omega(\mathbf{f}^{(i)}) > 0] + 3 + \max\{l : f_l^{(i)} \neq '0'\})}. \tag{5}$$

B_c and B_{nc} are obtained from (5) by selecting $l^{(i)}$ according to a c- and nc-station strategy, respectively. From a game theoretic perspective, ω is the stage payoff and B_x the player utility in a repeated $N \times E$ game; irreducibility precludes the existence of strategies known a priori to be overwhelmed [2] and non-triviality is related to the notion of a protective policy [12].

6 Proposed Scheduling Policy

The idea of the proposed policy, called EB/ECD-Δ, is to define ω so as to invoke a repetitive $N \times E$ game with a possibly fair and efficient outcome. The policy is configured with an integer parameter Δ from $0..E-1$ (EB/ECD-0 coincides with EB/ECD). For an observed channel feedback $\mathbf{f}$, denote $M=\max\Theta(\mathbf{f})$ (cf. Sec. 5), $J=\min\{\Delta, M-1\}$ and $\Xi(\mathbf{f})=\{l \in M-J..M: f_l='1'\}$; then $\omega(\mathbf{f})=\min\Xi(\mathbf{f})$. A possible implementation has a station sense other stations' bursts still in progress after termination of its own elimination burst, while counting successive slots. After the longest, M-slot elimination burst terminates (as detected upon an empty slot), a sequence of additional elimination and reaction slots starts. The first elimination slot is reserved for tentative packet transmissions of stations within J slots from the longest burst; this slot is left empty if there are no such stations, otherwise paired with a reaction slot. A reaction burst indicates that a winner is elected who resumes its packet transmission. If there is no reaction, the second elimination slot is reserved for stations within $J-1$ slots from the longest burst etc., and finally, the $(J+1)^{th}$ elimination slot is reserved for stations whose burst lengths equal M (again, positive reaction semantics is adopted). The resulting course of slots is illustrated in Fig. 3. Note that EB/ECD-Δ is both small-aperture-verifiable and non-deniable as well as feedback compatible, irreducible, decisive and nontrivial. Tuning of Δ is required and up to $2\Delta+2$ additional elimination slots have to be added (more precisely, the 3 in the denominator of (5) is to be replaced by $J+2+\#\{l \in M-J..min\Xi(\mathbf{f}): f_l \neq '0'\}$ which is usually much less than $2\Delta+2$). In return, no straightforward bandwidth stealing strategies seem to suggest themselves.

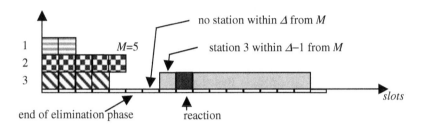

Fig. 3. EB/ECD-Δ protocol cycle ($\Delta=2$)

The station operation upon detection of a new protocol cycle is presented in Fig. 4 in a semiformal form. For simplicity and because we are primarily interested in heavy load conditions, the synchronisation after a longer idle spell is not considered. Two variables, M and *Counter*, are used, respectively, to store the maximum elimination burst observed and to count elimination slots beyond the Mth slot; another one allows to switch between various modes of operation in successive slots. The three vector counters, *fict_count*[], *own_count*[] and *other_count*[], may be used depending on the station strategy; their role will be explained later.

7 Performance Evaluation

In order to compare the performance of EB/ECD and EB/ECD-Δ in a non-cooperative MAC setting, a simulation model was used that featured: $N=10$ stations, including a varying number of nc-stations, $NC \in 0..N-1$, $L=50$ slots and symmetric heavy offered load meaning that each station always had a packet ready to transmit; the latter assumption created traffic conditions similar to a competing multimedia streams environment. Elimination burst lengths ranged from 1 to $E=12$. A few c- and nc-station strategies were modelled as described below.

A c-station model termed *Randomiser* used a truncated geometric pdf over $1..E$, with parameters 0.5, 1 or 2 corresponding to "gentle", "neutral" and "aggressive" play. Another model, called *Responsive Learner*, used instead what was believed to mimic best-response learning: based upon recent protocol cycles, it computed a histogram of

```
reset Counter;
select own burst length l from 1..E; transmit burst;
repeat for successive slots
 increment Counter
until slot sensed empty;
M := l+Counter; J :=min{Δ, M–1}; reset Counter;
for k∈ M+Δ+1..E do increment fict_count[k];
Mode := Recursion;
repeat for successive slots
 case Mode of
 Recursion:if l=M–J+Counter
                start tentative packet transmission;
                Mode := Tentative
            else case slot sensed
                empty: increment fict_count[M–J+Counter]
                busy:  increment fict_count[M–J+Counter]
                       increment other_count[M–J+Counter]
                       Mode := Reaction
                colliding: Mode := Pause;
            increment Counter
 Tentative: if slot sensed empty
                Mode := Recursion
            else
                increment fict_count[l];
                increment own_count[l];
                Mode := Packet
 Reaction: transmit one-slot reaction burst;
            Mode := Idle
 Pause:    Mode := Recursion
 Packet:   resume packet transmission;
            Mode := Idle
until (Counter=J) or (Mode := Idle)
```

Fig. 4. EB/ECD-Δ operation at a station

fictitious winning actions. Given **f**, *l* is a fictitious winning action if $f_l \neq$ '>1' and $\omega(f_1 \ldots f_{l-1}$ '1' $f_{l+1} \ldots f_E)=l$; thus action *l* either wins or would have won had it been taken. Referring to Fig. 3, suppose station 3 is doing the calculation. Because the 7th slot is empty, station 3 infers that no station transmitted a 3-slot burst which would have won, therefore it counts 3 as a fictitious winning action as it does its own winning action i.e., 4; if *E*=9 then 8 and 9 are counted too. For EB/ECD-0 it was found beneficial to count also *M*−1 in a no-winner situation. A Responsive Learner station used the vector counter *fict_count*[] to keep a count of fictitious winning actions in successive protocol cycles. After a number of protocol cycles (an update period), *fict_count*[] was reset, and a histogram of fictitious winning actions was built and averaged on a per update period basis using a linear autoregressive filter with a learning constant α. In each update period, an action was drawn from the calculated histogram and repeated consistently. To make the learning process realistically asynchronous across the set of stations, update periods were $UP+X$ protocol cycles long, with UP a constant and X drawn at random from $0..UP-1$. For the experiments, $UP=20$ and $\alpha=0.5$ were assumed.

For an nc-station, two models were adopted: Responsive Learner, acting as described above, and *Biased Randomiser* using the Randomiser pdf over $1..E$ modified by an upward bias $b \in 0..E-1$ (to be on the safe side, we assume that an nc-station has enough intelligence to adjust its bias in order to self-optimise its bandwidth share). Such strategies are arguably isolated, insistent, rational and statistically inconspicuous. Model homogeneity was assumed within each class of stations, leading to three realistic c- vs. nc-station model scenarios: Randomisers vs. Biased Randomisers/Responsive Learners, and Responsive Learners vs. Responsive Learners (we exclude the Responsive Learners vs. Biased Randomisers scenario since it seems irrational for an nc-station to consciously employ less intelligence than a c-station).

Under symmetric load, ideally $B_c = B_{nc} = 1/N$ (or 10%) times the total available bandwidth. Scheduling penalty causes this figure to drop below the 10% even in the cooperative MAC setting (as observed at $NC=0$), whereas bandwidth stealing in a non-cooperative setting (as observed at $NC>0$) may bring about a further decrease in B_c as well as discrepancies between B_c and B_{nc}. To learn how effectively these are prevented in EB/ECD-Δ, B_c was studied as a function of NC for EB/ECD-0 (i.e., our reference policy EB/ECD) and EB/ECD-8 in ways dependent on a particular scenario. $\Delta=8$ was found to be a good compromise between an increased scheduling penalty and the risk of a no-winner situation.

1. Randomisers vs. Biased Randomisers: taking a c-station's viewpoint, the worst-case scenario is for the nc-station strategies to reach an efficient Nash equilibrium with respect to b (as justified by their isolated and rational nature [6, 12]); what little bandwidth is then left for the c-stations can be regarded as the minimum guaranteed bandwidth. The corresponding B_c values (as percentages of the total available bandwidth) are shown in Fig. 5. Under EB/ECD-8, unless the c-stations play "gently", a Nash equilibrium can only be reached at $b=0$ regardless of NC, which is reflected by the two flat plots ("neutral" play is recommended). Note the distinct superiority of EB/ECD-8 to EB/ECD-0, for which a modest price is paid in the cooperative MAC setting if the c-stations play "gently".

2. Randomisers vs. Responsive Learners: as shown in Fig. 6, under EB/ECD-8 the nc-stations are unable to take full advantage of their increased intelligence, which they easily do under EB/ECD-0. Here, too, the nc-stations tend to reach a Nash equilibrium (with their averaged histograms of fictitious winning actions stabilising), which EB/ECD-8 prevents from being unfair to the c-stations provided the latter do not play too "aggressively" (again, "neutral" play is recommended). Note that the Nash equilibrium is not guaranteed to be unique. Interestingly enough, under EB/ECD-0 the c-stations enjoy a larger-than-fair bandwidth share when in the minority and playing "aggressively". This, however, comes at the cost of unacceptable performance for the cooperative MAC setting (cf. Fig. 2) and for smaller NC; it is also doubtful whether in this situation the nc-stations would feel much incentive to continue acting as such.

3. Responsive Learners vs. Responsive Learners: by learning to play effectively, the c-stations hope to induce desirable behaviour of the nc-stations (a "teach to learn" approach). What is feared now is that some nc-station might become a *sophisticated* player [10]. For example, it might attempt to be more consistent than other stations by lengthening its update periods whenever the latest selected action is deemed advantageous i.e., seek a Stackelberg equilibrium [2, 12], itself becoming the "leader". In this way the c-stations, instead of "teaching to learn" might themselves be "taught" to avoid certain advantageous actions (which is essentially what happened to the nc-stations under EB/ECD-0 in Fig. 6 when the c-stations played "aggressively"). In Fig. 7 and Fig. 8, after a third of the simulation run station 1 becomes the "leader" by increasing *UP* tenfold whenever the selected action is $E-\Delta$. It is then able to capture a significantly more than fair share of the total bandwidth. A form of protection is for a c-station to monitor, via a linear autoregressive filter, its own and other stations' winning rates associated with each action using *own_count*[] and *other_count*[]; a particular action is then favoured if own winning rate falls below, and other stations' remain above, a given threshold ε (assumed equal to 0.005). When the protection is switched on after another third of the simulation run, station 1's bandwidth share is supposed to drop down to approximately fair; this indeed happens under EB/ECD-8 in contrast with EB/ECD-0. Fig. 9 illustrates the insensitivity of EB/ECD-8 complete with the above protection to diverse values of *UP* (*UP* = 200 at the nc-stations). Note the difference in the Nash equilibrium efficiency for EB/ECD-0 and EB/ECD-8.

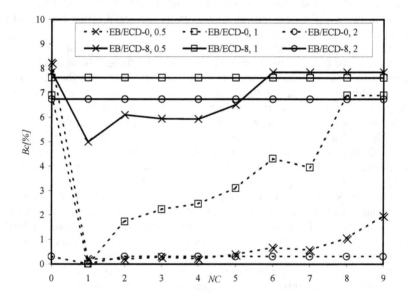

Fig. 5. Randomisers vs. Biased Randomisers, truncated geometric pdf with parameter indicated

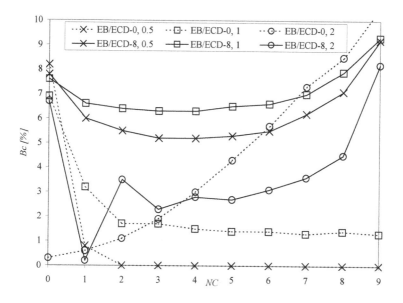

Fig. 6. Randomisers vs. Responsive Learners, truncated geometric pdf at c-stations with parameter indicated

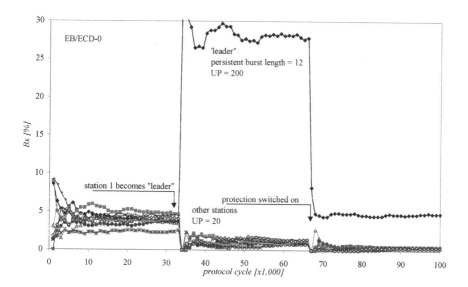

Fig. 7. Responsive Learners vs. Responsive Learners, station 1 plays "leader"; EB/ECD-0

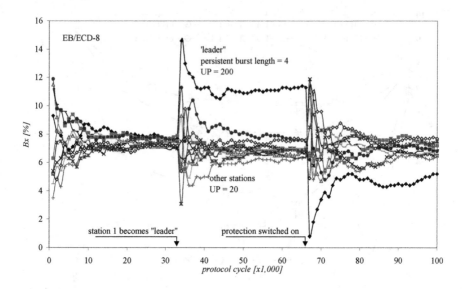

Fig. 8. Responsive Learners vs. Responsive Learners, station 1 plays "leader"; EB/ECD-8

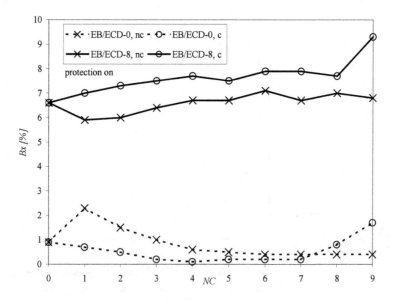

Fig. 9. Responsive Learners vs. Responsive Learners

8 Conclusion

In view of the non-cooperative paradigm gaining ground in the design of computer networks, non-cooperative scheduling policies at MAC level seem of interest, in particular in a wireless ad-hoc LANs where user volatility and the lack of tight administration (in particular, procedures to enforce prescribed bandwidth allocation) render c-stations prone to bandwidth stealing by nc-stations. The latter might feel particularly inclined to do so in a traffic environment where a number of multimedia streams i.e., long packet trains with minimum-bandwidth requirements compete for the channel bandwidth in an interleaved fashion. It is advisable in such an environment to design a scheduling policy so as to protect the c-stations' bandwidth share. One way of achieving that is to invoke a non-cooperative game with as fair and efficient a Nash equilibrium as possible. The presented EB/ECD-Δ policy provides a useful option though its significance is limited to the considered class of scheduling policies. Further research should extend this class as well as include a delay analysis.

References

1. ETSI TC Radio Equipment and Systems: High Performance Radio Local Area Network (HIPERLAN) Services and Facilities (1995)
2. Friedman E.J., Shenker S.: Synchronous and Asynchronous Learning by Responsive Learning Automata, Mimeo (1996)
3. Ha A.: Multimedia Applications Support for Wireless ATM Networks, Prentice Hall PTR (2000)
4. Heikkinen T.: On Learning and the Quality of Service in a Wireless Network, In: Proc. Int. Conf. Networking 2000, Lecture Notes in Computer Science 1815, Springer-Verlag, Berlin Heidelberg New York (2000) 679-688
5. IEEE Standard 802.11: Wireless LAN Media Access Control (MAC) and Physical Layer (PHY) Specifications (1999)
6. Kalai E., Lehrer E.: Rational Learning Leads to Nash Equilibrium, Econometrica 61 (1993) 1019-1045
7. Konorski J.: Packet Scheduling in Wireless LANs – A Framework for a Non-cooperative Paradigm, In: Proc. IFIP Int. Conf. on Personal Wireless Commun., Kluwer Academic (2000) 29-42
8. Korilis Y.A., Lazar A.A., Orda A.: Architecting Noncooperative Networks, IEEE J. Selected Areas Commun. 13 (1995) 1241-1251
9. Lazar A.A., Semret A.: Auctions for Network Resource Sharing, Tech. Rep. CU/CTR/TR 468-97-02, Columbia Univ. (1997)
10. Milgrom P., Roberts J..: Adaptive and Sophisticated Learning in Normal Form Games, Games and Economic Behaviour 3 (1991) 82-100
11. Sanders B.A.: An Incentive Compatible Flow Control Algorithm for Rate Allocation in Computer Networks, IEEE Trans. Comput. 37 (1988) 1067-1072
12. Shenker S.: Making Greed Work in Networks: A Game-Theoretic Analysis of Switch Service Disciplines, In: Proc. SIGCOMM'94 (1994)

Ad Hoc Routing in Bluetooth

Jeroen P.F. Willekens M.Sc.

Ericsson EuroLab Netherlands, Ericssonstraat 2, P.O.Box 8, 5120 AA Rijen,
The Netherlands
Jeroen.Willekens@eln.ericsson.se

Abstract. Bluetooth is a wireless, small, cheap and power efficient communication technology. It appears to be a candidate for building ad hoc networks. In this area some problems still have to be investigated, especially with respect to the ad hoc routing scheme to be used in these networks. In this paper the problem of ad hoc routing in Bluetooth networks is introduced and the results of a simulation study to determine the applicability of three existing ad hoc routing protocols in dynamic ad hoc networks are presented. The reactive protocol Ad-Hoc On Demand Vector Routing (AODV) is performing especially well in the simulations. A hybrid routing protocol, in this case the Zone Routing Protocol (ZRP), seems not to be as promising as expected. Proactive routing protocols function very poorly.

1 Introduction

Nowadays the availability of laptops, mobile phones, and for example handheld organizers is high. People like to have the capability to communicate with them and to connect them to data networks. Furthermore mobility is becoming more important. Communication facilities should be available always and everywhere. This is the context where both Bluetooth and ad hoc networks appear.

1.1 Bluetooth

In the 90s, some technologies appeared on the market to eliminate the cables around electronic devices such as computers. Wireless technologies were introduced to give peripheral equipment connectivity to the computer without using a separate data cable. An example of is the infrared interface.

Bluetooth has been designed to be an inexpensive, small, power efficient, short-range communication technology. It is operates in the "free" 2.4 GHz ISM band and uses a frequency hopping scheme through 79 1Mhz-wide bands. The gross bitrate is 1 Mbit/s and the radio range is about 10m - with power amplification 100m. Although it was first developed to be used only for cable replacement, already in an early stage of development networking facilities were incorporated. It was foreseen that people would have more digital devices in a small area, which would like to have the capability to communicate with each other.

M.J. van Sinderen and L.J.M. Nieuwenhuis (Eds.): PROMS 2001, LNCS 2213, pp. 130-144, 2001.
© Springer-Verlag Berlin Heidelberg 2001

A personal area network (PAN) is an example of them. All digital devices (mobile phone, laptop, organizer, wireless wallet, etc.) that a person is carrying around himself can form a network. Such PANs are foreseen to be an area where Bluetooth can play an important role.

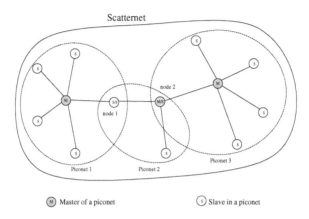

Fig. 1. A Bluetooth scatternet consisting of different piconets

To support these types of PANs Bluetooth nodes are able to form piconets. A piconet is a network of one master and up to seven (active) slaves, see Figure 1. All slaves are connected to the master by a bi-directional link. All the nodes in the piconet share a common radio channel with a gross bit rate of 1 Mbit/s – the channel is defined by a pseudo random frequency hopping scheme. On the radio channel the master addresses the slaves by a 7 bit temporary MAC-address and the slaves identify themselves to the master by this address; this leads to the logical topology of a star, because in this addressing scheme a slave can not address directly other slaves. The master controls the radio channel. Although synchronous and asynchronous communication is possible on the radio channel, this investigation concentrates only on the asynchronous communication. For asynchronous communication the master has to poll the slaves in order to give them the permission to send data back.

To make larger networks, either with more nodes or with an extended range, the Bluetooth specifications shortly describes the possibility to form a scatternet [1]. A scatternet is a group of piconets, interconnected by nodes which are a member of more than one piconet, see Figure 1. The scatternet has the shared node 1 and the shared node 2. Node 1 is a slave in two piconets. Node 2 is master of its own piconet and slave in another piconet as well. In the current specifications, only the principle of scatternets is introduced, without solving for example the problems of synchronization between the piconets and the problem of network topology construction and maintaining. It is still an important area for research.

1.2 Research Problem

To run ad hoc networks the problem of routing is one of the important problems to be solved. At the moment, no ad hoc routing protocols have been specified for Bluetooth networks. In a different context, some ad hoc routing protocols have been developed already. The research question addressed in this article is "Which (existing) ad hoc routing protocol seems to be most promising in dynamic Bluetooth networks?"

This research question has been answered by means of a simulation study. Three different existing ad hoc routing protocols have been selected for simulation in a dynamic Bluetooth network. For the dynamic Bluetooth network two different scenarios are defined that differ in size and mobility. A two-factor-full-factorial-design-with-replication, including the accompanying statistical methods, is applied.

1.3 Existing Work

In the IETF MANET (Mobile Ad Hoc Networks) working group, work is ongoing on ad hoc networking technology in general and the ad hoc routing protocols in particular. All discussed protocols were developed for IP networks, although some of them can be deployed in other networks as well. Without going into details, some of the recently discussed protocols are:

- Ad Hoc On-Demand Vector Routing (AODV) [2]
- Zone Routing Protocol (ZRP) [3]
- Adaptive Demand-Driven Multicast Routing Protocol (ADMR) [4]
- Dynamic Source Routing and Flow State in Dynamic Source Routing (DSR)[5, 6]
- Fisheye State Routing Protocol (FSR) [7]
- Landmark Routing Protocol (LANMAR) [8]
- Optimized Link State Routing Protocol (OLSR) [9]
- Topology Broadcast Based on Reverse-Path Forwarding (TBRPF) [10]
- Temporally-Ordered Routing Algorithm (TORA) [11]

They all have their own characteristics, but some general approached can be distinguished. They are discussed later in the paper.

Some more information about ad hoc routing has been published outside MANET. For example the protocol Destination-Sequence Distance Vector Routing (DSDV) [12]. In the articles of Royer [13] and of Misra [14] many other routing protocols are discussed. In total 21 existing ad hoc routing protocols were found.

Concerning Bluetooth routing a proposal for a routing scheme is given by Bhagwat et al. [15]. They focused on a source routing scheme in which the paths are decoded by routing vectors. The scheme can be deployed in Bluetooth scatternets. Unfortunately, a good comparison with other schemes based on empirical research is not given.

Some research has been done to ad hoc routing protocols without making assumptions on the communication technology. Some comparative studies to mention are: Larsson [16], Johansson [17] and Das [18]. Their results are discussed in the next section of this article.

The contribution of this paper is that it compares different types of ad-hoc routing protocols, assuming Bluetooth as the underlying communication technology and assuming an environment typical for Bluetooth networks.

1.4 Structure of the Article

An the remainder of this paper an introduction is given first to ad hoc routing in general and the possibilities of the application of ad hoc routing in Bluetooth more specifically. Bluetooth, scatternet forming, routing, user behavior and the scenarios were modeled in order to be able to implement and simulate ad hoc routing in those highly dynamic networks. This is explained in the next section. Thereafter the results of the simulations are presented and discussed. Finally the conclusions and some recommendations for further work are given.

2 Ad Hoc Networking

An ad hoc network is a network, which always can be formed, everywhere, independent of fixed infrastructure, and without central entities. This is in contrast to most networks, which are built up very carefully, with fixed devices and fixed infrastructure. There are special (central) nodes like routers and name servers.

Because Bluetooth is a communication technology that is independent of fixed infrastructure, and which has been developed especially for mobile devices, it should be suitable to make ad hoc networks.

In ad hoc networking with Bluetooth two questions are very important. The first one is "How is the scatternet formed and, therefore, how is the topology determined?" and the other one is "How is the routing carried out?" First an introduction to ad hoc routing is given and the topology formation is discussed later in the paper.

2.1 Ad Hoc Routing

Traditional routing protocols in general have some requirements on the underlying network. Known topologies, a few broken links per time unit, the number of new upcoming links per time unit and central entities are just some of the assumptions. Because in an ad hoc network most of the nodes will be moving, the topology is likely to change all the time. Further, it is not known which nodes will join the network; therefore, no well-known central control entities can be part of it.

The existing ad hoc routing protocols were designed to address these problems. A distinction into three categories can be made. The different types are the so called proactive, reactive, and hybrid ad hoc routing protocols. They are shown in Figure 2.

The first type (proactive) tries to gather all the routing information for all destinations before any packet to the destinations can be sent. In general this routing protocol has the same characteristics as the traditional ones, with some adaptations for ad hoc environments. Most well known in this category is DSDV (Destination-Sequenced Distance Vector Routing [12]). It is a distributed routing scheme, using hop-by-hop routing, based on distance vector routing. It is a unicast routing protocol and can be deployed on a network that exists of nodes with point-to-point links in between them (in contrast to networks in which the messages are broadcast).

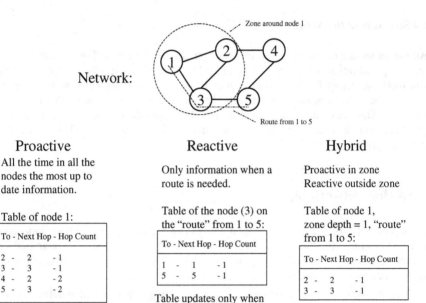

Network:

Proactive

All the time in all the
nodes the most up to
date information.

Table of node 1:

To - Next Hop - Hop Count		
2 -	2	- 1
3 -	3	- 1
4 -	2	- 2
5 -	3	- 2

Table updates via sending
routing tables to neighbors.

Reactive

Only information when a
route is needed.

Table of the node (3) on
the "route" from 1 to 5:

To - Next Hop - Hop Count		
1 -	1	- 1
5 -	5	- 1

Table updates only when
needed via route request
and route replies.

Hybrid

Proactive in zone
Reactive outside zone

Table of node 1,
zone depth = 1, "route"
from 1 to 5:

To - Next Hop - Hop Count		
2 -	2	- 1
3 -	3	- 1

To - Next Hop - Hop Count		
5 -	3	- 2

Fig. 2. Different types of ad hoc routing protocols

The second type, the reactive protocols, start gathering routing information for a specific location only if a route to that location is needed. This is done by sending a route request when a packet for an unknown location arrives. The route request spreads through the network and as soon as the destination is reached, this node sends back a route reply. Based on the route reply, the source-node is able to send the data packets in the right direction. Most prominent in this group is AODV (Ad-hoc On Demand Distance Vector Protocol, [2]). It is a protocol developed to be used in link-oriented ad hoc networks; it supports uni- and multi-cast and has the optional use of hello-messages (a sort of heart-beat mechanism to check if the neighbors are still active – alive); it introduces no hierarchy and has no other assumptions on the used communication technology.

The third type of routing protocol is the hybrid one. Hybrid, as the name suggests, means the protocol has a proactive part and a reactive part. In general the network is divided into zones or clusters. Within these zones, with a radius of only a few hops, a proactive protocol is used and for destination outside the zone a reactive protocol will be used. The protocol ZRP (Zone Routing Protocol, [3]) is a framework that can be used in hybrid routing. It defines zones, with a given zone-depth, around every node. For the proactive routing in the zone two recommendations are given, a link state and a distance vector implementation. For the reactive routing outside this zone only one recommendation is given. This all is combined with the so-called Bordercast Resolution Protocol, which provides some assistance functions, used particularly in the reactive part of the protocol.

Already some research has been done in the area of ad hoc routing protocols. The proactive protocols function well, but they generate a lot of overhead data and in cases of high mobility their performance decreases quickly. The reactive protocols function significantly better; but the delays are increasing because of the waiting time during a route request procedure [16, 18, 19]. At this moment there are a few publications about hybrid protocols available [3, 20]. Hybrid protocols are considered promising, when there are few changes in the topology in the local zone, and many more outside the zone. Good empirical comparisons between hybrid on the one hand and proactive and reactive on the other hand are not yet available.

At this moment no convergence to "the best" ad hoc routing protocol is seen. Some protocols function better in specific environments and scenario's; others have such specific characteristics that they can only be deployed in specific networks. Most of the protocols are only available as a description and as an implementation in a simulation tool. Real implementations are scarce and it is not yet known which protocol will function well in real networks. One can conclude that still a lot of work has to be done in this area.

2.2 Ad Hoc Routing Protocols for Bluetooth

The Bluetooth specifications [1] provide no specific solutions for ad hoc networking. Routing in Bluetooth is still an issue of research. It is foreseen that a routing mechanism must be incorporated in the Bluetooth stack. At least the master has to have the capability to route between its slaves. This is called piconet-routing. In the scenario of scatternet the shared nodes (slaves and masters) need a mechanism to route the packets between the piconets.

Bluetooth has some specific characteristics that do not allow the use of some ad hoc routing protocols. Some of these specific characteristics are discussed here.

Bluetooth is a link-oriented network. This in contrast to the broadcast oriented networks. In the first type links are created between nodes, and it takes some time to build the topology. In the second type, a node sends a radio-message and everyone who is able to hear the message is allowed to listen to, and process the message.

A second important characteristic is that Bluetooth is a radio technology with a small available bandwidth. In addition, nodes have to be small and cheap, which implies less electrical and computation power available. Therefore, things must be done as efficiently as possible. An example is the use of hello and/or beacon message. These messages are used to check the availability of a link and a neighbor. They create extra overhead and they are not necessary in Bluetooth. The lower layers control the links and detect errors on the links and the unavailability of the peer node – this information can be re-used in the routing protocol.

A very specific characteristic is the synchronizations which occur in a piconet and not among piconets. Consequently, within a piconet all nodes know the clock of the master and are synchronized to that clock – outside that specific piconet they know nothing of the other clocks in the network. Therefore, for example, routing protocols are not able to use timestamps.

Some routing protocols are based on the knowledge of the location of a node, which is another limitation. In Bluetooth this information is not available. Only some information on the signal strength of a node, to which one is already connected, can be used to deliver proximity services to the higher layers.

In a way, Bluetooth is a technology without hierarchy, because, in principle, all nodes are equal. Only after setting up a link, the roles of master and slave are given to the two nodes. In this way a form of hierarchy is introduced, but is very Bluetooth specific. On the other hand, this introduced hierarchy which is reused in every piconet does not introduce any limitations to the use of a not-hierarchical routing scheme.

The Bluetooth addresses are given to the nodes without any specific scheme. Therefore, if the ad hoc routing algorithm uses the Bluetooth address scheme, it should not assume any structure in the used address scheme.

In this research, the three most important representatives of the categories reactive, hybrid and proactive have been selected for simulation. They are, respectively, AODV (Ad hoc On Demand Distance Vector Protocol), ZRP (Zone Routing Protocol) and DSDV (Destination-Sequenced Distance Vector Routing). With all factors accounted for, it is decided to use these protocols for testing ad hoc routing in Bluetooth.

3 Modeling

3.1 Bluetooth

Bluetooth is a technology with a complicated baseband structure. In the specifications most of this is described [1], but some specific characteristics can be vendor dependent. Because of these two factors it was decided to make a macro model of the Bluetooth technology. In the next paragraphs some characteristics of the nodes are discussed: the source, the scatternet forming algorithm, the routing algorithms, and the movement pattern of the nodes. The other basic ingredients of the model are nodes that have a specific role (a slave, a master or idle/not connected). Every node has a unique address. Between the nodes there are links, of which the existence is determined by the scatternet forming algorithm. The links get a capacity, but only when this capacity was needed for that specific link – a capacity allocation algorithm allocates the total piconet capacity to the links in the piconet. The capacity was, per link, divided into an upstream and downstream bitrate, and some capacity was reserved as being "Bluetooth-overhead". The packets that are transferred over the links get a delay that is dependent on the capacity of that link and the size of the packet. Two types of packets were introduced: data packets and routing-algorithm-information-packets.

3.2 Scatternet Forming

Only the principle of Bluetooth scatternets has been introduced in the specifications [1], without defining the implementation and relevant protocols in detail. For the sake of this investigation some extra assumptions regarding the scatternet forming and maintenance algorithm have been made.

In this investigation only the macro-aspects of scatternetting were taken into account. These are the topology forming and maintenance (inclusive piconet forming). Other aspects are also related to scatternetting in Bluetooth. For example, the problem that a slave has to synchronize itself to different piconets on a time division multiplexed base. This baseband related problem is neither in the current specifications [1] nor in the implementations been addressed or solved and therefore this could not be modeled in the simulator. On the other hand, it was taken into account in the models at macro level.

Scatternet forming algorithms are not yet available. A scatternet-forming algorithm has been developed, which has some topology maintaining aspects in it. It is a lightweight solution and designed on basis of logical reasoning.

The algorithm strives for some network-related objectives. The first one is that all the nodes are connected to a single network. Another parameter is the robustness, which implies that the network is not allowed to be split up into separate parts because a crucial link was broken. After some logical reasoning these more general characteristics were translated in a set of measurable goals and in a set of executable priorities. These goals were: A master strives for 4 slaves in its piconet – a slave strives for 3 masters – and between two interconnected piconets the nodes strive for two slaves that are shared by both piconets. The priorities were: first "connecting unconnected nodes", the next one was "to get 4 slaves per master" and last "to have 3 master per slave" and "to have two different shared slaves between two piconets". The shared role of being a master and a slave was not allowed. The distributed algorithm was executed in every node at fixed intervals. At that moment a procedure was executed to find other nodes in the radio range that were also searching for another node, and if according to their current role and characteristics, they did like to contact each other a new link was formed. Links were only broken when the two nodes moved out of each others radio range. The radio range was set to 10 meters.

This algorithm was tested in a small simulator. It is very successful in contacting all the nodes and forming a single network. For small amounts of time some nodes were not connected or the network was split up into separate scatternets.

3.3 Routing Protocols

DSDV was modeled according to the specifications given in [12]. Some choices had to be made for the parameters in the protocol. This was done on basis of information in literature [17] and on basis of some preliminary tests of the algorithm in simulations. The most important parameter in the simulations is the time in between complete table broadcasts to neighbors. This parameter was set to 3 seconds. Another parameter is the time a route has to be stored in the table, although it became inactive. This time was set to 30 seconds.

AODV was modeled according to the specifications given in the Internet draft [2] that was posted to the MANET workgroup of the IETF. Values for the parameters in the algorithm are recommended in this document. After some preliminary simulations with these parameters and some small adaptations that perform best in the simulated network, the values mentioned in Table 1 were used in the simulations (RREQ = Route Request – TTL = Time to Live, expressed in number of hops).

The multicast options and optional use of hello-messages were not implemented.

Table 1. Parameters in the Simulated AODV Algorithm

parameter	value
Remember RREQ's	30 [s]
Time per TTL before RREQ retry	0.05 [s]
Maximum RREQ retries	3
RREQ TTL start	10
RREQ TTL increase	10
RREQ TTL max	40
Route Active	3 [s]

ZRP was modeled and implemented according to the specifications given in the Internet draft [3]. There the protocol is split up into two different "geographical" parts. One is the zone directly around a node, the geographical area where proactive routing has to be executed. It was decided to implement the link state solution for the proactive part of the algorithm, because its performance, within the zone, is comparable with the proactive DSDV protocol. The routing protocol that was used outside the zone was implemented similar to the implementation of the AODV protocol. The optional use of source routing for specific sections of the whole path was not implemented. The internet draft included a pseudo-code implementation as well. This was not used, because it was not easy to implement it in that way in the simulator.

One of the main parameters of ZRP is the zone depth. All the nodes in a Bluetooth network do already know their neighbors. Therefore, they have, at a lower Bluetooth level, already created a proactive knowledge about all the nodes one hop away. In this simulation, this information was not directly used in the routing protocols, but it is expected that ZRP could use this if the zone-depth was set to 1 hop. Therefore, in this experiment the zone depth was chosen to be 1.

3.4 User(s) of the Network

User behavior was modeled in two ways. One was the movement pattern of the nodes. At the beginning of the simulation some nodes get a given and randomly chosen speed and they start moving in a randomly chosen direction. When they arrive at a wall they change their direction according to the rule "the angle of incidence is the angle of reflection". All the nodes are moving independently of each other.

The parameters of the data-sources are another part of user behavior. These parameters reflect the expected type of data-traffic: a combination of internet applications and LAN communication (printer – file server – etc.). The most important corresponding characteristic is the burstiness of these completely different types of traffic. Another choice concerning LAN-traffic is the size of a data packet, they are modeled as packets of 1500 bytes, the standard size on an Ethernet.

The sources were modeled as a bursty ON/OFF source. It was a discrete-time Markov source with two states: sending a burst of packets or being idle (see Figure 3). The possible transitions between the states were made at fixed moments, with an time interval equal to the transmission time of a data packet.

In this research a LAN access scenario was foreseen. Two types of sources were introduced: a "normal" node, which sometimes sends a small train of packets and is quiet for a much longer time, and a "LAN-access" node that sends substantially more trains of packets to the nodes in the network. These trains of packets are on an average basis longer than the trains from the nodes in the network. All packets in one train are addressed to the same node. The LAN-access nodes address only the other nodes in the network, randomly chosen and uniformly distributed. The "normal" nodes in the network address a LAN-access point with 80% certainty, randomly chosen and uniformly spread, and for the other 20% another node in the network.

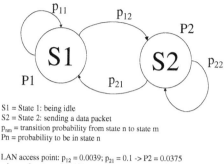

S1 = State 1: being idle
S2 = State 2: sending a data packet
p_{nm} = transition probability from state n to state m
P_n = probability to be in state n

LAN access point: p_{12} = 0.0039; p_{21} = 0.1 -> P2 = 0.0375
other nodes: p_{12} = 0.00039; p_{21} = 0.3 -> P2 = 0.0013

Fig. 3. The model of the sources

3.5 Scenarios for Simulation

Two scenarios that are foreseen to be realistic in the near future were drawn up. In both situations the purpose of the formed ad hoc network is to give people access to a LAN in the building.

The first one is an office scenario in which about four to eight people are working. Some people have a personal area network. Therefore 20 Bluetooth nodes are in this area, but because of the relative static situation in an office only 5 are moving.

The second one is that of an exhibition hall. In this larger hall there are more people: there are 80 Bluetooth nodes. Of this group of Bluetooth nodes, more nodes are moving and the distribution of the speeds of the nodes is a little bit larger. All the details about these two scenarios can be found in table 2.

Table 2. The parameters of the different scenarios

parameter	Office scenario	Exhibition hall scenario
area size	10x20m	20x40m
number of nodes	20	80
number of LAN access points	2	8
number of moving nodes	5	60
speeds of the moving nodes	uniformly distributed throughout the interval 0.9 – 1.1 m/s	uniformly distributed throughout the interval 0.8 – 1.4 m/s

In both scenarios the LAN access points are located at the walls. These nodes are equally spread over the four walls of the rectangle area.

4 Experiment

The experiment to test the suitability of the protocols in Bluetooth ad hoc networks was carried out as a simulation study. In the simulations only two variables were changed during the different executions of the simulations. They are the two different simulated scenarios and the different routing protocols. Therefore there were 6 different simulations. Every simulation was done 5 times in order to find an average behavior. All simulations were executed for a simulated time of 500 seconds.

In these experiments three different parameters were constantly measured. They are throughput, delay, and generated overhead percentage. See Table 3 for more details.

Table 3. The measured parameters in the simulations

parameter	description	unit
throughput	the percentage of all the user data that arrived at the destination	[%]
delay	the average of the times between generation of a data packet at a source and the arrival at a destination	[s]
overhead as a percentage of total transmitted user data	the amount of generated routing algorithm data divided by the total amount of transmitted user data	[%]

The "Theory of design of experiments" influenced the analysis of the measurements. More information on this theory and the used statistical analysis can be found in [21]. In this theory the two-factor-full-factorial-design-with-replication did fit exactly on the above-mentioned experimental design. This resulted in an experiment that could be analyzed with a set of statistical technologies. A statistical model was applied in which the influence of all input variables and the interaction effects between the input variables were calculated. The relevance of these parameters was calculated. On basis of the calculated model parameters one was able to calculate the percentage of explained variation as the result of a change in the input parameter "Routing protocol", "scenario" or the "interaction effect". The remainder of 100% variation is the experimental error.

During the preliminary simulations a dependency of ZRP on the zone depth was noticed. This is expected, because at a zone depth of 0 the algorithm has to function as a pure reactive protocol, and at a zone depth of infinite the algorithm has to function as a pure proactive protocol. At other zone-depths it is expected the performance of the ZRP algorithm is just a combination of the proactive and reactive part or it combines best of both and functions significantly better.

Therefore, some extra simulations were done on the ZRP algorithm in which the zone-depths was varied. This was done in the exhibition hall scenario, for a simulated time of 50 seconds, and every simulation at a given zone-depth was repeated two times.

4.1 Results and Discussion

The measured results for all combinations of scenario and routing algorithm are presented in combination with a discussion of these results. In Tables 4, 5 and 6 the average values of the five measurements for the specific combinations are presented. The small printed number right below the average is the standard deviation on that average. The calculated values concerning the explained variations are given in the same tables. In Table 7 the results of ZRP as function of the zone-depth are given.

4.2 Throughput

All the routing algorithms perform quite well concerning throughput. In the office scenario DSDV has a (little) larger packet loss than AODV and ZRP. The largest difference between the routing algorithms can be found in the exhibition hall scenario. In this situation DSDV is not able to handle the larger mobility of the nodes.

The variation is explained for a large part by the routing algorithm, because DSDV is in general not performing as well. The explained variance by the interaction effects is large because in general all throughput was above 96% but only in one specific situation, DSDV and the exhibition hall scenario, the measured result is much lower.

Table 4. Results of the simulation concerning throughput

Throughput			
	AODV (reactive)	ZRP (hybrid)	DSDV (proactive)
office scenario	99.9% 0.12	99.9% 0.07	96.6% 4.82
exhibition hall scenario	98.9% 0.19	98.6% 0.24	49.2% 0.24

type of effect	explained variation	relevance
scenario	19.8%	relevant
routing protocol	44.9%	relevant
interaction effects	34.4%	relevant
unexplained (experimental error)	0.9%	

4.3 Delay

The routing algorithms explain the variation in the delay only partly. The explained variation originates for more than 95% from the change in scenario. This can be explained by the fact that the average path length between two nodes is larger in the exhibition hall scenario.

If, on the other hand, one compares the measured delay of the different algorithms it is clear that DSDV always has a shorter or equal delay, compared with AODV. This is as expected because in the DSDV routing table all the routing information is already available. Therefore, a packet does not have to wait for an answer on a route request.

In the exhibition hall scenario, ZRP still has a better performance than DSDV due to the lower overhead percentage for ZRP. In this specific scenario DSDV generates about 20 times more overhead data. This data fills up queues and increases the waiting times of packets.

Table 5. Results of the simulation concerning delay

Delay			
	AODV (reactive)	ZRP (hybrid)	DSDV (proactive)
office scenario	0.12s 0.013	0.13s 0.014	0.12 0.031
exhibition hall scenario	0.54s 0.085	0.47s 0.023	0.50 0.011

type of effect	explained variation	relevance
scenario	95.6%	relevant
routing protocol	0.5%	not relevant
interaction effects	0.6%	not relevant
unexplained (experimental error)	3.3%	

4.4 Overhead Data

In all the scenarios, evaluated here, DSDV is rather inefficient. It generates so much overhead data that the data transmission through the network consists largely of overhead data (especially in the case of the exhibition hall scenario). AODV performs best and ZRP has, concerning overhead data, a performance that is in between that of proactive and reactive. These observations are seen in both scenarios, but in the exhibition hall scenario the differences are larger because of the larger mobility.

The values of the explained variation confirm this. A relative small proportion of the variation is explained by the change of scenario. A larger part is explained by the change of routing protocol. Moreover, a large part of the variation originates from the interaction effect between DSDV and the exhibition hall scenario in particular.

Table 6. Results of the simulation concerning overhead, as percentage of the rransmitted user data

Overhead, as Percentage of the Transmitted User Data						
	AODV (reactive)		ZRP (hybrid)		DSDV (proactive)	
office scenario	15.6%		58.4%		169.7%	
		1.83		5.97		24.5
exhibition hall scenario	53.2%		271.2%		5400%	
		1.7		18.5		203.7
type of effect		explained variation		relevance		
scenario		21.4%		relevant		
routing protocol		41.2%		relevant		
interaction effects		37.2%		relevant		
unexplained (experimental error)		0.1%				

4.5 The Performance of ZRP as Function of the Zone-Depth

As expected the performance of ZRP inclines towards that of a reactive protocol ($\approx$AODV) if the zone depth is going to 0 and to that of a proactive one ($\approx$DSDV) in the case the zone depth increases to "infinity". It was expected that there would be a point for this algorithm where the performance of ZRP is even better than that of AODV and DSDV. This is not observed in the measurements if one analyses the measured overhead percentage. The throughput is slightly better in the case of zone depth 1, but this could be coincidental because the average is based on two measurements. Concerning delay it seems that zone-depth 1 is a good choice, but this comes at the cost of more overhead.

Table 7. The Average of 2 measurements of the ZRP algorithm at different zone depths

zone depth	throughput	delay [s]	overhead
0	96.6%	0.69	335.8%
1	96.9%	0.49	354.8%
3	96.4%	0.59	754.9%
6	95.3%	0.74	2985.1%
10	86.7%	1.59	3774.8%
15	88.0%	1.61	2937.7%
20	82.5%	1.65	3863.7%

5 Conclusions

Within the limits of this research it can be concluded that AODV performs best in a Bluetooth environment. In accordance with the information given in literature DSDV is not able to handle an increase of mobility. ZRP performs on some parameters just as a combination of DSDV and AODV, but concerning delay it performs better when the mobility was much higher.

In ZRP the zone depth is probably the most important parameter when configuring this algorithm, no optimum was found in which the algorithm performs much better than a purely reactive or a purely proactive protocol. Only at zone-depth 1 is the performance better concerning delay.

5.1 Further Work

In this investigation only some conclusions can be drawn on basis of the chosen scenarios and simulated ad hoc routing protocols. Therefore more work should be done. First of all this includes simulations of other available ad hoc routing protocols and Bluetooth specific protocols. Further, varying the mobility scenarios and traffic conditions can give more insight in the specific differences between proactive and reactive in Bluetooth networks. In the paper the models that are used in the simulations are mentioned. Some choices in these models are rather arbitrary. The scatternet-forming algorithm, for example, is kept constant in this investigation. Changing the topology of the network can effect the performance of the different ad hoc routing protocols. Therefore, more work should be done on investigating the specific dependencies on the Bluetooth-specific characteristics.

References

1. Bluetooth Special Interest Group," Specification of the Bluetooth System, v1.1B, volume 1 and 2", February 22nd 2001, available at: http://www.bluetooth.com/ (20 March 2001)
2. Charles E. Perkins et al.; "Ad Hoc On-Demand Distance Vector (AODV) Routing", *IETF Internet Draft*, http://www.ietf.org/internet-drafts/draft-ietf-manet-aodv-05.txt (20 March 2000)
3. Zygmunt J. Haas and Marc R. Pearlman, "The Zone Routing Protocol (ZRP) for Ad Hoc Networks", *IETF Internet Draft*, http://www.ietf.org/internet-drafts/draft-ietf-manet-zone-zrp-04.txt (June 1999)
4. Jetchevan, Jorjeta G. and David B. Johnson, "The Adaptive Demand-Driven Multicast Routing Protocol", *IETF Internet Draft*, http://www.ietf.org/internet-drafts/draft-ietf-manet-admr-00.txt (13 July 2001)
5. Johnson, David B. Johnson, et al., "The Dynamic Source Routing Protocol for Mobile Ad Hoc Networks", *IETF Internet Draft*, http://www.ietf.org/internet-drafts/draft-ietf-manet-dsr-05.txt (2 March 2001)
6. Hu, Yih-Chun Hu, et al., "Flow State in the Dynamic Source Routing Protocol for Mobile Ad Hoc Networks", *IETF Internet Draft*, http://www.ietf.org/internet-drafts/draft-ietf-manet-dsrflow-00.txt (23 February 2001)
7. Gerla, Mario, et al., "Fisheye State Routing Protocol (FSR) for Ad Hoc Networks", *IETF Internet Draft*, http://www.ietf.org/internet-drafts/draft-ietf-manet-fsr-01.txt (17 November 2000)
8. Gerla, Mario, et al., "Landmark Routing Protocol (LANMAR) for Large Scale Ad Hoc Networks", *IETF Internet Draft*, http://www.ietf.org/internet-drafts/draft-ietf-manet-lanmar-02.txt (17 May 2001)
9. Jacquet, Philippe, et al., "Optimized Link State Routing Protocol", *IETF Internet Draft*, http://www.ietf.org/internet-drafts/draft-ietf-manet-olsr-04.txt (2 March 2001)

10. Bellur, Bhargav, et al., "Topology Broadcast Based on Reverse-Path Forwarding (TBRPF)", *IETF Internet Draft*, http://www.ietf.org/internet-drafts/draft-ietf-manet-tbrpf-01.txt (2 March 2001)
11. Park, V., et al., "Temporally-Ordered Routing Algorithm (TORA) Version 1", *IETF Internet Draft*, http://www.ietf.org/internet-drafts/draft-ietf-manet-tora-spec-03.txt (24 November 2000)
12. Charles E. Perkins, Praving Bhagwat, "Highly Dynamic Destination-Sequenced Distance-Vector Routing (DSDV) for Mobile Computers" In *Proceedings of the SIGCOM '94 Conference on Communications Architecture, Protocols and Applications*, pages 234-244, August 1994. A revised version of the paper is available from http://www.cs.umd.edu/projects/mcml/papers/Sigcomm94.ps (20 November 2000)
13. Royer, Elizabeth M., et al., "A Review of Current Routing Protocols for Ad Hoc Mobile Wireless Networks", IEEE Personal Communications, April 1999, p46-55
14. Misra, Padmini, "Routing Protocols for Ad Hoc Mobile Wireless Networks", http://www.cis.ohio-state.edu/~misra (July 2000)
15. Bhagwat, Pravin and Segall, Adrian, "A Routing Vector Method (RVM) for Rotuing in Bluetooth Scatternets", *The Sixth IEEE International Workshop on Mobile Multimedia Communications (MOMUC'99)*, Nov 1999
16. T Larsson and N. Hedman, "Routing Protocols in Wireless Ad-hoc Networks – A Simulation Study", Graduation study at the Luleå University of Technology and Ericsson SwitchLab, Department of Computer Science and Electrical Engineering, Luleå University of Technology.
17. Per Johansson et al., "Scenario-based Performance Analysis of Routing Protocols for Mobile Ad-hoc Networks." *Proceedings Mobicom 1999*, Pages: 1414-1420.
18. Das, Samir R., et al., "Comprarative Performance Evaluation of Routing Protocols for Mobile, Ad hoc Networks*", Proceedings of 7th Int. Conf. on Computer Communications and Networks (IC3N)*, Lafayette, LA, October, 1998, pages 153-161
19. Sung-Ju Lee *et. al.*, "A Simulation Study of Table-Driven and On-Demand Routing Protocols for Mobile Ad Hoc Networks", IEEE Network, July-Aug 1999 , p48 –54
20. Jiang, Mingliang, et al., "Cluster Based Routing Protocol (CBRP)", *IETF Internet Draft*, http://www.ietf.org/internet-drafts/draft-ietf-manet-cbrp-spec-01.txt (14 August 1999)
21. R. Jain, "The Art of Computer Systems Performance Analysis, Techniques for Experimental Design, Measurement, Simulation and Modeling", John Wiley & Sons, New York, 1991

An Open Signaling Protocol for Wireless Host Mobility

George Kormentzas, D. Vergados, J. Soldatos, and G. Stassinopoulos

National Technical University of Athens,
Electrical & Computer Eng. Dept.,
Computer Science Division,
9 HEROON POLYTECHNEIOU STR., GR-15773 ZOGRAFOU, GREECE
{gkorm, vergados, jsoldat, stassin}@telecom.ntua.gr

Abstract. The paper presents a distributed multi-agent system designed to give flexible, scaleable, robust and efficient connection management of WATM networks. The presented system includes distributed software entities (i.e., agents) that provide a virtual environment for deploying management and control operations, and generic interfaces between agents complying with the programmable network interfaces specified in the emerging P1520 reference model. Given that conventional ATM signaling protocols can not support the functionality offered by the discussed system, the paper proposes and describes an open signaling protocol for efficiently and effectively supporting host mobility in a WATM network.

1 Introduction

With more and more computing devices becoming portable and lightweight in design, the concept of Wireless ATM (WATM) is emerged as a potential framework for next-generation wireless communication networks [1,2]. WATM combines the advantages of freedom of movement for end users (which wireless networks provide) and the statistical multiplexing (allowing for flexible bandwidth allocation and efficient utilization of network resources) and Quality of Service (QoS) guarantees (which wired ATM networks offer) [3,4]. The said qualities are not supported in the existing Wireless Local Area Networks (WLANs), which were designed focusing mainly on conventional LAN data traffic. Emerging standards, such as IEEE 802.11, have been designed to provide wireless access to corporate networks, but do not incorporate ATM technology over the air interface [5,6].

Wireless ATM concept brings with it several open issues need to be solved in the prospect of having commercialized WATM networks in the near future. Among these issues, the paper deals with the Virtual Channel (VC) connection management [7]. In a WATM network VC connections are available to both the wired and wireless hosts. The difference between the hosts is that a wireless host can move from one wireless Access Point (AP) or "cell" coverage area to another. From the VC connection management point of view mobility means that extra signaling for location management

M.J. van Sinderen and L.J.M. Nieuwenhuis (Eds.): PROMS 2001, LNCS 2213, pp. 145-154, 2001.
© Springer-Verlag Berlin Heidelberg 2001

and hand-off must be provided to enable new VCs to be set up in the new location and old ones torn down whenever a wireless host moves within the network [8].

The paper presents an open signaling protocol, which supports an agents-based software system suitable for connection management of WATM networks. (An overview of applying the agent technology towards tackling with network management and control tasks is given to [9].) The system's software agents, as well as the interfaces between these agents comply with the P1520 reference model depicted in Figure 1 [10]. The said model has been developed in the context of the IEEE P1520 standards development project [11], with the aim of standardizing an open programmable network management/control framework.

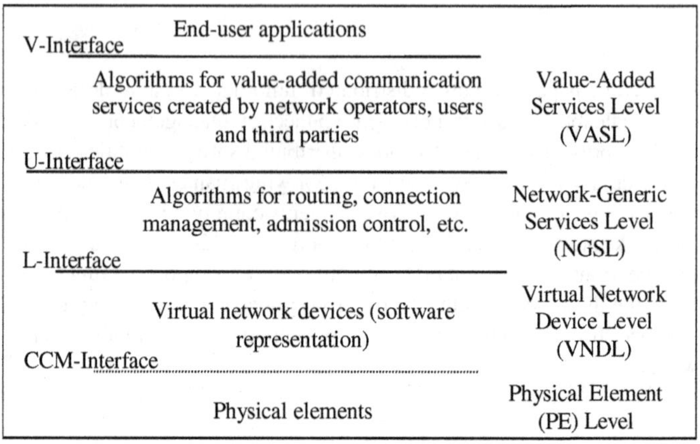

V-Interface End-user applications	
Algorithms for value-added communication services created by network operators, users and third parties	Value-Added Services Level (VASL)
U-Interface	
Algorithms for routing, connection management, admission control, etc.	Network-Generic Services Level (NGSL)
L-Interface	
Virtual network devices (software representation)	Virtual Network Device Level (VNDL)
CCM-Interface	
Physical elements	Physical Element (PE) Level

Fig. 1. The P1520 reference model

The rest of the paper is organized as follows: Section II outlines the architecture of the presented distributed multi-agent system. Section III briefly discusses a suitable for the described system open signalling protocol. The next Section IV presents a prototype implementation of the system. Lastly, Section V concludes the paper, outlining also some plans for future work.

2 The Proposed Software Multi-agent System

Figure 2 depicts the proposed software system for accomplishing connection management tasks in WATM networks. As shown in this figure, the system consists of a number of distributed software entities (i.e., agents). Three different types of agents may be identified:

- the *Terminal Agents* (TAs) that provide a virtual representation of ATM fixed and mobile terminal devices;
- the *Switch Wrapper Agents* (SWAs) that furnish an abstract software environment for performing management/control operations on ATM switches; and
- the *Connection Management Agents* (CMAs).

CMAs express in abstract and portable terms a set of management/control procedures, which are activated each time a fixed or a mobile ATM terminal requests a connection. This request can refer either to a new call (originated by a fixed/mobile terminal), or can be the result of a handover process taking place when the mobile terminal decides to move from one cell to another. The CMAs' procedures include the discovery of the ATM terminal (which requests the connection), the connection admission control (CAC), the routing, and lastly the establishment, maintenance and release of terminals' connections. Different subagents of CMAs can undertake the independently performance of these procedures. For example, Figure 3 depicts a totally "distributed" realization of CMA, where separate subagents perform individual control/management functions. In this arrangement, three different types of subagents (modules) can be identified:

- the *Connection Admission Control Agent* (CACA), which decides to either accept or reject a connection request following the rules of a CAC scheme;
- the *Routing Agent* (RA), which accomplishes for each connection request a routing algorithm in order to compute a path that connects the connection's source and destination; and
- the *Connection Agent* (CA), which is responsible for establishing, maintaining and releasing the ATM switches' Virtual Channels Crossconnections (VCCs), which are involved in the requested connection.

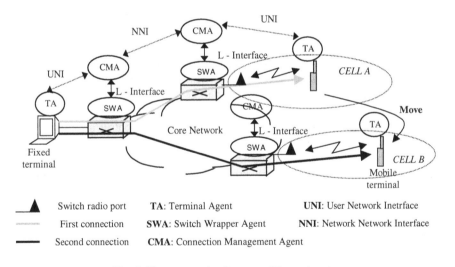

Fig. 2. The proposed software multi-agent system

Returning to Figure 2, in terms of the P1520 initiative, SWAs and TAs correspond to VNDL, while CMAs belong to NGSL. Clearly, there is always an one-to-one correspondence between ATM switches and SWAs; the same holds for the relationship between TAs and ATM terminal devices (both fixed and mobile). In contrast, the "distribution" of CMAs within the system can be more flexible. Normally, a network

of significant size would employ one CMA per ATM switch. This arrangement offers
the highest potential for scalability.

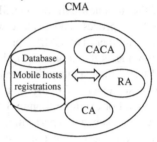

Fig. 3. CMA subagents

However, when implementing the presented software system to support a WATM
network known to be small in size, several - or all - ATM switches may be chosen to
share a single CMA. This arrangement can be achieved at a lower implementation cost
and may turn out to be more efficient in terms of the exchange of control information
between different switches.

A CMA communicates with the respective SWA at a virtual level through a switch-
independent interface, called an L-Interface, in terms of P1520. The L interface is
programmable and allows a CMA to access the abstract software version of the switch
representation within the SWA. Matching the real status of the switch to the abstract
counterpart maintained within the SWA is achieved through a switch-specific interface (a CCM-Interface, in terms of P1520). The CCM interface is *not* programmable,
but a collection of switch-specific protocols or software drivers that enable exchange
of state (and management/control information in general) at a very low level between
a switch and the respective SWA.

Given the proposed multi-agent system, the exchange of control information (i.e.,
connection requests, topology updates, etc.) between switches can not take place
through control paths/channels established by fixed standards signaling protocols, as
these protocols do not support externally defined control/management functionality.
Therefore, it is necessary an open signaling protocol, which will ensure that the enhanced functionality supported by the presented software multi-agent system, can be
communicated between different switches. Addressing this issue, the next section
presents a signaling protocol appropriate for the proposed software system.

3 An Open Signaling Protocol for Wireless Host Mobility

This section discusses an open signaling protocol appropriate for the software multi-
agent system presented in the previous section. To help understand this protocol better,
it follows a simple example of how the software entities of the proposed system handle a call request for setting up a point-to-point connection between a fixed and a

mobile terminal. Note that the discussed scenario involves a handover process when the mobile host decides to move from one cell to another.

According to the scenario depicted in Figure 4a, the fixed host (i.e., source) sends a call request message with parameters {source, destination} to the CMA (called SrcCMA), which controls the ATM switch located at the UNI boundary of the source. Receiving the call request message, the SrcCMA firstly checks whether the destination belongs to the cell area defined by the radio port of the ATM switch. The check involves the examination of the registrations of the radio port database. The said database includes all the mobile hosts that are served by the source ATM switch. Note that each network mobile host is registered to a specific radio port database. The mobile host registration is based on signal "evaluation metrics", which can include criteria like signal strength and bit error rate.

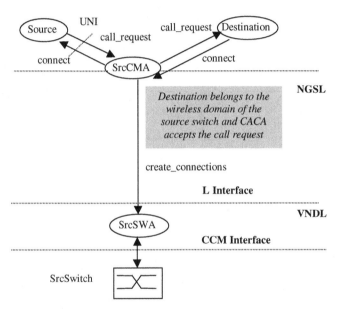

Fig. 4a. One-hop process

Returning to the examination of the call request message procedure (Figure 4a), provided that the destination belongs to the wireless domain of the source switch, the SrcCMA (through its CACA subagent) performs a CAC scheme in order to accept or reject the call request. Given that it accepts the call, it informs the destination for the new call request. Considering that the destination also accepts the call, the CA subagent creates in the source switch the appropriate VCC between the source and the destination. It also notifies the source for the call acceptance.

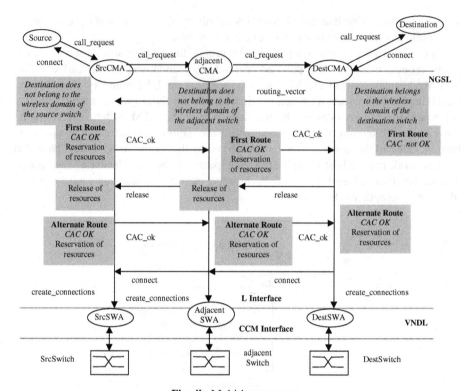

Fig. 4b. Multi-hop process

Assuming in the sequel (Figure 4b) that the destination does not belong to the source switch cell area, the SrcCMA initializes a searching process for tracking down the destination. This process involves a form of broadcast in which the whole network is queried for the destination of the call request. Specifically, the SrcCMA (through its RA subagent) broadcasts the call request message to all the CMAs, which control the ATM switches that are connected with the source ATM switch. In their turn, these switches also broadcast the call request message and so on. Sometime, a CMA (called DestCMA) finds that the destination (i.e., the mobile terminal) belongs to its radio port database. Then, the DestCMA sends to the SrcCMA a message, which encapsulates a routing vector containing the whole path between the source and the destination. In the scenario depicted in Figure 4b, the routing vector message contains the path {SrcCMA, adjacentCMA, DestCMA}.

In a time-window, the SrcCMA is possible to receive from the DestCMA more than one different routing vectors. For the firstly received routing vector, the SrcCMA initializes a per-hop CAC process. For each ATM switch hop, the corresponding CACA subagent performs a CAC scheme in order to accept or reject the call request. As long as the call is accepted, the required resources for each hop are reserved and the CAC check is passed to the next hop. If in a hop, the corresponding CACA subagent rejects the call request, the SrcCMA is informed in order to proceed to examine a different (if there is) routing vector. The reserved resources are released as the message encapsulating the call rejection travels to the SrcCMA from the CMA, which rejects (through its CACA subagent) the call request.

Assuming now that all involved in a routing path CMAs, as well as the destination accepts the call request, then in a back-to-forward process all the required VCCs are established in the ATM switches by the corresponding CA subagents.

Coming in the sequel to discuss how the proposed signaling protocol covers handover. Whenever a host moves among the APs of a WATM network, a handover process takes place. For a WATM network, the handover process involves two steps: handover at the VC level and at the wireless or Radio Frequency (RF) level. Wireless handover involves the underlying hardware switching to the new AP's (ATM switch's radio port) frequency and establishing a communication channel with it. This process is relatively simple compared with the VC-level handover, where new VCs have to be routed, negotiated and set-up and the old VCs have to be deleted.

Focusing on the VC-level handover, let assume that the mobile terminal (i.e., the destination) of the previous discussed scenario moves and a stronger signal "beacon" is detected by a radio port of a different ATM switch. Immediately, the terminal is registered to the database of the new radio port, while its registration to the database of the old port is deleted. The CMA controlling the "old" ATM switch takes over to delete the old VCs. Towards this direction it broadcasts an appropriate message to each CMA involved in the routing path between the source and the destination.

The CMA controlling the "new" ATM switch takes over to establish the new VCs. In this context, it follows the process described in the beginning of the section. In other words, it firstly defines an appropriate routing path between the destination (which is now the source of the connection message) and the source (which now plays the role of the destination). For this path, it performs the required CAC checks (and reserves the corresponding resources) and finally in a back-to-forward process establishes the appropriate VCCs. Note the difference between the set-up and the release of the VCCs, where the set-up involves a back-to-forward process, while the release a forward-to-back..

Note that this section presented only a "top" view of the proposed open signaling protocol. A full description of the protocol including messages' semantics will be published in the near future.

4 A Prototype Implementation

This section discusses the implementation of a prototype system that follows the general architectural framework of two previous sections and makes use of intelligent software agents Currently the implemented prototype covers only the fixed part of a WATM network. However it is expected that in the near future a full prototype system will be implemented.

Although not mandated by the design, and for the purpose of facilitating the implementation process, the software entities of the prototype system have been built on top of an agent platform [12] that supports communication primitives according to the ontology specified by the FIPA organization [13]; therefore communication between the various distributed software entities in the prototype is achieved by means of an Agent Communication Language (ACL). The underlying agent platform used in the implementation was based on background work, conducted in the scope of the IMPACT[1] research project [14]. Again, this choice was made for achieving a faster development cycle, without being forced by design or other constraints.

Figure 5 outlines the structure of the implemented software infrastructure. Two different types of agents can be identified: the *Switch Wrapper Agent* (SWA) that furnishes an abstract software environment for performing management and control operations on an ATM switch; and the *CAC & Routing Agent* (CRA), which is the software entity expressing in abstract and portable terms CAC and routing algorithms. (An in depth description of these two agents can be found elsewhere [15].)

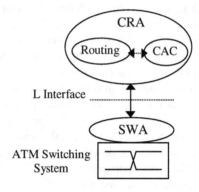

Fig. 5. Structure of the implemented prototype

The core components of the SWA are:
- an abstract information model (called *Switch-Independent Management Information Base* (SI-MIB)) that provides an abstract virtual representation of the resources and traffic load conditions within an ATM switch [16]; and
- a library, consisting of a set of software drivers, for accessing the low-level management facilities of an ATM switch.

In the prototype, the low-level library has been implemented using the Java Management API (JMAPI). Currently there are vendor-specific versions for three models of ATM switches, specifically: FORE ASX-200, CISCO LS1010 and Flextel WSS 1200. Porting the library to other devices is easy, since the task involves only the mapping of the abstract objects in SI-MIB to the counterparts in the specific MIBs of the target switch.

---

[1] The IMPACT project (Implementation of Agents for CAC on an ATM Testbed—AC324) was funded by the European Commission under the Advanced Communications Technologies and Services (ACTS) Research Programme.

5 Conclusions

Following recent proposals for open programmable network management/control infrastructures, the paper presents a distributed multi-agent system for flexible and efficient connection management of WATM networks. The system includes distributed abstract software entities (i.e., agents) and generic interfaces between entities, both complying with the emerging P1520 reference model. Moreover, the presented system adopts an open signaling protocol, which leads to many advantages over the existing standard solutions proposed by the ATM Forum.

An implemented prototype that has been installed on top of a small experimental fixed ATM network provides a first evidence for the correctness of the system's design. We plan to check the whole design by implementing a full prototype system operated in a WATM network in the near future. Furthermore, we plan to extend our work in the directions of system's performance and security issues.

References

1. ATM Forum, Wireless ATM WG, *Doc. no. LTD-WATM-01.02*, 1997.
2. D. Raychaudhuri, "Wireless ATM Networks: Architecture, System Design and Prototyping", *IEEE Personal Communications*, pp. 42-49, Aug. 1996.
3. E. Ayanoglu, K. Eng, and M. Karol, "Wireless ATM: Limits, Challenges and Proposals", *IEEE Personal Communications*, Aug. 1996.
4. A. Acampora, "Wireless ATM: A Perspective on Issues and Prospects", *IEEE Personal Communications*, Aug. 1996.
5. T. Saadawi, M. Ammar, and A. Hakeem, *Fundamentals of Telecommunication Networks*, Wiley, 1994.
6. A. Acampora, *An Introduction to Broadband Networks*, Plenum Press, 1994.
7. L. Ngoh, H. Li, and W. Wang, "An Integrated Multicast Connection Management Solution for Wired and Wireless ATM Networks", *IEEE Communications Magazine*, pp. 50-58, Nov. 1997.
8. A. Acharya, J. Li, B. Rajagopalan, and D. Raychaudhuri, "Mobility Management in Wireless ATM Networks", *IEEE Communications Magazine*, pp. 100-109, Nov. 1997.
9. A. Hayzelden, and J. Bigham, "Agent Technology in Communications Systems: An Overview", *Knowledge Engineering Review*, Vol. 14, No 3, pp. 1-35, 1999.
10. J. Biswas, A. Lazar, S. Mahjoub, L.-F. Pau, M. Suzuki, S. Torstensson, W. Wang and S. Weinstein, "The IEEE P1520 Standards Initiative for Programmable Network Interfaces", *IEEE Communications Magazine*, pp. 64-70, October 1998.
11. Information electronically available from http://www.ieee-pin.org/ and http://stdsbbs.ieee.org/groups/.
12. J. Bigham, L.G. Cuthbert, A.L.G. Hayzelden, Z. Luo and H. Almiladi, "Agent Interaction for Network Resource Management". In Proc. *Intelligence in Services and Networks '99 (IS&N99) Conference*, Barcelona, April 1999.
13. Foundation for Intelligent Physical Agents, *FIPA 97 Specification, Part 2: Agent Communication Language (ACL)*, 1997. Electronically available from http://www.fipa.org/ or http://drogo.cselt.stet.it/fipa.

14. MPACT AC324, Technical Annex, March 1998. See also `http://www.acts-impact.org/`.

15. J.Soldatos, G. Kormentzas, E.Vayias, K.Kontovassilis, N.Mitrou, "An Intelligent Agents-Based Prototype Implementation of an Open Platform Supporting Portable Deployment of Traffic Control Algorithms in ATM networks", In Proc. 7th *COMCON Conference*, Athens, Greece July 1999.

16. G. Kormentzas, J. Soldatos, E. Vayias, K. Kontovasilis, and N. Mitrou, "An ATM Switch-Independent MIB for Portable Deployment of Traffic Control Algorithms", In Proc. 7th *COMCON Conference*, Athens, Greece July 1999.

TCP/IP Protocol Engine System Simulation

M. Benz[1], K. Feske[2], U. Hatnik[2], and P. Schwarz[2]

[1] Department of Computer Science,
Dresden University of Technology, Germany
[2] Fraunhofer Institute for Integrated Circuits
Design Automation Department EAS Dresden, Germany

Abstract. General transport layer protocols like TCP/IP are relatively complex because they have to deal with very different and dynamic application requirements and networking conditions. In this paper, we present an approach for hardware support of such protocols using FPGAs. We outline a hardware/software partitioning, a heterogeneous protocol engine for protocol processing acceleration and describe its transparent integration into standard systems. For the design, development and verification of such communication systems extensive simulation support is required. We describe how protocol engine VHDL models, a network simulator and existing networking applications were integrated to support this process. For this to be accomplished, object oriented techniques were applied. We present our approach for the simulation of communication systems and discuss the object structure and implementation details. As a result, the simulation enables to evaluate different configurations, modifications or the influence of system dynamics like network transmission errors on protocol processing and achievable performance.

1 Introduction

Today's communication environments are mainly influenced by the tremendous success of the Internet. As a result, the Internet Protocol (IP) and standard layers above - especially TCP -are now the common denominator. This means that although these protocols have a number of limitations concerning functionality, flexibility and performance other protocol approaches like XTP [7] have failed to gain broad acceptance. This is also partly true for other superior technologies like ATM, which compete with IP. Hence, it is important to transfer the alternatives and ideas developed in various research projects to improve implementations of these standard protocols.

On the other hand, the Internet has encouraged huge investments in fibre optical networks and technologies to exploit them more efficiently like Wave Division Multiplex (WDM). Furthermore, new technologies like xDSL and cable modems will also provide high-speed communication in the access networks. Altogether, this will contribute to an emerging global high-speed networking infrastructure based on IP.

In contrast to using the same base protocol everywhere, communication devices are extremely diversified. This includes standard workstation and server

M.J. van Sinderen and L.J.M. Nieuwenhuis (Eds.): PROMS 2001, LNCS 2213, pp. 155–164, 2001.
© Springer-Verlag Berlin Heidelberg 2001

class computers as well as notebooks up to Wireless Application Protocol (WAP) mobile phones. Therefore, architectures for protocol processing acceleration have to be adaptive to various network interfaces, their properties as well as processor architectures or optimisation goals concerning performance as well as memory, CPU and power limitations.

The ongoing research and deployment of WDM technologies and the direct transmission of IP datagrams over specific wavelengths, will contribute to very high bandwidth capacities at low error rates. These optical networks will again shift the protocol processing overhead to the access routers and into the end systems. On the other hand they will probably provide no or only limited quality of service (QoS) features. Combined with data touching intensive or real time requirements of specific services and applications this adds to processing power that is required within end systems. Hence, flexible architectures for protocol processing acceleration are necessary to cope with these conditions.

Such large heterogeneous systems require extensive simulation support during the development process. First it is used to clarify communication relations and interactions in general. Since our protocol partitioning approach assumes low error rates a goal was to find reasonable limits for the error probability of the target network to improve the efficiency compared with existing solutions. Then we wanted to evaluate the impact of network dynamics like congestion or transient loss. Furthermore, we aspired to evaluate the integration within an embedded processor based system-on-chip. Here the utilisation of different components like buffers, the on-chip bus or the memory interface is interesting to allow bottleneck detection and early performance predictions. On the other hand the simulation environment can be used for configuration or customisation as well as optimisation when targeting production releases.

In the following section, we give an overview of our hardware/software partitioning of the TCP/IP protocol stack, which allows to take advantage of existing software implementations. The extracted hardware partition and the synchronisation are discussed in more detail. The utilised high level design flow is outlined and initial synthesis results are presented. In section 3.1 we introduce our object oriented communication system simulation approach. Here we also address the object structure and implementation details. Afterwards, we conclude our results and address future work.

2   Protocol Engine

The Protocol Engine is an integrated hardware/software architecture for protocol processing acceleration. Although it is generally protocol-independent we currently focus on TCP/IP as an implementation example. The work includes a partitioning of the protocol where non-real-time parts like connection management are still performed in software. On the other hand, the fast path which has to be processed for every packet is accelerated. The basic approach and the integration in a standard operating system are described in [4]. A prototype implementation based on an intelligent network adapter is presented in [6]. In [5] we outline a FPGA-based hardware implementation of the fast path for TCP/IP receive path processing.

There are various requirements like performance, power usage or price that have to be met. Furthermore, different network environments like Ethernet LANs or wireless networks may require adaptations. Thus, many implementation alternatives and configurations have to be considered. As a consequence extensive simulation support of the entire network and especially of the protocol engine itself is required. The next chapter describes a system-on-chip architecture for TCP acceleration. Then we will shortly describe TCP fast path protocol processing and the developed accelerator. Afterwards we will outline our distributed simulation environment and explain its use for functional validation and error simulation.

2.1 System-on-Chip Architecture

Due to the complexity of transport layer protocols, it is usually not beneficial to perform the entire protocol processing in specialised components. Hence, we use a general purpose processor, which runs a modified software TCP/IP stack. The processor core was developed by the European Space Agency is Sparc V8 compatible and is freely available as a synthesisable VHDL model [10]. It performs non real-time processing tasks like connection management or exception handling. Furthermore, it is responsible for efficient communication with the application on the host system. To avoid operating system overhead we use a modified implementation of the virtual interface architecture (VIA) for efficient communication [11]. This allows the application to directly communicate with the protocol engine bypassing the operating system. The Leon integer unit is

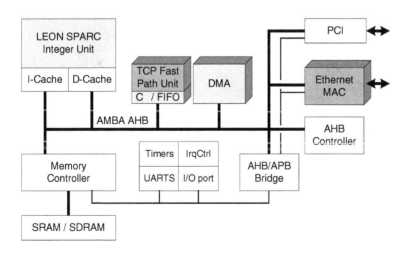

Fig. 1. Protocol Engine SoC Architecture

supported by on-chip AMBA AHB/APB buses [13]. The TCP accelerator is implemented as a slave and is attached to both busses. The APB bus is used to control the component while the AHB is responsible for data transfer.

2.2   Fast Path Protocol Processing

Figure 2 illustrates the tasks that are involved in the fast path processing for bulk data transmission. The sender accepts the application s data and transmits them if certain criteria are met. The receiving protocol instance takes and validates the data and eventually hands them over to the application. Both protocol instances are coupled by a window based flow control that ensures that enough buffer space is available at the receiver. Usually for every other received protocol data unit the receiver generates an acknowledgement. Based on this information the sender can release transmitted data that was saved for eventual retransmission. Furthermore, the transmission window is enlarged enabling the transmission of new data.

The fast path consists of three major components: TcpSend, TcpRecv and SendAck. These tasks may run concurrently but since they access shared context data, synchronisation has to be applied. Furthermore, they signal each other required processing like the receiver indicating necessity of sending an acknowledgement. Depending on the communication behaviour, only some tasks are active on each instance. The context data include information describing the connection and variables for flow and congestion control as well as for error detection. These data sets are kept separate for every connection. Hence, connections can be processed concurrently. Statistics data however, are gathered for every connection and thus have to be periodically synchronised with the software stack.

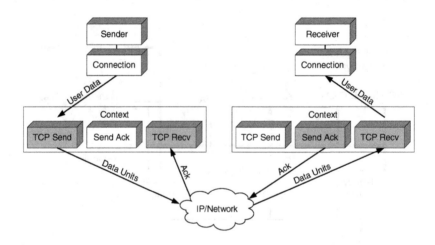

Fig. 2. TCP Fast Path Processing Flow for Bulk Data Transfer

2.3   Software Stack Synchronisation

According to the proposed partitioning the complex tasks of connection, management and error handling are still performed in software. Thus, we can benefit from existing well performing and stable implementations. Therefore, when an application initiates a connection establishment the software stack is invoked. On the receiving side the protocol data unit cannot be mapped onto a known fast path entry, therefore it is passed to the software stack. If the user decides to accept the communication, the context information for this connection is transferred to the fast path processing unit and marked active. The same happens on the client side. The number of connections that should be accelerated may be limited to participants of the same or corresponding networks because normally only here very high performance is required and the above-mentioned conditions are met. The data units that are exchanged afterwards are entirely processed by this unit and transferred directly to the application. This happens without invoking the operating system or the TCP/IP software stack. This means that no interrupts have to be dealt with, no operating system contexts or processor modes have to be changed and caches could remain intact. When a connection is idle for some time, errors occur or the user terminates it, the context information and remaining user data are transferred to the software stack. Then the communication is treated as it would have been without an accelerator. In case an error condition was successfully managed, the fast path unit could be reinitialised for this connection.

2.4   TCP/IP Fast Path Unit Specification and Implementation

Conventionally, the controller design of structured data stream processing is not well supported by EDA tools. So we are facing a bottleneck in the design process especially for protocol processing hardware components. To fill the gap, we incorporated modelling and synthesis facilities of the Protocol Compiler [12] into a proved FPGA based rapid prototyping (RPT) design flow. With the Protocol Compiler the high-level specification is graphically composed. Furthermore, it provides the following features: formal protocol analysis, back annotation simulation, controller logic partitioning and synthesis, and VHDL code generation. Figure 3 shows the start of the 32 bit implementation of the header analysis. A 32 bit wide register p_data_in is used to processes the data sequentially. First the checksum is computed. Here, within each cycle portions of 16 bit are added. Then the length of the IP header is extracted. Next we check whether the received data is a IPv4 fragment. Within the next step the pseudo header is initialised which is required for the checksum computations of higher layers. The next step calculates the number of 32 bit words (v_iplength) that have to be processed and determines eventually remaining bytes (p_rest). All these actions are performed within one clock cycle. Than the rest is read in units of 32 bytes. Within these steps header fields like the source IP address are extracted. Furthermore option fields are taken into account. After the header fields are extracted we perform

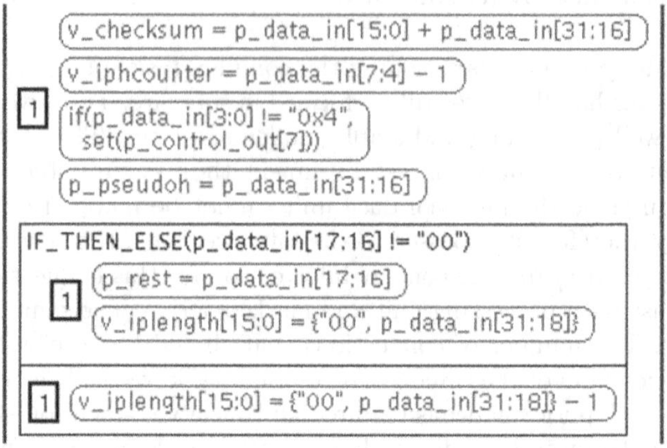

Fig. 3. Protocol Compiler IP Header Analysis Specification (excerpt, 32 bit)

validation operations as outlined in the previous section to verify the received fragment.

To evaluate the tradeoffs concerning device utilisation and performance implications of different bus widths the unit was implemented for 32 and 64 bit. Currently only the receive side is implemented. The 32 bit version utilises about 10 % of an Xilinx Virtex FPGA XV1000 device and runs at 25 MHz.

3   Communication System Simulation

Figure 4 shows a system top level view example. The system consists of clients and servers that are connected by the network. Each connection is a transmission line model with characteristic parameters (e.g. delay time) which connects one or several clients and servers. There are two different kinds of client and server models. Abstract client and server models (C_A, S_A) do not handle real user data. They only receive and send abstract data packets, which are characterized by typical parameters e.g. the packet size. The send and receive functions can be modeled very differently, depending on the simulation goal. For example a statistical function can be used to determine data volume and send time. If a network protocol has to be simulated, the client and server models also have to realize the protocol functionality. Contrary to abstract models, detailed client and server models work with real application data (C_D, S_D). In our scenario these are the VHDL protocol engine models. They interact with application models, e.g. a benchmark application which can be used to determine the transmission performance of the system. The system simulation allows the analysis of dependencies between network and client/server parameters. For our work especially the effect of different protocol engine configurations and parameters as well as network error rates is in the focus of interest. Additionally, the simulation framework allows a comfortable development of new protocol engine components, which can be tested using real application data. Therefore, the simulation and test conditions are close at the real system and the development time decreases.

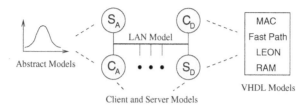

Fig. 4. Top Level System View (LAN Example)

3.1 Simulation Approach

Because the communication system simulation is very complex, we use an object oriented simulation approach. Object oriented simulation means that a system consists of subsystem, which are simulated autonomously. On top level, e.g. a client, server or network connection can be such a subsystem. A subsystems is named "object" and may contain other objects, so that an object hierarchy may be built, see figure 5. Each object includes a model and a simulation algorithm. The simulation algorithm can be a small code fragment but also a complex simulator and evaluate only the model of its object. Therefore, it can be optimized for the object's model and is independent of other objects. All implementation details are encapsulated by the object, only an interface allows data exchange and simulation control. Therefore it is possible to change the object implementation without influencing other system components. Even real hardware can be encapsulated by an object, hidden to the objects outside. More details about the inclusion of real hardware can be found in [1]. Furthermore the encapsulation allows a simple and effective intellectual property protection.

3.2 Object Structure

Figure 6 shows the object structure of the simulated communication system. The top level object contains the network model, for example a local area network (LAN). The network model describes the network topology, protocol, bandwidth, delay etc. It includes abstract and detailed client and server models as described in section 3.

The detailed client and server models use the described protocol engine (see section 2) which is available as VHDL code. Because the network simulator cannot handle VHDL code, each protocol engine is encapsulated in a separate object, which contains a VHDL simulator and the protocol engine model.

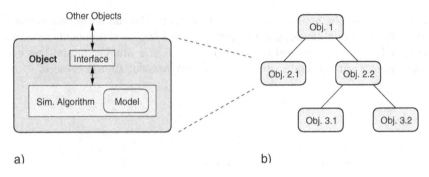

Other Objects

Fig. 5. Basic Object Structure (a) and Object Hierarchy (b)

Furthermore the protocol engine object uses another object that contains the application code. In addition, real hardware protocol engine components can be encapsulated as an object too.

3.3   Implementation Details

For the top level object we use the network simulator NSv2 [8]. The simulation bases on a scenario, which is a description of network topology, protocols, workload and control parameters. It produces an output statistic, e.g. the number of packets sent by each data source, the queuing delay at each queuing point, and the number of dropped and retransmitted packets.

For the simulation of the protocol engine VHDL components, any VHDL simulator may be applied. In our environment, we use ModelSim.

For the application objects real software components are encapsulated into objects. The software generates or consumes a data stream, which is sent to or received from the corresponding application.

The real hardware object encapsulates a FPGA based fast path prototype, as we have described in [1]. So already existing hardware components can be included and an efficient evaluation of the developed hardware is possible. To couple the objects an interface is needed. We developed a suitable interface for NS and use the ModelSim interface FLI (Foreign Language Interface). These interfaces provide all necessary initialization, data exchange and control functions.

The communication between the objects is implemented via CORBA (Common Object Request Broker Architecture) to guaranty maximum flexibility [9]. The simulation may run on a single host or distributed in a network.

4   Conclusions and Future Work

In this paper we introduced an architecture for the hardware-supported acceleration of transport layer protocols. Due to the various requirements of applications, environments and networks and the dynamics of protocol processing a major goal was flexibility and customisable configurations of the protocol engine. This was

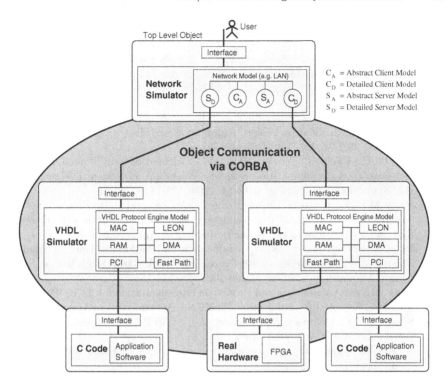

Fig. 6. Object Hierarchy

accomplished by exploiting existing software TCP/IP stacks and integrating additional hardware as required. Designing such protocol engines is a complex task. Hence, it is beneficial to have a far-reaching system design support. This includes the presented communication system simulation environment. It enables to integrate heterogeneous components which are modelled using different abstraction levels ranging from VHDL to real application layer software. Hence, different simulators were used and coupled. The use of CORBA as a means of communication in this context also facilitates distribution to improve simulation performance. The simulation helped us to understand the inherent dynamics and interactions within this complex communication system. Furthermore, functional validation was simplified and performance estimation and bottleneck detection before the entire implementation is completed are now possible. Based on these results we have implemented the receive part of the TCP fast path as a hardware component using high-level methods [6]. Currently we are working on an Ethernet MAC core and its connection to the described protocol engine. Other directions beyond the TCP fast path implementation will include quality of service and IP security acceleration. The presented simulation environment is generic and flexible enough to be useful within these scenarios as well. Moreover, we will evaluate different configurations of this protocol engine for such system-on-chip applications to foster design space exploration and automating system design for this domain.

References

[1] Hatnik, U.; Haufe, J.; Schwarz, P.: An innovative approach to couple EDA tools with reconfigurable hardware. 10th International Conference on Field Programmable Logic and Applications, FPL, Villach (Austria), 28.-30. Aug. 2000, 826-829

[2] Haufe, J.; Schwarz, P.; Berndt, T.; Große, J.: Accelerated Logic Simulation by Using Prototype Boards. Design, Automation and Test in Europe DATE 1998, Paris, 23.-26.2.98, 183–189 (Designer Track)

[3] Hatnik, U.; Haufe, J.; Schwarz, P.: Object Oriented System Simulation of Large Heterogeneous Communication Systems. Workshop on System Design Automation SDA 2000, Rathen, March 13-14, 2000, 178-184

[4] Benz, M.: The Protocol Engine Project - An Integrated Hardware / Software Architecture for Protocol Processing Acceleration , SDA 2000 - Workshop on System Design Automation, Rathen, March 2000, pp. 137-144

[5] Benz, M., Feske, K.: A Packet Classification and Validation Unit for Hardware Supported TCP/IP Receive Path Processing , SDA 2000 - Workshop on System Design Automation, Rathen, March 2000, pp. 145-151

[6] Benz, M.: An Architecture and Prototype Implementation for TCP/IP Hardware Support , accepted for publication, TERENA Networking Conference, 2001

[7] Strayer, W.T.; Dempsey, B.J.; Weaver, A.C.: "XTP - The Xpress Transfer Protocol", ADDISON-WESLEY, 1992

[8] K. Fall, K. Varadhan: "ns Notes and Documentation", January 2000, http://www.isi.edu/nsnam/ns/

[9] Free High Performance CORBA 2 ORB from AT&T Laboratories Cambridge http://www.uk.research.att.com/omniORB/

[10] European Space Agency, LEON-1 processor, http://www.estec.esa.nl/wsmwww/leon/, 2000

[11] Virtual Interface Architecture, specification version 1.0, www.viarch.org, 1999

[12] SYNOPSYS: "V1998.08 Protocol Compiler User's Guide", Synopsys Inc., 1998

[13] ARM: AMBA- Advanced Microcontroller Bus Architecture, Rev2.0, www.arm.com, 1999

Design and Implementation of a Transparent Forward Error Correction Coding Daemon for Unreliable Transports*

Albert K.T. Hui and Samuel T. Chanson

Department of Computer Science
Hong Kong University of Science & Technology
Clear Water Bay, Kowloon, Hong Kong

Abstract. In this paper we propose a novel approach to adding a forward error correction (FEC) code to UDP and other IP-based unreliable protocols. We call this Sub-socket FEC (SSF). Implemented below the socket interface, SSF provides universal and transparent FEC protection to any IP socket-based communication channels on which all existing IP applications can continue to work without any modication. A prototype system called the FEC Daemon (FECD) has been implemented using the SSF approach. It employs an erasure code based on XOR encoding, which can be extended to support Vandermonde matrix coding. Since the system is light-weight and does not use retransmission, it is particularly suitable for multimedia applications with real-time constraints. The design, implemenation and performance analysis of FECD are presented in this paper.

Keywords: Forward Error Correction, Erasure Code, Socket, TCP/IP, Multimedia Applications

1 Introduction

Data communications traditionally requires reliable data transmission. To achieve this goal, various error detection and correction techniques are employed at different layers to protect the integrity of the data as discussed below:

Bit Errors. At the data link layer, bit errors can be introduced by garbled signals or wrong timings. Upon detecting an Ethernet frame containing bit errors using its frame CRC checksum, receivers will drop it immediately.

Conventional physical media are so reliable that frame losses are almost never due to corrupted frames; hence TCP assumes that packet losses indicate congestions. This assumption no longer holds in wireless networks, causing standard TCP stacks to suffer from undue slow downs. To combat this, modern wireless

---

* This work was partially supported by a grant from the Hong Kong Research Grant Council (Number HKUST6080/97E).

M.J. van Sinderen and L.J.M. Nieuwenhuis (Eds.): PROMS 2001, LNCS 2213, pp. 165–179, 2001.

adapters generally have FEC in the physical layer to keep the error level down to that of wired networks.

These physical layer FEC systems deal with bit errors, and therefore cannot correct packet stream errors.

Packet Stream Errors. Because of link layer error detection, only frames passing the CRC are visible at the network layer. Network functions also introduce additional errors in the form of lost, duplicated or misordered packets. Ethernet and IP checksums, designed to detect errors in the individual frames and packets, are incapable of dealing with these packet-stream errors.

TCP/IP stacks silently discard packets failing the IP checksum check in an "all or nothing" manner—packets are either error free, or not seen at all. The users of network layer see "holes" of dropped packets in the packet stream, instead of seeing corrupted bits in a bit stream.

TCP tackles this problem with retransmission whereby lost packets are repaired, duplicate ones discarded and all the packets correctly ordered before the data stream is pushed out of sockets. This convenience introduces retransmission delay and does not support multicast communications. Applications using UDP or other non-reliable protocols have to deal with packet-stream errors themselves.

IP Multicast and Multimedia Applications. In an IP multicast [2] network, members of a multicast group can have paths exhibiting a wide range of network characteristics. TCP flow control will fail to work in this environment.

Reliable transports like TCP are best used for bulk data transfer where perfect transmission is required. For multimedia applications, TCP can be a very poor choice because while TCP retransmission guarantees packets are delivered to their destination reliably, it offers no guarantee regarding their timely delivery. This is a major problem for multimedia applications with real-time constraints such as video conferences. Packets in these applications have a time frame within which the packets are useful. Late coming packets that have already expired are useless and will have to be dropped; they may as well have never been sent. On the other hand, perfect delivery of data is generally not needed. Multimedia applications can usually tolerate some degree of errors, since errors in a multimedia stream typically have no long-lasting effects.

1.1 Related Works

RFC 2198 defines RTP payload types for redundant audio which allows for multiple encodings of the same data in a session. Most implementations limit themselves to the most simple form of FEC—data repetition in $n + 1$ frames. RAT [3], FreePhone [4] and Percept IP/TV are examples of these. CCFAudio [5] has a simplified design where the primary and secondary codecs are the same. In multimedia applications retransmission makes little sense, hence AQR is seldom used in conjunction with FEC.

New versions of Rendez-Vous [6] have a hierarchical FEC scheme where FEC codes of multiple coding rates are computed and multicast in such a way different levels of protection can be achieved by different combinations of groups of these FEC code sets.

RMDP [7], a reliable multicast protocol designed for bulk data transfer, uses an erasure code based on the Vandermonde matrix [8] to generate a large amount of redundant data for transmission to a multicast group. In spite of losses, the original data can be reconstructed as long as individual receivers have received an adequate number of packets.

1.2   Motivation

FEC techniques have not received much attention at the network layer, although their usefulness has been proven in mobile communications and information processing. On one hand, software-based FEC systems are believed to be too inefficient; on the other hand, hardware vendors are busy building FEC systems that focus on recovering bit level errors.

Traditionally packet losses are considered necessary for the proper functioning of the Internet by indicating congestions. However, we suggest that with the advent of new access technologies like wireless networks, increased use of real-time applications, and weighted-fair queueing switches, Internet applications need to work in a different way. For instance, in wireless networks or other noisy links where the quality of the media is intrinsically poor, the assumption that losses necessarily indicate congestion no longer holds. TCP traffics will crawl under this environment due to spurious slow-starts. UDP sessions, on the other hand, have to deal with excessive error rates.

By putting extra bandwidth to good use, one can actively control the quality of service offered by the channel. In this paper, we propose bringing FEC techniques to the network layer to correct packet losses.

2   Overview of the Proposed Design

2.1   Packet Loss Characteristics

To design an effective error correction code, the packet loss characteristics must first be considered.

Mbone, the IP multicast enabled portion of the Internet, covers network segments of varying qualities. Studies have shown that packet losses are inevitable in a multiparty conference, and that most receivers experience loss in the range of 2–5%, with a small number of receivers seeing significantly higher loss rates [9, 10,4].

Bolot [4] shows that consecutive packet losses are rare, and that most loss periods involve one or two packets only. Furthermore, the distribution of the number of consecutive packet losses is approximately geometric. His claim is supported by previous experimental [11] and analytical results [12].

2.2   Erasure Codes

Whereas traditional forward error correction codes can correct multiple errors in a code block, erasure codes are only capable of repairing losses if the location of losses are known in advance. The basic idea is that for every k packets, the sender generates n packets consisting of data from those k packets plus some redundant data, such that any subset of k packets within the encoded block of n packets suffice to reconstruct the original k packets at the receiver. Such a code is referred to as a (n, k) code and allows for up to $n - k$ packet losses within the block of n packets.

Let x be the source data consisting of k components, and y be the encoded data of n components where $n > k$. A *generator matrix* G of size $n \cdot k$ can be found such that $y = Gx$. This matrix G has the property that y', a subset of y, with k components of y, can be used to reconstruct x by inverting G and solving the set of linear equations corresponding to the location of the components of y' in y.

G can be built by interpreting the k source components as the coefficients of a polynomial of degree $k - 1$. Such a polynomial can be completely specified by its values at k different points. Thus we take the values of this polynomial at n different points. Any subset of these n values, with at least k elements can be used to reconstruct the polynomial. This type of generator matrix is known as a Vandermonde matrix. The reader is referred to [13] for details.

2.3   Design of the FEC System

We make use of an erasure code based on XOR encoding (extendible to the Vandermonde matrix) to compute FEC codes for every k blocks of packets. Such a system would allow the complete recovery of the entire block if no more than $n - k$ packets are lost.

Layer Consideration. Conventional FEC codes are attached to individual packets to protect their integrity; but this would not be suitable for the proposed packet stream FEC scheme because at the network layer, all the corrupted packets have already been taken care of by the checksum check, and the remaining packets are all good. Additional FEC protection applied after the checksum process will serve little purpose.

This means that within the TCP/IP framework, packet-protecting FEC codes must be implemented at or below the data link layer. However, this approach can only protect the integrity of individual packets, holes can still be observed in the packet stream. This is because though bit level error can be eliminated through the use of very strong FEC codes in the network adapter, network congestions, intermittent route changes, traffic shaping, and other abnormal behaviors can still cause packet losses. To correct network level errors, a network level solution is needed. It follows that a block of packets must be protected as a single unit. Redundant FEC data should be computed based on the contents of the packets in a block.

Packet stream level FEC protection has been implemented in applications like FreePhone and RMDP (refer to section 1.1 for details). However, they all use proprietary schemes and hence only support applications specifically designed to make use of them. Low-level packet mangling systems allow a generic packet stream protecting FEC system to be implemented below the socket interface. We call this approach Sub-socket FEC (SSF). SSF allows any application to take advantage of the added protection of FEC without having to change the source code.

Placement of FEC Data. If the redundant FEC data is to be transmitted to the receiver by attching itself to the source packet, in the case that a source packet is lost, the FEC data that can be used to recover it will also be lost. Therefore, the FEC data should be transmitted in its own packets (see Figure 1).

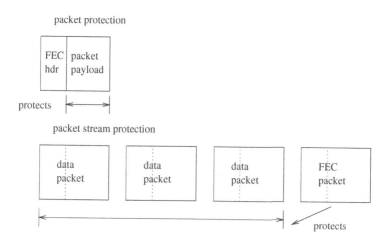

Fig. 1. Placement of FEC data.

Block Length Consideration. The proposed FEC system repairs packet loss within individual blocks. Due to the way it operates, the block length is directly related to the coding rate. For instance, when the coding rate in use is 3/4, 1 FEC packet is to be sent after every 3 data packets. Since repair can be applied to a block only after the entire block is received by the receiver, blocks that are too long can introduce too many delays. This rules out the use of long blocks and the associated coding rates, such as 13/14.

3   Implementation

A prototype system called Forward Error Correction Daemon (FECD) has been implemented. FECD is intended to satisfy 3 objectivs, viz. *transparency* which means existing programs can take advantage of the added features without change; *heterogeneity* meaning that the system is not tied to a particular operating environment; *and ease of use.*

We have opted for an in-stack packet mangling approach, whereby the system taps into the OS networking stack to intercept packets passing through it and reinject the modified packets back to the stack. The main advantage of this approach is transparency. Several implementation issues are tackled as follows:

Keeping Track of Data Packets. The location of packets within individual blocks need to be conveyed to the receiver side for the operation of erasure codes. This is achieved by storing in the redundant packet of each block the identifiers of the IP packets in the block.

Monitoring Data Packets. Linux Netfilter has been used to allow our daemon processes read packets passing through specific connections from the user space.

Sending Redundant Packets. Redundant packets must be sent to the receiver side. Since there is no provision under the Netfilter framework for inserting a packet into the stack in an arbitrary location, an ordinary UDP socket is used to transmit the redundant packets. Multiplexing on port numbers generally takes place on highly optimized code path in networking stacks, separating the data packets from the redundant packets by different port numbers is much more efficient than having them intermixed on the same socket to be demultiplexed at the receiver side.

Injecting Packets. Packets recovered at the receiver side need to be pushed up the networking stack. We have used the Linux Ethertap virtual interface for this.

3.1   Dynamic Coding Rate Adjustment

FECD as it stands can be used without a feedback channel. In this case, the coding rate would have to be manually set to cope with the channel condition. Table 1 provides a guideline for choosing an optimal coding rate, given the channel loss rate and the desired residual loss rate.

If, however, the channel condition fluctuates, dynamically adjusting the coding rate in response to the changing channel loss rate can potentially better utilize the network. A simple scheme for dynamically changing the coding rate to adapt to the channel condition has been implemented. When there are some packets that cannot be repaired, the coding rate is considered too low. Hence everytime a packet failed to be repaired, the block size is reduced by one, thus moving the coding rate up one level. For instance, if the original coding rate is 7/8, a packet beyond repair will move it up to 6/7. An additional QoS parameter *"target loss rate"* will determine the threshold below which the coding rate is allowed to move down.

From our observation, the packet loss rate over a given segment of network tends to follow a trend and moves slowly, hence a loss packet beyond repair often signals the beginning of a channel degrading period. A *good packet counter* has been introduced which keeps track of the number of successfully transmitted packets with or without repair. When the coding rate has been increased, the coding rate should stay at that level for some time. Only when the good packet counter reaches an assigned threshold will the system be allowed to move down the coding rate. Since the counter resets everytime a packet fails to be repaired, this mechanism serves to stabilize the coding rate as it adapts to the channel's condition.

This optional feature requires a feedback channel. In this case multicast transmission is not supported. In our scheme, every successful decoding of a block by the receiver, with or without repair, is reported to the sender to give it an idea of how well the present coding rate performs and whether adjustment is needed.

3.2   Protocol Stack

From the perspective of applications, once the end hosts have been configured to use FECD, nothing gets in the way of accessing the network via sockets. The system behaves as if an "FEC layer" has been inserted below the network layer (see Figure 2).

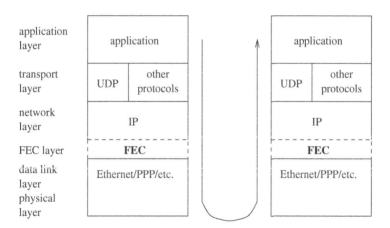

Fig. 2. Protocol Stack.

Because the FEC codec operates below the socket interface, applications are free to use any transport layer protocol. In practice, however, our system is most efficient when used with a low-overhead protocol like UDP. In fact, FECD was written with adaptive multimedia applications running over unreliable transport in mind. Although most of these applications use UDP, FECD can be used with transport protocols other than UDP.

The use of FECD with TCP, however, is not recommended, because the overhead of FEC and TCP combined will make the channel rather inefficient. On the other hand, from the perspective of TCP, the protected channel is of a better quality, albeit with a smaller bandwidth. There will be fewer incidences of packet loss, and therefore less frequent incidences of entering into slow-start mode. Interactive sessions will generally be more responsive.

Furthermore, FECD does not alter the original packet stream, and redundant packets are transmitted in a separate UDP channel. As such, even if the end hosts or tunnel end points have not been properly configured to use FECD, applications can still function normally. Although in this case the applications will not be FEC protected.

3.3   Coder Architecture

FEC Encoder. We can arrange for packets belonging to traffic flows needing protection to queue up for the encoder to grab a copy as they pass through. Everytime enough packets have been stashed up for a block (i.e. k packets), an FEC code packet will be computed and sent out of the FEC socket (refer to Figure 3).

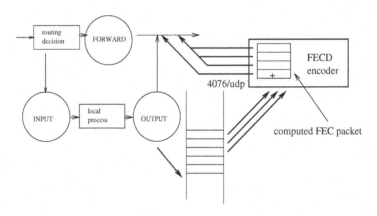

Fig. 3. Architecture of the FEC encoder.

FEC Decoder. Normally the decoder makes a copy of packets belonging to protected traffic flows as they enter the system. FEC code packets arriving on the FEC socket will trigger the FEC decoding process which will try to recover should it detect any packet loss in the corresponding block. Recovered packets are then pushed up the networking stack via the Ethertap virtual interface.

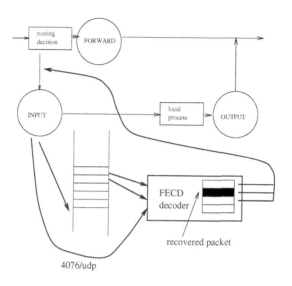

Fig. 4. Architecture of the FEC decoder.

This immediately-let-go policy is desirable as it reduces unnecessary delays. As UDP does not guarantee the in-sequence packet delivery , this policy is working within the specification. The packet recovery function offered by FECD in a sense trades "packet losses" for "recovered packets arriving out of order." To cater for certain broken applications which assume that UDP packes are arriving in sequence, a buffered mode is implemented, whereby an internal ring buffer is used to hold packets that come after the holes. Only when the holes are repaired or determined unrepairable will the entire block of packets be pushed up.

3.4   Usage

The SSF architecture per se only requires the end hosts to be FEC aware. However, the prototype implemenation FECD is written for the Linux firewall framework. The simplest configuration is shown on the left-hand side in Figure 5 where a server and client communicate over some network, both running Linux with FECD enabled. By inserting appropriate firewall rules and running the encoding daemon, the server can send redundant FEC data for all UDP traffic going to the client host. The client host should be configured likewise, inserting the firewall rules and running the decoding daemon, such that redundant FEC data are used to recover packet losses. Now extra protection are bestowed upon the path between the server and client, which is shown by the thick arrow.

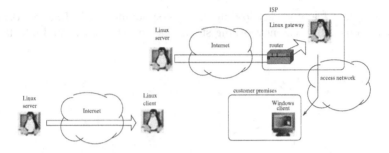

Fig. 5. Scenario: Linux server and client.

If communications with a non-Linux host is desired it can also be arranged to have a Linux host running FECD served as the gateway of that non-Linux host, as shown on the right-hand side of Figure 5. In this case the path between the 2 Linux hosts is protected by FEC.

4   Performance Analysis

4.1   Analytical Model

Residual Packet Loss Rate. If ϵ is the channel packet loss rate, then $(1-\epsilon)$ is the probability that a packet is not lost. For a block of n packets, the probability that i packets will be lost at specific locations (say the first i slots) is given by

$$\epsilon^i(1-\epsilon)^{n-i}. \tag{1}$$

A general equation for the probability that any i packets is lost in a block of n packets is given by

$$\binom{n}{i}\epsilon^i(1-\epsilon)^{n-i}. \tag{2}$$

The FECD system is capable of recovering all the packets in a block if it has no less than $n-1$ packets to work with. Hence a block containing zero or just one lost packet is considered perfect. Assume that a block with two lost packets gives $n-2$ "good" packets and 2 "bad" packets and so on. The residual packet loss rate can be computed by adding up the product of the bad packets proportion with the probability for such a block composition. The residual packet loss rate P_ϵ is given by

$$P_\epsilon = \sum_{i=2}^{n}\binom{n}{i}\epsilon^i(1-\epsilon)^{n-i}\cdot\frac{i-1}{n-1}. \tag{3}$$

However, this formula slightly underestimates the residual packet loss rate because if none of the i lost packets is the FEC packet, then all i data packets are bad. While certainly possible, a rigorous analysis aimed at correcting the errors is not warranted here because rough estimations are sufficient for the purpose of choosing the optimal coding rate. Since the probability of the FEC packet is $\frac{1}{n}$, raising P_ϵ by $\frac{1}{n}$ is a rough correction factor that gives close results to simulation data (see Figure 6). Although the error of this simplification gets larger as the channel error rate increases, a residual packet loss rate exceeding 15% is considered too high to be useful for most multimedia (especially audio) applications anyway. The refined formula is

$$P_\epsilon = \sum_{i=2}^{n} \binom{n}{i} \epsilon^i (1-\epsilon)^{n-i} \cdot \frac{i-1}{n-1} \cdot \frac{n+1}{n}. \tag{4}$$

Figure 6 shows the residual packet loss rate over a range of channel loss rates.

Equivalent Capacity. The equivalent capacity C_e is the the amount of bandwidth required to support a specific coding rate, such that the resulting throughput at a certain packet loss rate, protected by the code, will be the same as the bandwidth C requested. Note that $C_e \geq C$ since C_e must allow for lost packets and bandwidth to transmit the FEC codes.

Let C_e be the effective (total) bandwidth. A coding rate of r_c will result in a throughput of $C_e \cdot r_c$, which is the source data portion of the total bandwidth.

Since the probability that a packet is not lost is $(1-P_\epsilon)$, combining this factor with the throughput computed above gives the usable throughput C equal to $C_e \cdot r_c \cdot (1 - P_\epsilon)$. Therefore,

$$C_e = C \cdot \frac{1}{r_c \cdot (1 - P_\epsilon)}. \tag{5}$$

Figure 7 shows the computed equivalent capacity at different coding and packet loss rates.

4.2 Experimental Results

A series of experiments were carried out to investigate the performance of various coding rates over a range of channel error rates.

Experiment Setup. All the tests were performed over a 2-hop Ethernet network where MPEG1 layer 2 audio was sent via UDP from one host to the other host two hops away. Both hosts were running Linux 2.3 with FECD loaded. Although the traffic actually passed through an actively used web and mail server, the errors naturally produced were minimal. The "channel error rate" was artificially introduced by selectively dropping packets at the sender according to a standard C library random function.

Measurements. As can be seen in Figure 6, FECD improves the quality of service quite significantly even at low coding rates. For instance, in a channel with about 10% errors which is very poor for audio transmission, FECD running

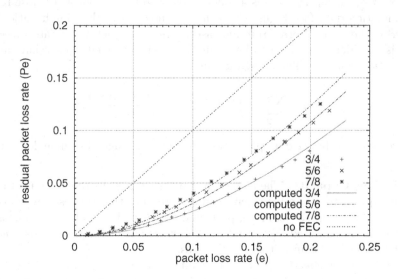

Fig. 6. Comparing computed with measured residual packet loss rates.

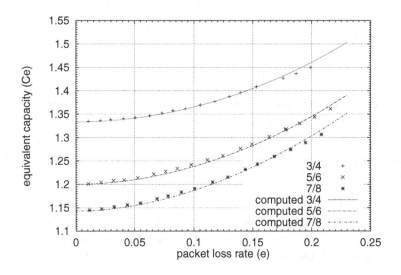

Fig. 7. Comparing computed with measured equivalent capacity.

at 7/8 coding rate can bring the error rate down to 4% which gives noticeably better audio quality. If a 3/4 coding rate is used, then the error rate can be reduced to 2.5%. As another example, a 3/4 coding rate can bring a 15% error rate down to 5%.

The experimental results confirm the validity of the analytic model. To facilitate capacity planning, the corresponding equivalent capacity as computed from the collected data is shown in Figure 7. The measured results compared closely with the analytic results.

Table 1. Optimal coding rate for various target packet loss rates.

target	packet loss rate of channel							
	2.5%	5%	7.5%	10%	12.5%	15%	17.5%	20%
2.5%		7/8	7/8	3/4				
5%				7/8	3/4	3/4		
7.5%					7/8	5/6	3/4	
10%						7/8	5/6	3/4
12.5%							7/8	5/6
15%								7/8

Table 2. Equivalent capacity of various target packet loss rates.

target	packet loss rate of channel							
	2.5%	5%	7.5%	10%	12.5%	15%	17.5%	20%
2.5%		1.16	1.235	1.36				
5%				1.21	1.265	1.4		
7.5%					1.25	1.29	1.425	
10%						1.27	1.32	1.47
12.5%							1.295	1.36
15%								1.35

Discussions about the Experimental Results. Figure 6 shows that the residual packet loss rate is low for all 3 coding rates until the channel packet loss rate reaches around 6%, after which the 3 curves take off and diverge. This suggests that when the channel is in a relatively good condition, the choice of coding rate does not have a large impact on the recovery power. In this case low rate coding is desirable as the bandwidth expansion is lower, as can be seen from Figure 7.

Beyond about 6% channel packet loss rate, the residual packet loss rate grows geometrically, approaching the channel packet loss rate. This suggests that the benefit gained from the use of the FEC system wanes off after about 20% channel packet loss rate.

Tables 1 and 2 list the optimum coding rates and the corresponding equivalent capacities under various channel conditions. The tables are useful for capacity planning. For example, if the channel is suffering from a 15% packet loss rate and 5% is required to satisfy the QoS requirement, 3/4 coding rate should be used. The use of the FEC system incurs a 40% overhead however. If the channel cannot support such a bandwidth expansion, then the user must back off and be satisfied with a more forgiving QoS guarantees of say, 10% packet loss rate with 27% overhead in required bandwidth.

5   Conclusions

A novel approach to building FEC techniques into the TCP/IP model called Sub-socket FEC (SSF) has been proposed. A prototype system has been built to demonstrate its feasibility. This approach is unique because existing packet stream level FEC systems operate above the network layer, thus limiting their application to a specific protocol or application. Previously if an Internet application wants to benefit from the use of FEC techniques, it has to implement its own version. The proposed FEC system operates below the socket layer, offering FEC protection transparently to any applications. Furthermore, the scheme can dynamically adjust to changing channel conditions by adopting different coding rates. The prototype system demonstrates that this is indeed a viable approach, as vast improvements can be observed from real-world applications using the system.

From experimental results, tables have been constructed suggesting optimal coding rates for achieving a certain loss rate given an original channel loss rate. We have shown that this mapping indeed follows our general equations for channels with evenly distributed packet losses.

5.1   Suggestions for Further Research

The prototype system only uses coding rates of the form $(k, k + 1)$. Hence it can correct only single packet loss in a block. While versatile and effective, the scheme can be extended to correct multiple packet losses in a block.

Also, the traffic model adopted assumes that packets losses are evenly distributed. Whereas this is indeed the case for such channels as those shaped under weighted-fair queueing, our scheme would presumably exhibit different characteristics under channels with sporadic losses. How well would the extended scheme capable of correcting consecutive packet losses operate under such channels has yet to be studied.

Finally, partial retransmission can be introduced to the system for non-interactive streaming applications where we can afford some delays with the use of buffering. This further reduces the packet loss rate by allowing packets an extra chance to recover in the exceptionally bad cases where the FEC scheme fails to recover all lost packets. The performance of such a hybrid FEC scheme coupled with partial retransmission is an interesting subject for further research.

References

1. Lixia Zhang and D. Clark, "Oscillating behavior of network traffic: A case study simulation," *Internetwork: Research and Experience*, vol. 1, no. 2, pp. 101–12, 1990.
2. S. Deering, *Multicast Routing in a Datagram Internetwork*, Ph.d. thesis, Stanford University, Palo Alto, CA, Dec. 1991.
3. Vicky Hardman, Angela Sasse, Mark Handley, and Anna Watson, "Reliable audio for use over the internet," in *Proceedings of INET'95, Honolulu, HI*, June 1995, pp. 171–8.
4. Jean-Chrysostome Bolot and Andres Vega-Garcia, "The case for fec-based error control for packet audio in the internet," to appear in ACM Multimedia Systems.
5. Sarah E. Chodrow, Michael D. Hirsch, Injong Rhee, and Shun Yan Cheung, "Design and implementation of a multicast audio conferencing tool for a collaborative computing framework," *Information Sciences*, vol. 7, no. 23, pp. 7–23, Jan. 1998.
6. Frank Lyonnet, *Support des applications multimedia sur l'Internet incluant des liens sans-fils*, these de doctorat, Universite de Nice, 1998.
7. Luigi Rizzo and Lorenzo Vicisano, "A reliable multicast data distribution protocol based on software fec techniques (rmdp)," in *Proceedings of Fourth IEEE HPCS'97 Workshop, Chalkidiki, Grece*, June 1997, pp. 115–24.
8. Luigi Rizzo, "Effective erasure codes for reliable computer communcation protocols," *ACM Computer Communication Review*, vol. 27, no. 2, pp. 24–36, Apr. 1997.
9. M. Handley, "An examination of mbone performance," Technical report, University of Southern California/Information Sciences Institute res. rep. ISI/RR-97-450, Apr. 1997.
10. Audio-Video Transport Working Group, H. Schulzrinne, S. Casner, R. Frederick, and V. Jacobson, "RFC 1889: RTP: A transport protocol for real-time applications," Jan. 1996, Status: PROPOSED STANDARD.
11. Jean-Chrysostome Bolot, "End-to-end packet delay and loss behavior in the internet," in *Proceedings of ACM SIGCOMM'93, San Francisco, CA*, Aug. 1993.
12. I. Norros and J. Virtamo, "Who loses cells in the case of burst scale congestion?," in *Proceedings of Thirteenth International Teletraffic Congress, North-Holland, Amsterdam*, June 1991, pp. 829–33.
13. W. H. Press, B. P. Flannery, S. A. Teukolsky, and W. T. Vetterling, *Vandermonde Matrices and Toeplitz Matrices*, Cambridge University Press, 1992.

An Analytical Study on TCP-friendly Congestion Control for Multimedia Streams

Wei Wu, Yong Ren, and Xiuming Shan

Tsinghua University, Beijing 100084, P. R. China
wuw99@mails.tsinghua.edu.cn

Abstract. The TCP-style AIMD congestion control principle can't meet the need of the upcoming multimedia applications. They demand smooth adjustment and congestion aware, thus recently many works design TCP-friendly congestion control algorithms. In this paper, we focus on understanding one class of TCP-friendly congestion control algorithms, adjustment-based congestion control, which adjust transmission rate when loss is detected and can generalize TCP-style additive-increase by increasing inversely proportional to a power k of the current window (for TCP, $k=0$) and generalize TCP-style multiplicative-decrease by decreasing proportional to a power l of the current window (for TCP, $l=1$). We discuss their global fairness and stability. We prove that such class of congestion control algorithms can achieve *(p, k+l+1)-proportional fairness* globally no matter the network topology is and how many users there are. We also study their dynamical behaviors through a control theoretical approach. The smoothness of the congestion control will result in a less stable system and slower convergence to the fair bandwidth allocation. The modeling and discussions in this paper are quite general and can be easily applied to equation-based TCP-friendly congestion control scheme, another category of TCP-friendly transport protocols.

1. Introduction

The significant success of Internet to date has in large part been due to the congestion control and avoidance algorithms [1] implemented in its dominant transport protocol, TCP. Based on the implicit congestion notification feedback from the network, TCP can adapt its transmission rate to match available capacity by the principle of additive-increase/multiplicative-decrease (AIMD) [2]. But increase-by-one decrease-to-half, the adaptation feature of TCP, is not quite suited for several emerging applications including streaming and real-time audio and video, most of which can't bear the transmission rate throttled half when congestion signal detected. However, to be safe for deployment in the Internet, the protocols used by these applications must implement "TCP-friendly" or "TCP-compatible" end-to-end congestion control algorithms, which can interact well with TCP and maintain the scalability and stability of current Internet [3]. The idea of "TCP-friendly" is to ensure fair resource allocation between these protocols and TCP [4]. In the past few years, many unicast congestion control schemes [5, 6, 7, 8, 9, 10, 11] have been proposed and designed to

M.J. van Sinderen and L.J.M. Nieuwenhuis (Eds.): PROMS 2001, LNCS 2213, pp. 180-191, 2001.

gain approximately the same throughput as that of TCP under same conditions of round-trip time and packet loss.

The proposed TCP-friendly congestion control algorithms can be mainly divided into two categories: equation-based and adjustment-based. Equation-based schemes use the equation that expresses the TCP sending rate as a function of packet loss rate, round-trip time and timeout. A coarse function was given in [4] using a deterministic model by omitting the effects of timeout and slow-start. It is shown as follows:

$$T_{coarse} = \frac{\sqrt{1.5}\,B}{R\sqrt{p}} \tag{1}$$

where R is the average round trip time, B is the packet size and p is the end-to-end loss probability.

In [12], authors provided a finer function by analyzing a stochastic model of TCP, which takes timeout into account. It can be expressed as follows:

$$T_{fine} = \frac{B}{R\sqrt{\frac{2p}{3}} + t_{RTO}\,(3\sqrt{\frac{3p}{8}})\,p\,(1 + 32\,p^2)} \tag{2}$$

where t_{RTO} is the TCP retransmit timeout value.

We should notice that the performance of equation-based approach largely depends on how well function (2) describes TCP throughput [12], actually the validation of (2) is still a problem: does it work for asymmetric links, satellite links or wireless links? Furthermore, The way to estimate loss event probability p in (2) and the resource allocation of multiple nodes case are still unsolved properly. These problems are reported in [13].

Adjustment-based schemes include those algorithms still based on AIMD principle, such as TEAR [7], RAP [8], LDA [9] and GAIMD [10] and more general one recently proposed by Deepak Bansal and Hari Balakrishnan, the binomial congestion control algorithm [11]. Adjustment-based algorithms increase the transmission rate when packets are successfully received and decrease its rate when congestion is detected. The general form of adjustment-based scheme can be expressed as

$$W(t+R) = \begin{cases} W(t) + \alpha/W^k(t) & \textit{no loss } \det\textit{ected in a round} \\ W(t) - \beta W^l(t) & \textit{loss is } \det\textit{ected in a round} \end{cases} \tag{3}$$

Especially when *k=0, l=1*, we get GAIMD discussed in [10] and more specially *α=1, β=0.5* for TCP.

In [11], authors mainly proposed the binomial congestion control algorithm, which satisfies *k+l=1* and discuss its convergence and fairness under synchronized-feedback assumption. With a view of fairness, the fairness discussed in [11] focused on the resource allocation in one bottleneck link, called local fairness. In this paper we will extend it to a global case under the framework of flow optimization problems proposed in [14, 15] by Kelly and [16] by S. H. Low and D. E. Lapsley. We will show the *(k,l)* congestion control defined in (3) is *(p,k+l+1)-proportional fair*, which is defined in [17]. We also study the transient behavior of adjustment-based algorithms like (3) through a control theoretic analysis and we give the effects of the parameters k, l, α and β on the stability of Internet and convergence speed.

The contribution of this paper can be outlined as follows:
1. Modeling the adjustment-based congestion control in differential equations;
2. The theoretic confirmation of the global fairness of those congestion control schemes;
3. A control theoretic approach to analyze the stability and convergence of the system, including both the end users and network routers, and the effects of the parameters used in the algorithms.

The rest of the paper is organized as follows. In section 2, we give a differential model of (3) to provide a basis for further discussion. In section 3, we discuss the global fairness of (k,l) congestion control and its utility functions under the framework of flow optimization. We prove that the binomial congestion control $(k+l=1)$ algorithms have the same utility function and achieve the minimum potential delay fairness as defined by [18]. In section 4 we focus on the stability of the network if those TCP-friendly algorithms are deployed. Section 5 concludes the work and gives a brief view for future work.

2. Differential Model for General (k,l) Congestion Control

In this section, we will describe approximately the discrete algorithms (3) by differential equations. Firstly we should notice that: (i) the window-adjustment policy is only one component of the complete congestion control protocol like (3). Other mechanism such as slow-start, timeout, retransmission (if required) and timer estimation can maintain the same as TCP. (ii) The rate-based adjustment schemes can also follow the mechanisms of (3) by using $W(t)=T(t)*R$, where $W(t)$ is congestion window size and $T(t)$ is the transmission rate, and the differential equation can be developed in the same way as the window-based schemes.

Like [11], we model the behavior of the algorithms like (3) in terms of "round". A round start with the back-to-back transmission of W packets, where W is the current congestion window size. Once all packets falling within the congestion window have been sent in this back-to-back manner, no packets are sent until ACKs are received for some or all of these W packets. We also assume that ACKs arrive in a burst manner. This burst ACK reception marks the end of the current round and the beginning of the next round. So the probability that no loss in a round trip time is $(1-p)^W$ and the probability that loss exist in a round is $1-(1-p)^W$. And the expected value of congestion window E[W] can be calculated:

$$E[W(t+R)] - E[W(t)] = (1-p)^{E[W]}\alpha E[W]^{-k} - [1-(1-p)^{E[W]}]\beta E[W]^l \qquad (4)$$

We assume p<<1, so that we can approximate (4) using $(1-p)^{E[W]} \approx 1 - E[W]p$ as follows:

$$\frac{dE[W(t+R)]}{dt} \approx \frac{E[W(t+R)] - E[W(t)]}{R} \approx \frac{(1-E[W]p)\alpha E[W]^{-k} - \beta p E[W]^{l+1}}{R} \qquad (5)$$

Further more, we assume $E[W]>>1$, then $\alpha p E[W]^{-k+1}$ can be neglected compared with $\beta p E[W]^{l+1}$. So (5) can be derived to a more simple form:

$$\frac{dE[W(t+R)]}{dt} \approx \frac{\alpha E[W]^{-k} - \beta p E[W]^{l+1}}{R} \tag{6}$$

Noting that when $E[W]$ is stabilized, $dE[W]/dt \to 0$, we can get the throughput

$$T_0 = \frac{E[W_0]}{R} = \frac{1}{R}(\frac{\alpha}{\beta p})^{\frac{1}{k+l+1}} \tag{7}$$

which is the same as the one derived in [11] (see (7) in [11]). From (7), we can see that when $k+l=1$ and $\alpha=2\beta$, the (k,l) congestion control scheme is TCP-friendly. Replacing $E[W]$ in (6) with $T*R$, we can get the adjustment differential equation of throughput (or rate)

$$\frac{dT(t+R)}{dt} = \alpha R^{-k-2} T^{-k} - \beta p R^{l-1} T^{l+1} \tag{8}$$

3. Fairness

Consider a network with a set of links L such that $l \in L$ has capacity C_l. The network is shared by a set of sources S, where source is characterized by a utility function $U_s(T_s)$ that is concave increasing in its transmission rate T_s. Associated with each source $s \in S$ is a route which is also denoted by s, and consists of a set of links $L(s) \subset L$. We also define the set of sources sharing link l as $S(l)$. Our objective is to choose source rates $T = (T_s, s \in S)$ so as to

$$P: \quad \max_{T_s} \sum_s U_s(T_s) \quad subject\ to\ \sum_{s \in S(l)} T_s \leq C_l, \forall l \in L. \tag{9}$$

In [16], The problem P is formulated into a dual problem:

$$D: \quad \min_{p \geq 0} \max_{T_s} D(p,T) \quad D(p,T) = \sum_s (U_s(T_s) - p^s T_s). \tag{10}$$

$$p^s = \sum_{l \in L(s)} p_l \tag{11}$$

where p_l is interpreted as price per unit bandwidth at link l and p^s is the path price of source s in [16]. Actually, under the background of congestion control, the price of link can be seen as the loss/mark (mark when ECN is enabled) probability of the link as a special case. So we denote p_l as the loss/mark probability of link l and p^s as the end-to-end loss/mark probability in the rest of this paper. From (10), we can also see that the optimization problem can be solved in a distributed way: each source tries to maximize $U_s(T_s) - p^s T_s$ based on the information p^s fed back from the network. So the behavior of the source depends on its utility function used to be optimized. Next we will give the utility function of the adjustment in (3).

Proposition 1: The congestion control like (3) solves the dual problem D (10) with the utility function

$$U_s(T_s) = \begin{cases} \dfrac{\alpha}{\beta R_s}\log T_s, & k+l = 0 \\[2ex] -\dfrac{\alpha}{\beta(k+l)R_s^{k+l+1}}\cdot\dfrac{1}{T_s^{k+l}}, & k+l \neq 0 \end{cases} \tag{12}$$

Proof: Solving the dual problem D (10) in a distributed way, each source regulate its rate to maximize $B_s(T_s)=U_s(T_s)-p^sT_s$. By applying Gradient Projection method, the maximum can be achieved by

$$\frac{dT_s}{dt} = \gamma\nabla D(p) = \gamma\frac{\partial B_s(T_s)}{\partial T_s} = \gamma(\frac{\partial U_s(T_s)}{\partial T_s} - p^s)$$

Let $\gamma = \beta T_s^{l+1}R_s^{l-1}$ here, we get following adjustment scheme:

$$\frac{dT_s}{dt} = \gamma\nabla D(p) = \gamma\frac{\partial B_s(T_s)}{\partial T_s} = \beta T_s^{l+1}R_s^{l-1}\frac{\partial U_s(T_s)}{\partial T_s} - \beta p^s T_s^{l+1}R_s^{l-1}) \tag{13}$$

Comparing (13) with (8) and omitting the transmission delay, we can get

$$\frac{\partial U_s(T_s)}{\partial T_s} = \frac{\alpha}{\beta(T_s R_s)^{k+l+1}}$$

and get the utility function shown in (12). □

Corollary 1: All TCP-friendly congestion control schemes (called binomial congestion control) adjusted like (3) have the same utility function

$$U_s(T_s) = -\frac{2}{R_s^2 T_s}$$

Proof: It can be easily reached by applying proposition 1 with k+l=1 and α=2β. □

In [17], authors introduced a class of fairness criteria: *(w, δ)-proportional fairness*. Let $w = (w_1,..., w_N)$ and δ be positive numbers, then a vector of rates T^* is *(w, δ)-proportional fairness* if it is feasible and for any other feasible vector T,

$$\sum_{s\in S} w_i \frac{T_s - T_s^*}{T_s^{*\delta}} \leq 0$$

Proposition 2: The congestion control like (3) can achieve a bandwidth allocation with *(w, k+l+1)-Proportional fair* with

$$w = (\frac{\alpha}{\beta}R_s^{-(k+l+1)}, s\in S)$$

Proof: Applying Lemma 2 in [17] and proposition 1 directly, the conclusion can be reached directly. □

As a special case, binomial congestion control algorithms achieve *(w, 2)-proportional fairness*, which is also defined as potential delay minimization in [18].
   Remarks:
   1.   One thing we should notice is that the utility function of the congestion control is dependent on round trip time of the path R_s. To some extent, it is reasonable because the longer the distance is; the more expensive the tariff is, just like telephone call. But it might be an unexpected feature when considering fairness in a Differentiated Services (DiffServ) domain. We propose here that selecting proper α, β can remove the effects of RTT on fairness.
   2.   We can also consider the fairness of equation-based congestion control schemes through the same approach above. T_{coarse} calculated in (1) can be viewed as the optimal rate T^* by maximizing $U_s(T_s) - p^s T_s$ and T_{fine} is a more precise one taking timeout into accounts in $U_s(T_s)$. The equation-based algorithms always transmit packets with the optimal rate based on current feedback p^s. This may refute some viewpoints in [13]. The main challenge of equation-based congestion control scheme is to estimate p^s accurately and robustly.

4. Stability

In the former section, we analyzed the fairness of a general class of congestion control with a view from resource optimization. The optimum point can be achieved in a distributed manner after a long enough period. It can be seen as a static analysis of the congestion control. In this section, we will consider the congestion control as a feedback control system and study its dynamical behavior, especially its stability and convergence speed to the equilibrium state.

4.1 Queue Dynamics Modeling

Before the discussion of stability, we first setup models to be studied. Considering the link l with loss/mark rate p_l, we can describe queue dynamics by a revised Lindley equation:

$$\frac{dq_l(t)}{dt} = \begin{cases} 0 & (1 - p_l) \sum_{s \in L(s)} T_s < C_l \text{ and } q_l = 0 \\ (1 - p_l) \sum_{s \in L(s)} T_s - C_l & other \ else \end{cases} \tag{14}$$

   The loss/mark rate (more generally, price) is determined differently for different buffer management schemes. For Droptail, it is determined by

$$p_l(t) = \begin{cases} 1 & q_l(t) > Q_l \\ 0 & q_l(t) \le Q_l \end{cases} \tag{15}$$

where Q_l is the buffer size of the queue in link l.

With the recommendation to use active queue management (AQM) in IETF [3], some AQM algorithms, e.g. *Random Early Detection* (RED) [19], will be widely deployed. As an example, RED can be modeled as follows [20]:

$$\frac{d\bar{q}_l(t)}{dt} \approx -C_l w \bar{q}_l(t) + C_l w q_l(t)' \text{ and}$$

$$p_l(\bar{q}_l) = \begin{cases} 0 & \bar{q}_l < Q_{min} \\ \dfrac{\bar{q}_l - Q_{min}}{Q_{max} - Q_{min}} p_{max} & Q_{min} < \bar{q} < Q_{max} \\ 1 & \bar{q}_l > Q_{max} \end{cases} \tag{16}$$

where $\bar{q}_{l(t)}$ is exponentially weighted average queue, w is its weight; Q_{min}, Q_{max} is the minimum threshold, maximum threshold of queue size respectively, which is used to control the average queuing delay and p_{max} is the threshold of loss/mark probability. Details of the meaning of these parameters can be referred to [19].

So the dynamical behavior of the link l can be described by (14) and (15) (for Droptail) or (16) (for RED) and the dynamical behavior of the source s can be described by (8). Furthermore, the dynamics of the whole network can be characterized by those $|S| + 2|L|$ differential equations. In the rest of this paper, we use RED as the queue management algorithm.

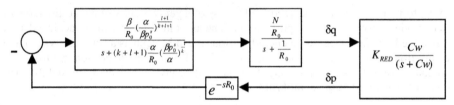

Fig. 1. Block-diagram of the linearized close-loop system

4.2. Local Stability

From the subsection above, we can model the dynamical behavior of the network by a set of $(|S| + 2|L|)$ nonlinear delay differential equations. It is tractable to study the stability of the systems theoretically in the classical control theory. By linearizing those nonlinear differential equations near the equilibrium point, we can get a set of linear local differential equations, which can be denoted as follows:

$$\delta \dot{X} = A(\delta X)$$
$$X = (T_1, T_2, \cdots, T_S, q_1, q_2, \cdots, q_L, \bar{q}_1, \bar{q}_2, \cdots, \bar{q}_L)$$
$$\delta X = X - X_0$$

where X_0 is the equilibrium point of the dynamical system where fair bandwidth allocation is achieved and network utility functions are maximized, which is discussed in section 2 above; matrix A is the coefficient matrix of the linearized differential equations. According to the classical control theory, the dynamical system can obtain asymptotic stability if and only if all $S+2L$ eigenvalues of A are all in the left part of complex plane: *Real(s)<0 for all s suffice* $|A - sI| = 0$. But it is difficult in reality for the computation complexity involved and it is also not helpful to understand the congestion control schemes. Trying to shed some light on understanding the effects of different parameters, we will focus on the mechanism of the congestion control like (3) at sources and then discuss the stability of the network under a simple network scenario.

Linearizing (6), we can get

$$\delta E[\dot{W}_s(t + R_0)] = -(k + l + 1)\frac{\beta p_0^s}{R_0}(\frac{\alpha}{\beta p_0^s})^{\frac{l}{k+l+1}} \delta E[W] - \frac{\beta}{R_0}(\frac{\alpha}{\beta p_0^s})^{\frac{l+1}{k+l+1}} \delta p^s \qquad (17)$$

Applying Laplace transform, we can obtain the transfer function of congestion control, $H_{cc}(s)$:

$$H_{cc}(s) = \frac{H_p(s)}{H_W(s)} = -\frac{\frac{\beta}{R_0}(\frac{\alpha}{\beta p_0^s})^{\frac{l+1}{k+l+1}}}{s + (k + l + 1)\frac{\alpha}{R_0}(\frac{\beta p_0^s}{\alpha})^{\frac{k+1}{k+l+1}}} = -\frac{\frac{1}{(k+l+1)p_0^s}(\frac{\alpha}{\beta p_0^s})^{\frac{1}{k+l+1}}}{\frac{s}{P_{cc}} + 1} \qquad (18)$$

where $P_{cc} = (k + l + 1)\frac{\beta p_0^s}{R_0}(\frac{\alpha}{\beta p_0^s})^{\frac{l}{k+l+1}}$ is the pole of $H_{cc}(s)$.

Remarks:

a) For those congestion control algorithms, which satisfy α/β=constant, $k+l$=constant, they have a common utility function according to proposition 1, and a common gain according to (18). The difference is their pole P_{cc}.

b) For the binomial congestion control schemes, α/β=2, $k+l=1$, thus the gain $\propto (p_0^s)^{-\frac{3}{2}}$, $P_{cc} \propto (p_0^s)^{\frac{1}{2}}$. The gain decreases with the increase of the path loss/mark probability, which infers the system may be more stable; while the pole increases with the increase of the probability, which infers the congestion control may be more responsive.

c) For GAIMD (k=0,l=1) in [10], the decrease of α, β will cause the decrease of the pole proportionally, thus slow down the response of the congestion control. Also in the binomial congestion control (k+l=1), higher k will make the control more smoothly, but it also results in the decrease of the pole and the increase of the response time. Obviously there exists the tradeoff between smoothness and responsiveness. We will study the tradeoff quantitatively in the later part of the paper.

4.3. Comparison in a Simple Case

Now we will consider the stability in a simple network scenario: *N* same sources with same parameters, e.g. window size *W*, propagation delay d (also round trip time R=d+q/C), share resources at a bottleneck router (queue size *q*, capacity *C*, loss/mark probability *p*), which is called *dumbbell* and is widely used by Internet communities of congestion control research. We rewrite our differential equations (14) in a more simple form according to such a topology as follows:

$$\frac{dq(t)}{dt} = \frac{NW}{R} - C \tag{19}$$

By linearizing (19), we can get

$$H_{queue}(s) = \frac{H_q(s)}{H_w(s)} = \frac{N/R_0}{(s+1/R_0)} = \frac{N}{(s/P_{queue}+1)} \tag{20}$$

where $P_{queue} = 1/R_0$.

The queue management scheme, RED, can be modeled as a control block with the transfer function by the work done in [21]:

$$H_{RED} = K_{RED}\frac{Cw}{(s+Cw)} = \frac{K_{RED}}{(\frac{s}{P_{RED}}+1)} \tag{21}$$

where $P_{RED} = Cw$.

What we are interested in here is the dynamical behavior of the close-loop system when different TCP-friendly congestion control schemes (also called binomial congestion control) are applied. We can study it through the poles of the close-loop transfer function, which are the roots of the equation

$$H_{cc}(s) \cdot H_{queue}(s) \cdot H_{RED}(s) = -1 \tag{22}$$

The dynamical behavior of the system is dominated by the main pole, which is also the root with the largest real part in (22). If the main pole has a real part no less than zero, the system will become oscillated thus can't achieve the fairness point we discussed in last section. When the main pole has a real part less than zero, the system can reach the equilibrium point asymptotically and the less its real part, the faster the system can converge. Next we will discuss the effects of α, β, k and l on the dynamical behavior by examples.

Example: $C=2500packets/s$ $(10Mbps)$, $w=0.002$, $Q_{min}=50$, $Q_{max}=150$, $p_{max}=0.1$, $C=2500$, $d=120ms$

In this example, we change the network load N to show the effects of the network and change α, β, k and l, to compare the effects of different adjustment congestion control schemes. We increase N from 30 to 100 (increase 5 connections each time) thus p_0 ranges from 1% to 10% approximately. Fig.2 shows the root-locus of the system when different congestion control algorithms are applied. We can find following properties:

1. When the network load increases thus loss rate p_0 increases, the system will become more stable and converge much faster than light-loaded condition.
2. Comparing TCP(1,0.5) (TCP Reno) with TCP(0.5,0.25) ($\alpha=0.5$, $\beta=0.25$) and TCP(0.25,0.125) ($\alpha=0.25$, $\beta=0.125$), the smaller α is, the less stable and slower convergence speed is. This also happens on SQRT ($\alpha=1$, $\beta=0.5$, $k=0.5,l=0.5$) and IIAD ($\alpha=1$, $\beta=0.5$, $k=1,l=0$). Things go worse when network load decreases. As an example, when N=30 ($p_0=1.4\%$), the roots go very close to imaginary axis thus the system need far more time to converge to the equilibrium point.

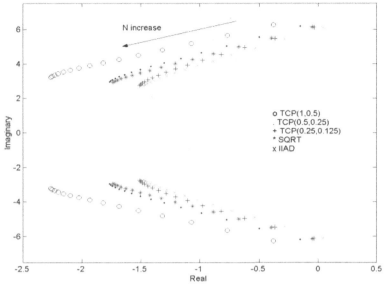

Fig. 2. Root-locus of adjustment-based congestion control algorithms (N ranges from 30 to 100)

3. The introduction of k and l to the congestion control like (3) makes the rate adjustment depend on the network load comparing with AIMD principles: the performance of SQRT is more like that of TCP(0.5,0.25) when network load is high and more like TCP(0.25,0.125) when load is low. And IIAD has a slower response in a low network load condition while it has almost the same response in higher network load compared with TCP(0.25,0.125).

4. The key problem of the smoother adjustment-based algorithms is the slow response at a low network load, which can be observed in both model calculation (solving the differential equation numerically by a math program, DE-solver, developed in Matlab) and simulation in ns2, a widely used network simulator. In the experiments, we use IIAD as our congestion control algorithm and let N=100, 20, 150, 40 at t=0, 25, 50, 75 respectively and draw the dynamics of the averaged queue size and instantaneous queue size of RED in fig.3. We can see it takes nearly 20s to achieve the equilibrium point after N switches from 100 to 20.

The fairness between TCP and its variants like TCP(α β), IIAD and SQRT, may be affected by the response of the algorithms: a slow responsive scheme may share unfair bandwidth allocation before it reaches the equilibrium. Such unfairness may become obvious when network load is low.

5. Conclusion

In this paper, we study the fairness and stability of the adjustment-based TCP-friendly congestion control analytically. We first model the dynamical behavior of adjustment-

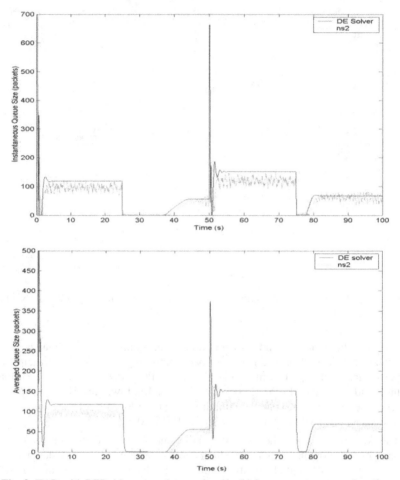

Fig. 3. IIAD with RED (a) averaged queue length; (b) Instantaneous queue length

based congestion control by differential equations. Using the model, we prove their fairness under the framework of global flow control optimization. We prove that the class of congestion control can achieve *(p, k+l+1)-proportional fairness* to optimize the aggregate of the network utility functions and as a special case, TCP-friendly binomial congestion control can achieve potential delay minimization. The fairness can be viewed as the static property of the schemes while the stability can be seen as their dynamical property. We study their stability generally first and discuss and experiment its details in a simple network scenario. By linearizing a set of differential equations, we formulate the system as a close-loop plant through a control theoretic approach. Then we study its stability and convergence qualitatively by drawing root-locus of the control system. A brief discussion and observation is given to help us understand the behavior of binomial congestion control.

References

[1] V. Jacobson, "Congestion Avoidance and Control," in Proc. ACM SIGCOMM, August 1988, pp. 314-329

[2] D-M. Chiu and R. Jain, "Analysis of the Increase and Decrease Algorithms for Congestion Avoidance in Computer Networks," Computer Networks and ISDN Systems, vol. 17, pp. 1-14, 1989.

[3] B. Braden, D. Clark, J. Crowcroft, B. Davie, S. Deering, D. Estrin, S. Floyd, V. Jacobson, G. Minshall, C. Patridge, K. Ramakrishnan, S. Shenker, J. Wroclawski, and L. Zhang, "Recommendations on Queue Management and Congestion Avoidance in the Internet," Internet Engineering Task Force, April 1998, RFC 2309.

[4] S. Floyd and K. Fall, "Promoting the Use of End-to-End Congestion Control in the Internet," IEEE/ACM Transactions on Networking, vol.7, No.4, August 1999.

[5] J. Padhye, J. Kurose, D. Towsley, and R. Koodi, "A Model Based TCP-Friendly Rate Control Protocol," Proc NOSSDAV'99, 1999.

[6] S. Floyd, M. Handley, J. Padhye, and J. Widmer, "Equation-based Congestion Control for Unicast Applications," Proc ACM SIGCOMM 2000, August 2000.

[7] Injong Rhee, Volkan Ozdemir, and Yung Yi, "TEAR: TCP emulation at receivers -- flow control for multimedia streaming," Technical Report, Department of Computer Science, NCSU.

[8] R. Rejaie, Mark Handley and D. Estrin, "RAP: An End-to-End Rate-based Congestion Control Mechanism for Realtime Streams in the Internet," Proc IEEE Infocom'99, pp. 1337-1345

[9] D. Sisalem and H. Schulzrinne, "The Loss-Delay based Adjustment Algorithm: A TCP-Friendly Adaptation Scheme," Proc NOSSDAV'98, July 1998.

[10] Y. R. Yang and S. S. Lam, "General AIMD Congestion Control," Proc ICNP'2000, Japan, Nov. 2000.

[11] Deepak Bansal and Hari Balakrishnan, "Binomial Congestion Control Algorithms," Proc IEEE INFOCOM'2001, April 2001.

[12] J. Padhye, V. Firoiu, D. Towsley, and J. Kurose, "Modeling TCP throughput: A Simple Model and its Expirical Validation," Proc ACM SIGCOMM'98, Vancouver, Canada, 1998.

[13] Sridhar Ramesh and Injong Rhee, "Issues on Equation-based Flow Control", http://www.csc.ncsu.edu/faculty/rhee/ export/tear_page/tcl_model.pdf.

[14] F. P. Kelly, "Charging and Rate Control for Elastic Traffic," Euro. Trans. Telecommun., vol.8, pp. 33-37, 1997.

[15] F. P. Kelly, A. Maulloo, and D. Tan, "Rate Control for Communication Networks: Shadow prices, Proportional Fairness and stability

[16] Steven H. Low and David E. Lapsley, "Optimization Flow Control ----I: Basic Algorithm and Convergence," IEEE/ACM Transactions on Networking, vol. 7, no. 6, Dec 1999.

[17] J. Mo and J. Walrand, "Fair End-to-End Window-Based Congestion Control," IEEE/ACM Transactions on Networking, vol.8, no. 5, Oct 2000.

[18] L. Massoulie and J. Roberts, "Bandwidth Sharing: Objectives and Algorithms," Proc IEEE INFOCOM'99.

[19] S. Floyd and V. Jacobson, "Random Early Detection Gateways for Congestion Avoidence", IEEE/ACM Transactions on Networking, vol. 1, no. 4, August 1993, pp. 397-413.

[20] Vishal Misra, Wei-Bo Gong and Don Towsley, "Fluid-based Analysis of a Network of AQM Routers Supporting TCP Flows with an Application to RED", ACM SIGCOMM 2000.

[21] C.V. Hollot, Vishal Misra, Don Towsley and Wei-Bo Gong, "A Control Theoretic Analysis of RED", in Proceedings of IEEE INFOCOM'2001, April 2001.

Model-Based Service Creation in the Friends Project

Wouter B. Teeuw[1] and Dick A.C. Quartel[2]

[1] Telematica Instituut, P.O. Box 589, 7500 AN Enschede, The Netherlands
teeuw@telin.nl

[2] CTIT-University of Twente, P.O. Box 217, 7500 AN Enschede, The Netherlands
quartel@cs.utwente.nl

Abstract. This paper presents a model-based approach to service creation. We observe that the complexity of software services increases. To manage this complexity, and to quickly create specific services in an efficient and cost-effective way upon user request, models are used, going towards 'higher-level' programming. A service creation environment is developed that supports the modelling of services at successive abstraction levels, the analysis of service models, their actual implementation, and the testing and deployment of service implementations. Services are assumed to be developed from existing or newly developed software components. Components are modelled by describing their external behaviour, rather than their interface(s) only. This provides additional design information facilitating a systematic approach to service creation. This paper shows how we model services and their constituent components, and how we use these models.

1 Introduction

In the Friends project, a middleware platform has been built to support the development, deployment and management of distributed services [11]. An important new feature of this platform is the integrated support for service creation, providing a so-called *service creation environment*. Upon user demand, the service creation environment enables a service developer to design and implement the requested service in an efficient and cost-effective way. A service is assumed to be composed from software components that conform to the middleware platform's underlying component architecture. The service creation environment promotes the re-use of existing components and supports the development of new components if needed. To enable rapid service development, the FRIENDS platform includes generic components supporting access control, authentication (PKI), accounting, performance monitoring, and QoS management, and multimedia components supporting Audio/Video streaming and CSCW services.

A model-based approach underlies the service creation environment. We observe that the complexity of software services increases and the allowed development time of services becomes shorter. A model-based approach helps to manage this complexity, to structure and facilitate service development —going towards 'higher-level' programming— and to validate services at design time. An important characteristic of

M.J. van Sinderen and L.J.M. Nieuwenhuis (Eds.): PROMS 2001, LNCS 2213, pp. 192-209, 2001.

our approach is to model the complete external behaviour of a component, defining both the operations that can be invoked on its interfaces and the operations invoked by this component on interfaces of other components, as well as the relationships between these operations and their parameters.

The purpose of this paper is twofold: to describe our model-based approach and to present the tool architecture of the service creation environment supporting our approach. A key element of this tool architecture is the modelling tool Testbed Studio [10,12]. This paper describes how we use this tool to specify and analyse the behaviour of services and components, and how this tool is integrated in the service creation environment. This paper is further structured as follows: section 2 describes the Friends middleware platform, section 3 motivates and introduces our model-based approach to service creation, section 4 presents the tool architecture of the service creation environment and illustrates the use of the tools identified in this architecture with examples, and section 5 presents our conclusions and future work.

2   The Friends Middleware Platform

Middleware platforms shield the heterogeneity of underlying operating systems and networks and provide distribution transparencies to applications [3]. Building such a platform, Friends does not start from scratch but uses the results of the Mesh project [2]. Mesh built a CSCW platform, which complies with the TINA service architecture. Among its features are network independence, user and session mobility, and the support for multimedia stream bindings. In Friends, the functionality of this middleware platform is extended and improved to support not only CSCW applications, but also applications in the area of E-commerce, entertainment and content engineering.

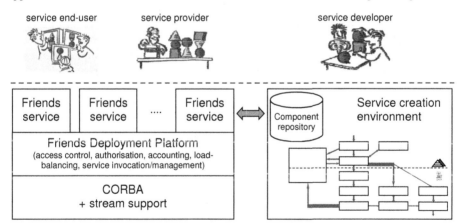

Fig. 1. Friends integrated platform approach.

Characteristic for the Friends platform is an *integrated* approach to support service users, providers, and developers (see Fig. 1). Given an arbitrary application, e.g., a CSCW environment for project co-operation, an electronic 'Game Hall' for entertainment, or an e-commerce environment for B2B transactions, FRIENDS offers services to all three categories of stake-holders. Video-conferencing, chat, messaging and application sharing are typical examples of functionality that supports the end-users. Service management, accounting and billing functionality typically supports the service providers. The functionality provided by the service creation environment to support service developers is the subject of this paper.

An Internet Service Provider (ISP) typically exploits the Friends Deployment Platform. Alternatively, a retailer (E-tailer) or Application Service Provider (ASP) may exploit the Friends Platform as a whole, including the Friends services on top of it. An Independent Software vendor (ISV) typically exploits the service creation environment. In principle, Friends services may be provided by third parties because they only need to use the deployment platform APIs.

The Friends Deployment Platform is based on component software [18]. Its underlying Distributed Software Component (DSC) *architecture* defines the minimal rules and constraints a component should adhere to, to achieve some minimal level of interoperability with other components [1]. DSC was developed as a proprietary component architecture because at that time no alternative existed. Recently the CORBA Component Model emerged [7], and DSC will be migrated to this component architecture. The DSC *framework* implements the DSC architecture. The framework defines amongst others the representation in which the component stores its implementation and its specification. The Friends Deployment Platform has been implemented in Java and uses CORBA to support the interaction between distributed components.

3   Service Creation: The Need for a Model-Based Approach

We define a *service* as the external observable behaviour of a system, which consists of the interactions between the system and its environment and the relationships between these interactions. Typical examples of systems are applications and software components, with operations invoked on/by components being examples of interactions. Applications are composed from one or more software components, where each component is either an atomic component or a compound component. Consequently, the service provided by an application is composed from the services provided by its constituent components. The term *Friends service* is used to denote the service provided by an application that is deployed by a service provider on the Friends deployment platform.

3.1   Limitations of Component-Based Design

One of the promises of component-based design is the quick introduction of new applications through re-use of software components. Ideally, an application can be developed by selecting available components and composing them such that the requested service is provided. Still many problems need to be solved, however, to realize this ideal picture, most of them originating from a need for methodological support. We mention some of these problems.

Finding components. Components are stored in libraries or repositories. In case repositories are not organised according to proper *classification criteria* it is difficult to find the software one is looking for. Furthermore, standard rules for documenting components in repositories are needed in order to support intelligent *search methods*.

Understanding components. Components are commonly described in terms of interface definitions, one for each component interface, using an Interface Definition Language (IDL). These interface definitions generally describe only the signatures (names and types) of the component's properties, operations and operation arguments. A list of operation's signatures, however, does not completely define how the component behaves. As a consequence, different implementations of the same interface definition may show different behaviours.

Architectural design. Designing a proper composition of components that provides the requested service is a non-trivial task, especially for more complex services. Starting from a specification of the requested service, multiple designs of the requested service at successively, related abstraction levels may precede the final design in order to manage the design complexity. Incorporation of available components in the early design steps shortens the entire design process. Therefore, methodological support is needed that combines a top-down design approach, including specification techniques and decomposition guidelines (e.g., design patterns), with bottom-up knowledge about available software components.

Correctness. Since IDL specifications incompletely define a component's behaviour, it is difficult, actually impossible, to assess the correctness of this component. At best, test runs obtained by executing a component implementation can be used to determine whether the actual (executed) behaviour corresponds to the "expected" behaviour. Many errors found in component implementations can however already be detected during the specification and design phases. Since adaptations in the implementation phase can be very expensive, service specifications and designs should be analysed and validated before.

3.2   Model-Based Service Creation

To tackle the problems as described in the previous section, we propose a model-based approach to service creation [16]. Modelling is an essential activity when dealing with the inherent complexity of systems. We observe that services become progressively larger and more complex. Models help us to understand services by representing only their *essentials*, i.e., by eliminating everything we consider irrelevant to what we want to consider.

A model-based approach supports *architectural design*, through structuring the service creation process into multiple design steps. Starting from an abstract specification of the requested service, each step delivers a more refined design modelling those service characteristics that are considered relevant at the respective abstraction (or refinement) levels. In this way, separation of concerns is achieved to manage the design complexity. Use of bottom-up knowledge should guide the design (or refinement) steps to optimise re-use of software components and to obtain the final design in a fast and effective way.

Modelling services (applications) at successively, related abstraction levels, enables validation of the *correctness* of designs. Each successive design step should produce a design that conforms to the designs defined in previous steps. Techniques can be developed to verify this conformance relation (semi-)automatically. The modelling of services also makes the testing of implementations more meaningful, by providing some reference against which the validity of test runs can be checked.

Modelling helps designers to *understand* services and components by representing only their essentials, i.e., the characteristics considered relevant at a certain abstraction level. E.g., a service specification should define completely and unambiguously the external behaviour of an application or component. In this way, for example, a service designer can determine the composite behaviour of a certain composition of components and thus decide whether this composition provides the requested behaviour.

Modelling the external behaviour of components can be extended with information about the environment (or context) in which the component can be used and the problems it solves. This resembles the idea of a design pattern [13]: a specification in terms of a problem, a context, and the (partial) solution as provided by the component. Modelling components this way not only supports a proper *understanding* of components, but also supports the process of *finding components* in a problem-oriented way. For example, it facilitates a problem-oriented categorisation of components and the identification of keywords to be used by component search engines.

3.3   Behaviour Specification

To support component-based design, it is generally recognised that the external (operational) behaviour of a component should be defined and, furthermore, be added to the component [18]. A modelling language is needed that allows one to express the relevant behaviours characteristics of components, with a formal semantics to support analysis and validation. Furthermore, tool support should be available to facilitate the use of such a modelling language. We investigated the following alternatives.

Java. In the Friends project, Java is used as implementation language. Java visual assemblers [8], like Inprise JBuilder, Symantec Visual Cafe, IBM Visual Age, or NetBeans, have simple component assembly features. In addition, extensions to the Java language may be defined to specify the behaviour of components. A straightforward way seems to add pre- and post-conditions to the operation signatures. Some examples already exist, like Biscotti, an extension of Java in which method specifications are extended with (Eiffel-style) preconditions, postconditions and invariants [6]. The specification of preconditions, postconditions and invariants can be used for runtime checks performed by either the caller (client) or the called (server) component [4]. However, the combination of Java visual assemblers with Java language extensions does do not support the *abstract* modelling of the behaviours of individual or compositions of software components. Therefore, they are not suited for model-based service creation, but are solely used at implementation level.

UML. UML-based tools support notations for describing different aspects of the structure and behaviour of software, and often suggest methodologies for applying these notations throughout the software development process [19]. However, UML is not very suited for modelling and relating the behaviour of components at successive (higher) abstraction levels. Furthermore, UML lacks a formal semantics that supports analysis and validation of behaviour specifications.

Formal Description Techniques (FDTs). To support the modelling and design-time analysis of components at higher abstraction levels, other specification techniques need to be considered. In the last decades, many (formal) specification languages have been developed supporting varying conceptual models. FDTs that support an asynchronous interaction model, like Estelle or SDL, are particularly suited for representing designs at the lower abstraction levels [15]. To support different and related abstraction levels or constraint-oriented specification styles, a synchronous interaction model is more suited, like in LOTOS [5] or AMBER [10].

The use of formal specification languages in distributed systems design is however not widely accepted. The primary reason for this seems to be the required effort to specify designs, which is considerable compared to the effort needed to actually implement the design. We believe the use of a specification (modelling) technique does pay off in terms of improved efficiency of the service creation process and quality of the resulting designs, if providing an integrated tool environment supporting the specification, systematic design, analysis, verification and testing of services.

Amber and Testbed Studio. In the Friends project we have chosen AMBER [10] as the modelling language, which is supported by an integrated tool environment, called Testbed Studio [12]. Strong points of AMBER are its expressiveness (allowing those behaviour characteristics to be modelled we consider relevant for service creation), its underlying formalisms (enabling different types of analysis), and its graphical representation. Testbed Studio supports the editing of AMBER specifications, including syntax and semantics checking, and adds a number of analysis tools, such as stepwise simulation, quantitative analysis, integrated use of the model checker SPIN [14], and several kinds of generated views on a model. An additional important factor favouring the choice of AMBER is that the Telematics Institute developed Testbed Studio in the Testbed project [12]. Therefore, as opposed to other tools, we are able to influence the further development of Testbed Studio.

4   Architecture of the Friends Service Creation Environment

Fig. 2 depicts the tool architecture of the Friends service creation environment, identifying the tools supported by this environment and their relationships. The upper part of the figure shows the tools related to the specification and design of services using the modelling language AMBER. The lower part of the figure shows the tools related to the implementation of components in Java and their assembly into deployable services.

This section further explains the tools identified in Fig. 2. The tools are divided into the following categories: design tools, implementation tools, analysis tools and deployment tools. Existing (market) tools are used for 'design-time analysis' and 'component implementation'. The 'method support' (guide) and 'packaging' (manual) are done by hand. All other tools have been implemented by the Friends project.

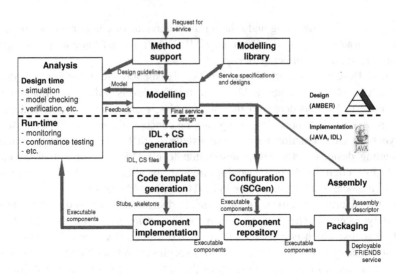

Fig. 2. Architecture of the Friends service creation environment.

4.1   Design Tools

Design tools assist the service developer in modelling and designing services (applications) at different abstraction levels. The following design tools are distinguished: modelling tool, modelling library and method support.

4.1.1   Modelling Tool

Testbed Studio is used to edit AMBER models. To support the service developer in the modelling process, a mapping is defined between concepts from the DSC component architecture and AMBER concepts. This mapping describes how a DSC concept, such as, e.g., an interface, operation or event, can be modelled in AMBER [17].

An Amber model consists of three sub-models: (i) an *actor model*, which defines the actors, involved, e.g., software components or functional application parts for which the assignment to components is yet undefined, and how they are interconnected, (ii) a *behaviour model*, which defines the behaviour (functionality) of each actor, and (iii) an *item model*, which defines the objects or data being manipulated by the actors through their behaviour.

Actor model. Fig. 3 depicts an actor model representing a design of the Friends Shared White Board service. In AMBER, components are modelled by actors (represented as octagons) and interfaces are modelled by interaction points (represented as ovals) [17].

The design of a Friends service should conform to the TINA service layer architecture. A service is decomposed into a service session User Application (ssUAP) function, which presents the service to the end-user, a Service Session Manager (SSM) function, which maintains the global view of a service session in terms of the parties, stream bindings and resources involved, and a User Session Manager (USM) function, which serves as a security guard between the ssUAP and SSM function to guarantee controlled access to the SSM. Each of these functions is assigned to a separate software component. The entire service is implemented by one instance of the SSM component, and multiple instances of the ssUAP and USM components, one per end-user. Each ssUAP, USM and SSM component is further decomposed into a *generic sub-component*, providing generic management functionality, such as starting and deleting service sessions and adding participants and streambindings to a service session, and *a service specific sub-component*. Consequently, a Friends service is built by extending the generic ssUAP, SSM and USM sub-components with service specific functionality, assigned to the SWB-ssUAP, SWB-SSM and SWB-USM [20].

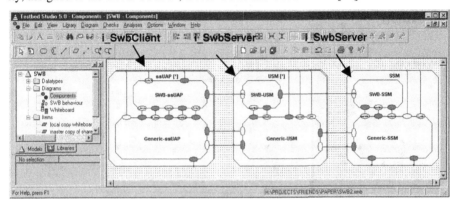

Fig. 3. SWB actor model

Behaviour model. Fig. 4 depicts the behaviour models of the SWB-ssUAP, SWB-SSM and SWB-USM, which only consider the i_SwbClient and i_SwbServer interface and abstract from generic service functionality.

Interface i_SwbClient provides a single operation startService(). This operation is called upon initialisation of the ssUAP. After startService is called:

- the ssUAP updates the whiteboard via operation (USM) getBoard, which is modelled by a sequence of two interactions (USM) getBoard invocation and (USM) getBoard return, which represent the operation invocation and the returning of its result, respectively;
- the ssUAP registers itself via operation (USM) subscribe to listen to so-called SwbEvents, which indicate an update of the shared whiteboard due to a drawing activity by another user. Subsequently, in an end-less loop, the interface listens to shared whiteboard update events (fired by the USM). On receiving a SwbEvent via operation (USM) notifyEvent, the ssUAP updates the whiteboard via operation USM getBoard;
- some drawing functionality is enabled. This functionality is part of the SWB-ssUAP behaviour, but is not part of the i_SwbClient interface. The drawing functionality is modelled as the repeated execution of a draw operation. Each draw operation is followed by updating the shared whiteboard through operation (USM) setBoard.

Interface i_SwbServer provided by the USM merely forwards getBoard and set-Board invocations of the ssUAP to the SSM, as well as forwards the return messages in opposite direction. Similarly, the USM forwards events between ssUAP and SSM.

Interface i_SwbServer provided by the SSM returns the shared whiteboard status upon a getBoard invocation or updates the status upon a setBoard invocation. The shared whiteboard status is represented by the item master copy of shared white-board. In case the status is updated an event is fired to notify all USMs involved (the replication of operation notifyEvent models that several listeners are notified). The firing and accepting events is modelled as an announcement. Iteration (loops) are used to model that operations can be invoked repeatedly.

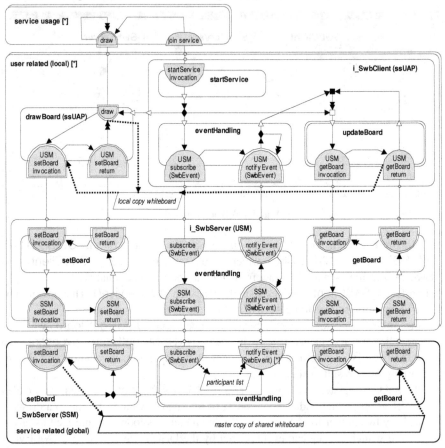

Fig. 4. SWB behaviour model

Component composition. The behaviour model of each component in Fig. 4 not only models the operations that can be invoked on its interface, which is denoted as the *invoked interface* (facet), but also the invocation of operations on the interface of another component, which is denoted as *the invoking interface* (receptacle). Compo-nents are graphically composed in Amber by connecting the interaction points model-ling the corresponding invoking (colored grey) and invoked (coloured white) interfaces. The correctness of such a composition, i.e., whether operations of the invoking and invoked interface match, are defined in terms of (static) semantics checks on interactions and interaction points in Amber.

4.1.2   Method Support

Having only a modelling tool (editor), i.e., a language and tool support for it, is not enough to create services. One also needs methodological support that tells us how to use the concepts of the language to build services. Methodological support is captured into guidelines and heuristics, service architectures (high-level software and its application to problems), and design methods.

The Friends service creation process consists of the following phases. Starting point is the user's request for service.

1. *Specification.* In this phase, a specification of the FRIENDS service is made. The main activity is scoping: deciding on what is "inside" or "outside" the service. The service specification defines the external observable application behaviour and should not define internal behaviour aspects. A well-specified service is one that is both desirable (client satisfaction) and feasible (builder feasibility). This phase also involves the determination of service objectives, service requirements, and use-cases.

2. *Design.* This phase considers the Friends service (application) from the internal perspective, by decomposing the service into multiple related functional parts. This decomposition step may be applied recursively to the identified parts, resulting into designs at successive abstraction levels. It is an episodic process of grouping versus separation of related solutions and problems, until a design is obtained that allows a direct mapping of the identified functional past onto existing or implementable software components. This design is called the *final design*. A well-designed service conforms to proven architectures or patterns, and maximises the re-use of existing software components. This phase includes issues like the use of patterns, searching for re-usable components, and design-time validation (see section 4.2.1).

3. *Implementation.* The components needed for service implementation either exist or need to be developed. In the former case they are retrieved from the component repository and configured. In the latter case, interface definitions (IDL) and component structure (CS) are derived from the final design, and the components are implemented. A well-implemented service meets its specification - no more and no less. The implementation tools of section 4.3 support the implementation process.

4. *Testing.* During the test phase, the implementation is certified to meet its specification. This certification may range from on the one hand common test practices relying on judgement and experience, to on the other hand a formal proof that the system as implemented possesses the desired properties. Friends currently develops a validation tool that checks whether test runs conform to the service specification (see section 4.2.2).

5. *Deployment.* In this final phase, the deployment tools described in section 4.4 are used to deliver a deployable Friends service.

The phases, though presented in a linear way, will be performed in iteration. Notice, however, the explicit distinction between design and implementation activities. This is reflected in the tool architecture of the Friends service creation environment, as shown in Fig. 2 (the right part of Fig. 1 in detail).

4.1.3   Modelling Library

Experience obtained with designing services leads to the recognition of re-usable components as well as *patterns* (sometimes called architectures). These components and patterns are stored in a modelling library. Testbed Studio supports the sharing of library elements (components) between several models.

Figure 5 shows an example: the ssUAP-USM-SSM pattern that has to be taken into account by each Friends service. To create different Friends services, the three basic components are extended with service specific components. Due

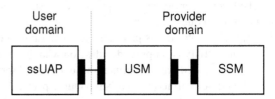

Fig. 5. Friends service session pattern

to the used architecture the SSM is the logical component to implement the basic service management functions. The ssUAP components are extended with the graphical user interface elements, like e.g. the display of a video conferencing component or the interface of a shared whiteboard.

4.2   Analysis Tools

Analysis tools assist the service developer in analysing the properties of services as represented in service models *at design time*, and the properties of services as exhibited by service implementations *at run-time*.

4.2.1   Design Time Analysis

Testbed Studio includes tools supporting step-wise simulation and functional analysis of behaviour models.

Simulation. The complete specification of the behaviours of components allows one to simulate the service provided by individual components as well as the service provided by a composition of components. For example, simulation of the shared whiteboard behaviour model has shown that updates of the whiteboard may be lost in case of two simultaneous setBoard invocations by different ssUAPs. The reason is that an ssUAP may invoke a

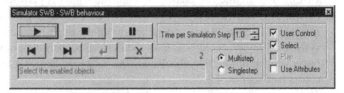

Fig. 6. Simulator control window

setBoard operation before the event notification of a previous setBoard from another ssUAP has been properly processed. The later setBoard simply overwrites the previous ones. Such design errors are typically detected during simulation. Figure 6 depicts the simulator control window.

Functional analysis. Testbed Studio enables a service designer to perform the following functional analyses on a behaviour model:

- *tracing*: checks whether a certain sequence of operations is always/ever/never executed;
- *liveness*: checks whether one, all or at least one operation invocation from a certain set of operations causes the invocation of at least one or all operations from another set;
- *combined occurrence*: checks whether the invocation of the operations from a certain set either exclude each other, or always/sometimes/never happen all together;
- *safety*: checks whether the invocation of each, all or at least one operation from a certain set requires the invocation of at least one or all operations from another set.

Verification. Based on the conceptual model underlying Amber, a general technique has been developed to enforce the correct replacement of an abstract behaviour by a more concrete behaviour, called *behaviour refinement*. A conformance relation defines which concrete behaviours are valid refinements (implementations) of the abstract behaviour, while it guarantees that the behaviour characteristics prescribed in the abstract behaviour are preserved by the concrete behaviour. For a further reading on this technique, we refer to [16]. Since this technique can in principle be automated, tools are planned that support conformance assessment after each design step.

4.2.2   Run-Time Analysis

Besides the common debug facilities provided by (Java) implementation environments, the Friends service creation environment adds two powerful techniques to test the actual implementation of a Friends service at run-time.

Monitoring. A monitoring framework is developed that enables the monitoring of interactions between distributed components [9]. Components interact by invoking operations on each other via a CORBA-compliant middleware platform. Operations can be synchronous (called interrogations), in which case a result is returned, or asynchronous (called notifications), in case no result is returned. An operation invo-

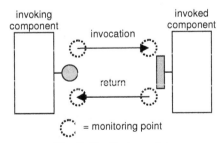

Fig. 7. Monitoring points

cation (and the return of its result) involves the transmission of a so-called request object between the invoking and invoked component. The request object contains the operation name, operation arguments, results and other (e.g., context) information. Figure 7 depicts the monitoring points of a synchronous operation.

When the operation is being executed, each monitoring point produces a so-called *interaction event* that is recorded. In this way, the monitoring framework is able to monitor the (real-)time ordering of interaction events. The interaction events are graphically represented using Message Sequence Charts (MSCs). Figure 8 depicts an MSC representing an execution of the SWB service.

The monitoring framework is also able to reconstruct the causal relationship between operations. For this purpose, monitoring information is sent between components using the context field of the CORBA request object, and is propagated through components by tagging threads of execution that process the operation.

A prototype of the monitoring framework exists. The monitoring framework is integrated into the component framework, such that the application (service) developer is not burdened with monitoring issues. Currently, the monitoring framework is developed further to support different types of events, e.g., life-cylce events, QoS events and user-defined events, which can be used for different purposes, such as accounting, load-balancing, QoS control and testing.

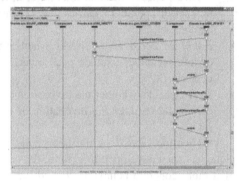

Fig. 8. Message sequence chart

Conformance testing. Based on the MSCs obtained using the monitoring framework, a technique for conformance testing is developed. This technique allows a service developer to check whether individual runs (executions) of a service implementation conforms to an Amber model of the service, which either represents the external specification of the service or one of its designs. The following steps are distinguished (see Figure 9):

1. *monitoring*: a single run of the service implementation is monitored using the monitoring framework described above. The obtained MSC represents a partial order of interaction events, which is called a *real trace*;

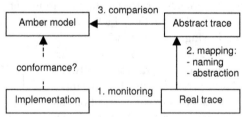

Fig. 9. Conformance testing steps

2. *mapping*: the real trace is transformed into an *abstract trace* that can be compared to the Amber model. This transformation involves, amongst others, the abstraction (removal) of operations that where not considered yet at modelling level. Furthermore, differences between naming conventions used at modelling and implementation level may have to be resolved, in case the generation tools as explained in section 4.3.1 and 4.3.2 were not used;

3. *comparison*: the abstract trace is compared with the Amber model, using the simulator of Testbed Studio. Successive operation invocations defined by the abstract trace should also be allowed by a step-wise simulation of the Amber model.

A tool supporting these steps has been developed. The kind of automated support provided in the mapping step strongly depends on the assumptions that can be made on the type of refinements made during the design process. This will be elaborated in a forthcoming paper dedicated to this conformancing testing technique.

4.3   Implementation Tools

Implementation tools assist the service developer in implementing (compositions of) components that provide the requested services.

4.3.1   IDL and CS Generation

The 'final service design' specifies a Friends service in terms of an assembly of components. Some components may already be available, others may be missing. The latter components need to be implemented. The first step in the implementation process is a (black-box) specification of the functionality of the component. Such a specification is already part of the final service design.

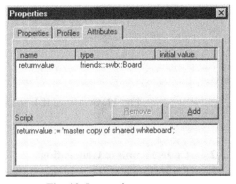

Fig. 10. Interaction parameters

Referring to the so-called Service Session Manager component of Figure 3 and 4 (SWB-SSM), the interface i_SwbServer provides two operations, called setBoard and getBoard. Each operation is specified as a *behaviour block* containing an invocation and a return *interaction*. Additionally, an exception interaction may be specified (not shown in the figure). For each interaction parameters can be specified, as shown in Figure 10 for the interaction getBoard return. The parameters of an invocation interaction and a return interaction model the input and output parameters of the corresponding operation, respectively. Modelling interactions and their parameters in this way, interface descriptions (CORBA IDL) and 'component specifications' (CS; description of subcomponents and the relation between invoking and invoked interfaces) can be generated. This functionality has been implemented, including the reverse engineering. Fig. 11 shows the resulting IDL for the SWB-SSM component.

```
// This file was generated by IDLGen
// Source file: D:\friends\src\friends\tools\IDLGen\SWB.xmb
// Date: 13-mrt-00 12:18:27

#ifndef SWB-SSM_IDL
#define SWB-SSM_IDL

// IDL file for component SWB-SSM
module friends {
    module swb {
        struct i_SwbServer {
            string itfType;
        };
        struct Board {
            integer version;
        };
    }; //swb
}; //friends

module SWB-SSM {
    interface i_SwbServer {
        void setBoard(in friends::swb::Board board);
        // invoke: board := 'setBoard invocation'.board;
        // 'master copy of shared whiteboard'.update(board);
        friends::swb::Board getBoard();
        // return: returnvalue := 'master copy of shared whiteboard';
    }; //i_SwbServer
}; //SWB-SSM

#endif
```

Fig. 11. Generated IDL specification of the SWB-SSM.

4.3.2   Code Template Generation

IDL and CS specifications can in turn be used to generate stubs or skeletons, as a next step in component implementation. For this purpose, Friends (DSC) tools already exist as described by Batteram et al. [2]. In this stage, CORBA Component Descriptors (CCD, as defined by the CORBA Component Model [7]) are generated as well.

4.3.3   Component Implementation (Atomic Components)

Standard (Java) development environments are used to implement components. Notice that interface descriptions (IDL) are part of the specification of the component, but are not enough. To support a proper implementation, behavioural specifications are required as well. The AMBER specifications (as a communication means) can be used for this purpose. In current practice, message sequence diagrams are commonly used to support component design. These message sequences are often made by hand. However, message sequences can be derived from the service specification of a component. A tool has been implemented to generate message sequence diagrams from AMBER specifications. The step-wise simulator of Testbed Studio generates a trace from a model (already implemented), and converts this trace to standardised message sequence formats to be visualised.

4.3.4   Configuration (SCGen)

Functionality related to, e.g., access control, authorisation, accounting and service invocation are identical for each Friends service. Aiming at service creation, i.e., the fast and flexible creation of new service running on this platform, one wishes to abstract from such generic functionality and to focus on the service-specific functionality only. The integration of generic functionality should be handled automatically, or at least not being the concern of the service developer.

A tool has been built, called SCGen, that automatically relates the Friends services to already available generic functionality. The tool is described by Verhoosel et al. [20]. As shown in Figure 12, all kind of parameter options can be specified in AMBER models (in so-called *profiles* of an *entity*), whereupon the code generator SCGen uses this information.

4.3.5   Component Repository

The component repository contains the (binary) components, which are stored as a zip-archive. Complying with the CORBA Component Model [7], a Software Package Descriptor (SPD) is part of this archive.

Fig. 12. Configuration parameters for generic service functionality

4.4   Deployment Tools

4.4.1   Assembly

Components are composed into larger ones, providing services to be deployed. In Friends, we migrated to the OMG CORBA Component Model (CCM) standard and the corresponding formats [7, chapter 10]. CMM prescribes that for a compound component we not only need a CORBA Component Descriptor (see section 4.3.2), but also a Component Assembly Descriptor (CAD). This CAD can be generated from the AMBER models, and has been implemented.

4.4.2   Packaging

To be deployed, a component has to be packaged according to formats as required by the deployment platform. Identical to 'atomic' components, compound components are stored as a zip-archive as described in section 4.3.5. Tools for automated packaging still have to be implemented. The CORBA Component Model allows the inclusion of (formal) behaviour descriptions in the software package, which we obviously intend to do.

5   Conclusions

In this paper, we sketched our ideas about model-based service creation and illustrated them in the context of the Friends project. Many of these ideas have already been implemented in the Friends platform, such as a graphical language for high-level component assembly, code generation from component specifications, and analysis tools. Through implementation of the service creation environment, we aim at proving the applicability of our approach, and in particular the added value of behaviour specifications.

Other ideas need further elaboration before they can be implemented. Some short term research issues are the extension of AMBER with concepts tailored to service creation, parameterisation of model-components to support model-based customisation, and searching components based on functionality. Research issues on the long(er) term are mainly in the area of analysis techniques, such as improved model checking support, verification techniques to assess the conformance between service designs defined at successive abstraction levels, and the modelling and analysis of performance aspects.

Concluding, we believe that our research contributes to the goal of developing a platform supporting rapid and correct service creation. In particular, the application of high-level specification languages and supporting (analysis) tools should enable the service developer to build a service from software components that can be considered at high(er) abstraction levels, and to assess the correctness of these components and their composition.

References

1. Bakker, J.-L., and H.J. Batteram, Design and evaluation of the Distributed Software Component framework for distributed communication architectures, In: Proc. Of the 2nd Int. Workshop on Enterprise Distributed Object Computing (EDOC'98), November 1998, p. 282-288.
2. Batteram, H.J., J.-L. Bakker, J.P.C. Verhoosel and N.K. Diakov, 'Design and implementation of the MESH service platform', In: Proceedings of TINA'99 Telecommunications Information Networking Architecture Conference, Oahu, Hawaii, USA, 12-15 April 1999.
3. Bernstein, P.A., "Middleware: A Model for Distributed Services." Communications of the ACM 39, 2, February 1996, pp. 86-97.
4. Beugnard, A., J.-M. Jézéquel, N. Plouzeau and D. Watkins, 'Making components contract aware'. IEEE Computer (July 1999), p. 38-45.
5. Bolognesi, T., J. van der Lagemaat and C.A. Vissers (eds.), LOTOSphere: Software development with LOTOS. Kluwer Academic Publishers, Dordrecht, The Netherlands, 1995.
6. Cicalese, C.D.T. and S. Rotenstreich, 'Behavioral specification of distributed software component interfaces'. IEEE Computer (July 1999), p. 46-53.
7. CORBA Components - Volume I, OMG TC Document orbos/99-07-01, August 2, 1999, http://www.omg.org/docs/orbos/99-07-01.pdf.

8. Diakov, N., Survey on products for visual assembly tools for Java, Amidst document WP1/N007, University of Twente, Enschede, The Netherlands, 3 June 1999, http://amidst.ctit.utwente.nl/workpackages/wp1/documents/wp1n007v01.pdf

9. Diakov, N.K., H.J. Batteram, H. Zandbelt and M.J. van Sinderen, 'Monitoring of distributed component interactions'. In Proceedings of 7th Int. Conf. on Interactive Distributed Multimedia Systems and Telecommunication Services (IDMS 2000) in Enschede, The Netherlands, October 2000.

10. Eertink, H., W.P.M. Janssen, P.H.W.M Oude Luttighuis, W.B. Teeuw, C.A. Vissers, 'A Business Process Design language', Proceedings World Congress on Formal Methods (FM'99), 1999.

11. FRIENDS, http://friends.gigaport.nl/; http://friends.telin.nl/

12. H.M. Franken and W. Janssen, 'Get a grip on changing business processes Results from the Testbed-project', Knowledge & Process Management (Wiley), vol. 5, no. 4, December 1998, p. 208-215.

13. Gamma, E., R. Helm, R. Johnson and J. Vlissides, "Design patterns : elements of reusable object-oriented software". Addison-Wesley, Reading, MA, 1995.

14. Holzmann, G.J., 'The model checker SPIN'. IEEE Trans. on Soft. Eng., vol. 23, no. 5, May 1997.

15. Quartel, D.A.C., L. Ferreira Pires, M.J. van Sinderen, H.M. Franken and C.A. Vissers, "On the role of basic design concepts in behaviour structuring", Computer Networks and ISDN Systems, vol. 29, no. 4, March 1997, 413-436.

16. Quartel, D.A.C., M.J. van Sinderen, and L. Ferreira Pires, "A model-based approach to service creation", In: Proceedings of the Seventh IEEE Computer Society Workshop on Future Trends of Distributed Computing Systems, IEEE Computer Society, 1999, 102-110.

17. Quartel, D.A.C., and W.B. Teeuw (Ed.), Modelling FRIENDS components in the language AMBER, Report FRIENDS/WP3/N012/V01, Telematics Institute, Enschede, The Netherlands, 21 June 2000.

18. C. Szyperski, Component Software, Beyond Object-Oriented Programming, Addison-Wesley, ACM Press, New York, 1998.

19. UML, http://www.rational.com/uml/resources/documentation/

20. Verhoosel, J.P.C., M. Wibbels, H.J. Batteram and J.-L. Bakker, 'Rapid service development on a TINA-based service deployment platform'. In: Proceedings of TINA'99 Telecommunications Information Networking Architecture Conference, Oahu, Hawaii, USA, 12-15 April 1999.

Validation of the Open Service Access API for UMTS Application Provisioning

Maarten Wegdam[1,3], Dirk-Jaap Plas[1], and Musa Unmehopa[2]

[1]Lucent Technologies,
Bell Labs Twente
Capitool 5, 7521 PL,
Enschede,
The Netherlands
[2]Lucent Technologies, UMTS Standards,
Larenseweg 50,
P.O. Box 1168, 1200 BD,
Hilversum, The Netherlands
[3]Centre for Telematics and Information Technology,
University of Twente
P.O. Box 217,
7500 AE, Enschede, The Netherlands

{wegdam, dplas, unmehopa}@lucent.com

Abstract. UMTS networks will allow the deployment of new types of applications, that are rich, interactive and multimedia capable, because of increased bandwidth, richer devices and location awareness. These applications are not necessarily provided by the network operator, but can be created and deployed by any third party. However, these third parties will need access to the UMTS core network capabilities, especially when it comes to call related services, location based services and services that charge for certain content. Intelligent Network (IN) based service creation and delivery platforms deployed in current 2G and 2.5G networks do not offer suitable interfaces for this, since third parties need to have detailed knowledge and expertise of low level, telecommunication specific protocols and can jeopardize the integrity of the network. The recent activities within the standardization bodies 3GPP and ETSI SPAN, and the industry forums Parlay and JAIN show an increased interest in the area of open network Application Programming Interfaces (APIs). The Open Service Access (OSA) specification is a collection of open network APIs for UMTS application provisioning defined by 3GPP. OSA is meant to allow third party application development and deployment by means of open, secure, and standardized access to core network capabilities, while preserving the integrity of the underlying network. We describe a prototype implementation, and list the possibilities and limitations of the OSA specification.

1   Introduction

The upcoming third generation (3G) mobile networks, such as UMTS networks, will be capable of providing much more powerful services than the regular, voice-related services. They will provide an always-on, relatively high bandwidth and packet-based

M.J. van Sinderen and L.J.M. Nieuwenhuis (Eds.): PROMS 2001, LNCS 2213, pp. 210–221, 2001.
© Springer-Verlag Berlin Heidelberg 2001

connection that allows a wide variety of Mobile Internet type of applications. Examples of these types of services are multi-media messaging applications, m-commerce type of applications, and location based applications. The promise of revenues created by these applications explains the enormous investments that operators and vendors of 3G networks are making in this area.

With the arrival of 3G networks, we will see a real convergence of the Intelligent Networking and the (Mobile) Internet type of service provisioning. Applications will not only be provided by the network operator, but also by third parties – like on the Internet – and they will be able to use capabilities provided by the 3G networks to provide these applications. The capabilities we focus on in this paper are the possibility to control the call setup, to determine the location of a user and to charge a user through his operator. Although the operator will not necessarily provide the application himself, his involvement in the delivery and provisioning of the application goes beyond providing the basic IP connectivity [Unmehopa01]. The 3G standardization body 3GPP has defined interfaces to access the service capabilities of the UMTS network, called the Open Services Access (OSA) API [3G 23.127].

In Section 2 we give an overview of the OSA specification, its architecture, and related standards. Section 3 describes the OSA Framework, the service independent part of the OSA. Sections 4, 5 and 6 describe three services that are part of the OSA, respectively Call Control, User Location and Charging Service. Section 7 describes the prototype of OSA we built to validate the specification. Section 8 lists the main issues and risks we found, based on our prototyping experience. Section 9 contains the conclusions and future work.

2   Open Service Access

This section focuses on the Open Service Access (OSA) specification and its architecture. The aim is to provide background information to support the focal point of the paper, i.e. the capability of third parties to make use of the core network functionalities Call Control, User Location and Network Charging offered by this 3G application delivery mechanism.

2.1 Business Model

Service delivery to roaming mobile subscribers in 2G network technology has been achieved by standardizing service logic behavior on every network node that serves the subscriber. Apart from the lengthy, laborious, and often strenuous process of standardizing every possible service, the impact of service deployment on every network node is quite severe. The Intelligent Network (IN) concept was a first attempt at overcoming these drawbacks, by introducing a clean separation between core switching functionality and value added service logic. This separation of concerns allows service logic to be developed and deployed with minimal impact on the switching and transport functionality of the operational network. Although the issue of smooth service introduction and deployment has been properly addressed by IN technology, service creation requires very skilled and specific telecommunications expertise. This slows down the service development process, whereas market requirements demand rapid service development as can be seen on the Internet today. Industry initiatives such as JAIN and Parlay [Parlay/JAIN] have demonstrated that the paradigm of open network Application Programming Interfaces (APIs) provides rapid service development by abstracting from telecommunication specific details. The business model for services and applications in 3G networks, through the introduction of network APIs, is now centered around shorter development cycles, third party Independent Software Vendors (ISVs) and the marriage of Internet content and mobile telecommunication networks [Unmehopa01].

2.2 Architecture

The Open Service Access API is an open network API that provides the application developer with an abstract view of the core network functionality. In this way, the application developer is shielded from the specific details of the underlying network technology. The OSA APIs are specified in OMG IDL [CORBA]. The gain for the network operator lies in the fact that the API provides secure and standardized access so that network integrity and security can be preserved, supports rapid service development, and is network independent – allowing easier service migration. An introductory overview of OSA and its capabilities can be found in [Unmehopa02]. [Torabi01] describes the applicability of OSA in an all-IP network architecture using the SIP protocol as an example of a network technology other than the GSM evolved UMTS network technology.

Abstractions of core network capabilities are offered to application developers as generic service building blocks, and are referred to as OSA services. Although OSA is network technology independent, 3GPP does provide optional mapping recommendations to CAMEL-based [3G TR 29.998] mobile networks. CAMEL is the collection of SS7 IN protocols used in 2G and 3G mobile networks. Fig. 1 gives a global overview of OSA.

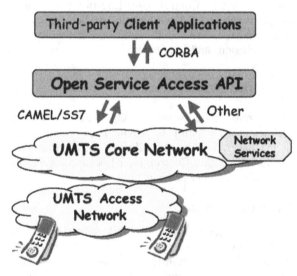

Fig. 1. OSA Overview

The Framework provides the functionality required to use the OSA services and the mechanisms to offer these to third parties. For a more detailed description on the general functionality of the Framework the reader is referred to [Bakker], [Yates], and [Stretch]. An assessment of the Framework functionality is provided in Section 3 of this paper. The Network Services targeted in the remainder of this paper are Call Control (Section 4), User Location (Section 5) and Charging (Section 6). In addition, the set of OSA specifications includes interface definitions for the following Network Services:

o Data Session Control - provides an OSA client application with the means to manage control functions related to data sessions, known as Packet Data Protocol sessions in the GPRS network.

o User Interaction - allows an OSA client application to instruct the network to engage in an interaction with the end-user on its behalf. Examples of these user interactions include voice-recorded announcements and Short Message Service (SMS) messages.

o User Status - offers the means for an OSA client application to check whether the terminal e.g. is attached to or detached from the network, or if the terminal is Network Determined User Busy.

o Terminal Capabilities - permits the OSA client application to acquire device capabilities and user preference information from the network. This information may be exploited to adapt content and content delivery mechanisms to best match the capabilities of the end-user terminal equipment.

3 Framework

Two of the key issues of providing third parties access to core network functionality are security and integrity management of the network. Only authenticated applications should be allowed access to the OSA services. Also the usage of the OSA services should be controlled, as intended or unintended misusage of the services can seriously disturb the integrity of the network. The OSA framework addresses these two issues, which are described in the next two sections.

3.1 Secure Access

All the security aspects of OSA are the responsibility of the framework. Two authentication types have been defined: OSA Authentication and CORBA Security. The OSA Authentication interface supports the usage of multiple encryption methods. The authentication process is based on a challenge/response protocol. The challenge mechanism used is in accordance with [RFC1994]. Before a client application gets access to a specific OSA service, the application and the framework must also (digitally) sign a service agreement. The exact text of these service agreements should be agreed upon off-line by the parties involved.

Limitations

The OSA Authentication on itself only defines authentication and does not address other security aspects like availability, integrity, privacy, and non-repudiation. In addition, the current specification remains unclear. For example, it does not exactly define how different authentication methods and encryption techniques should be used. This makes the specification ambiguous and difficult to implement, and may lead to portability and interoperability problems.

The OSA specification itself mentions that the middleware and lower layer protocols, on which the OSA API is based, should provide security mechanisms to encrypt data. One of the proposed mechanisms is the CORBA Security Service. However, the OSA specification does not clearly define how to use the CORBA Security Service in combination with the OSA, which again may lead to interoperability problems. Although the OSA specification does not mention it, other security mechanisms (e.g. SSL, IPsec, etc.) may well be used together with OSA Authentication to provide the required level of security.

3.2 Integrity Management

The Framework specifies capabilities for integrity management. Integrity in this context is much more general than integrity in the security context (see Section 3), and should deal with the performance and availability aspects of the OSA.

The integrity management capabilities of OSA consist of the following interfaces:

- Heartbeat interfaces, to have the client application and the framework exchange heartbeat messages.
- Load management interfaces, to get load information, both on the client application and the framework.
- Fault management interfaces, to monitor faults that occur at either the framework or the services.

Heartbeat Management

The heartbeat interfaces are symmetrical: Both the client application and the server side can be supervised through periodically sent heartbeats. The party receiving the heartbeat triggers the heartbeat.

Load Management

The load management interfaces offer capabilities for load management on both the client application and the server side. It allows a client application to request load control for certain services, to get load statistics or notifications when the load changes. What the capabilities of a load controller should be is not specified. Neither is specified what the threshold for load change is to inform the application about. Also, the use case behind a periodic notification of load statistics is unclear. In case of an overload of a certain service, the only possible action seems to be to stop using it until the overload has passed. This is of course not acceptable in most cases, for example it would be more appropriate to redirect the load to another service or host. However, there is nothing specified that addresses, preferably transparent, load balancing, limiting the possibility to use standard mechanisms that are present in the object middleware, and instantiation time load balancing [Othman01].

Fault Management

The main capability of the fault management interfaces is for the client application to get information about faults occurring in the framework and the services. The client application can explicitly ask the framework for this, or can be notified by the framework. These interfaces are mostly symmetrical, thus the framework can also ask the client applications if it is functioning correctly. A capability offered by the framework but not by the client application is to provide fault statistics. The fault management only deals with fault detection and notification. Nothing is specified about fault recovery or masking. This should be part of an OSA product though. E.g. the CORBA specification for Fault Tolerance could be used for this [CORBA FT]. In this specification replication is used to achieve a higher availability.

Relation to Business Model

In the OSA/Parlay business model, the framework and the different services may be developed by different vendors, but the interface between the framework and services is limited to service registration type of functionality. No functionality for integrity management is present, making it impossible to implement the integrity management interfaces without using proprietary interfaces. This is not consistent.

All the integrity interfaces are located between client application and server side. However, it is questionable if a client application should be able to control or even inspect, for example, the load on the server side. This is a responsibility of whoever is managing the server side, not the 3rd party. For the same reason the server side should also not have control over the load on the client application.

4   Call Control Service

One of the obvious capabilities of the UMTS network will be to establish a call. The OSA Call Control service provides functionality to monitor and control two party call setup, over both circuit and packet switched bearers.

4.1 Functionalities

The main capabilities of this service are that a client application can be notified of certain call events (e.g. call initiated, call ended, etc.), can control the routing of calls, and supervise charging parameters for calls. The new release of this service (release 4) will also have capabilities for multi-party calls.

4.2 Architecture

The Call Control service interacts with the underlying UMTS network. To support roaming end users, this interaction has to be performed through a standardized protocol for the delivery of operator specific services, which in the case of UMTS networks is CAMEL [3G TR 29.078]. CAMEL is a SS7 based protocol that is used in 2G and will also be used for 3G call control signaling. 3GPP describes an optional mapping recommendation for the call control API to CAMEL messages in [3G TR 29.998]. When UMTS networks migrate to an all-IP architecture (SIP), CAMEL will have to support the used VoIP protocol (SIP), or the Call Control service will have to be mapped on top of a SIP server. Similar the Call Control service can also support different types of mobile or fixed networks, such as H.323. Our prototype implements both the mapping on CAMEL and the mapping on a SoftSwitch that supports H.323, see Section 7.

4.3 Limitations

The current version of the specification basically assumes a circuit switched network. There are for example no possibilities to influence the Quality of Service (QoS) that a call in a packet-based network would receive.

The Call Control service suffers from the same feature interaction problems as IN services do. Only one client application can be in control of a call. In case of multiple interest for the same call, the specification prescribes a 'first come, first serve' policy, thus rejecting the second client application. This policy could quite easily be relaxed to allow two or more client applications to monitor a call, as long as one has actual control over it.

The initiation of calls by the client application is not possible in the current version of CAMEL, although it is expected to be supported in release 4. This is a much-desired functionality though.

5   User Location Service

New UMTS applications will increasingly require the support of location awareness. Being able to determine the geographical location of a mobile subscriber will enable the application to offer personalized and location relevant information and functionality. The set of OSA specifications therefore includes the User Location service, which defines the interface to obtain the mobile subscriber's location.

5.1 Functionalities

The User Location service provides an interface that can be used to request the location of a user. A client application can request the location of a specific user, or can ask for triggered or periodic reports of the location of the user. The accuracy and data type of the location reports can be the geographical position including an indication of its accuracy, but also more UMTS network oriented and by definition less accurate data types like an identification of the radio cell currently serving the mobile terminal.

5.2 Limitations

An issue that is not addressed in the OSA specification is that of the user privacy. Although mechanisms are in place to restrict access to the User Location service itself, this is not enough. Some mechanism needs to be in place to enforce per-user policies on what application can access exactly the location information from a certain user. The end-user should be able to set these policies, preferably directly and on-line. Also if a certain applications requests location information, the end user should be notified so he can deny or grant permission. All this is not addressed in the User Location specification, and it is thus left to the implementer of the User Location service.

At some places the OSA specification is ambiguous. For example, the timestamp parameter is not properly defined, leading to ambiguity between different implementations.

Except for geographical position, the data type definitions for location information in the current specification are predominantly applicable to the circuit switched domain instead of the packet-based domain. We expect that client application developers will usually prefer geographical position above the other data types.

6   Charging Service

The OSA specification contains two charging possibilities, call (or data session) related, or more general charging for a certain non-call/data session related service. The call related charging is primarily modeled after the charging functionality provided by the CAP protocol [3G TS 29.078], and is based on the duration of the call or the volume of transferred traffic in a session. In this section we will only cover the non-call/session related service based charging, which is intended for content based charging, with typically small amounts. The Charging service is a relatively new part of the OSA specification, as was proposed in December 2000 by the authors of this paper based on prototyping efforts [Charging].

6.1   Functionalities

The basic functionalities of the Charging service are to check if a charge can be covered by the users account or credit limit, to reserve a charge in the subscriber's account, and to deduct an amount from the subscriber's account. This is for both pre-paid and post-paid billing.

Certain operations have been considered more privacy sensitive, and are offered though a separate interface. This interface can be used to query the balance, monitor an account or get a history of transactions.

6.2   Limitations

This specification is aimed at micro payments, which is expected to be very important for content charging. However, for larger amounts the usage of a two-phase commit transaction mechanism should be considered, which is not in the specification. It has a similar issue as the User Location service in that it does not prescribe a method for the operator to give the user control over the payment. Although there is a trust relation between the third party and the operator, keeping final control over payments with the user is highly desirable. The specification does not inhibit proprietary solutions to address this issue; it is thus left to the implementer.

7   Prototype

Lucent Technologies Bell Labs Advanced Technologies, in conjunction with the Lucent Technologies UMTS Applications Development group have built a prototype of the OSA framework, the Call Control service, the User Location service and the Charging service. Fig. 2 depicts the prototype. It shows besides the OSA services and framework, also the back-end systems, and some generic OMG services we used such as the Naming and Event service. The Monitoring service is used to create Message Sequence Diagrams during run-time [Diakov].

The Call Control service is mapped upon two network technologies, a CAMEL based network and a H323 network. For the latter we use the Lucent SoftSwitch [Pluss01]. We did not implement the whole framework; especially the fault management and load management interfaces are not implemented.

We have built two different client applications. The first type is an application that performs location based and charged call forwarding, for example a caller is forwarded to the nearest Pizza restaurant if he calls 1-800-PIZZA and is charged for it. This application – a typical IN service – shows how IN type of services can easily be implemented on top of the OSA API.

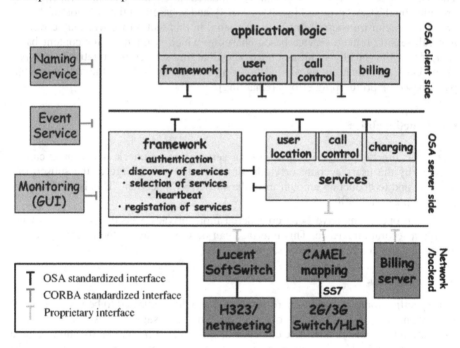

Fig. 2. High level view on prototype architecture

The second application assumes that the user has mobile terminal with web browsing capabilities, instead of just voice capabilities. The client application is in this case implemented as a Java Server Page, and after determining the location of a user it displays the local weather, and charges the user for it. It is possible to think of much more applications in this area of location-aware, personalized services, such as nearest restaurant, reserving movie tickets etc.

Due to the absence of real UMTS terminals and real UMTS network connectivity, we use pocket PCs connected through WaveLAN to simulate their characteristics. Network elements and protocols to provide the call control, user location, and charging functionality are supported by simulators and by real products.

8   Evaluation

Based on our prototyping efforts, we list here the main issues we found for OSA to fulfill to become the open API for UMTS application provisioning.

OSA as it is now is mainly aimed at IN type of services. For a more general service platform for mobile Internet type of services, OSA offers some interfaces such as

User Location and Charging, but that is not enough. Examples of what is also needed to make a more complete service-provisioning platform are interfaces to authenticate the end-user, to store user profiles, to do terminal adaptation and to deal with QoS issues. Preferably existing standards outside the telecom domain could be re-used for this, but they have to be integrated in the overall platform. Exactly what interfaces and how to integrate them into one platform is outside the scope of this paper.

Guaranteeing security and network integrity is of the utmost importance for an open API based approach like OSA. Not only because opening up a public network can potentially mean that anyone can cause major disruptions, but also because the privacy of the subscribers can be violated. We found the current security interfaces to be somewhat incomplete, which will result in implementations that are not portable. A second issue related to this, is that even if a certain party is sufficiently authenticated and authorized for a certain service, this party can still intentionally or unintentionally disrupt the network or violate the privacy of subscribers. This requires precise policies on what a certain party is and is not authorized to do. For an OSA product to be successful, it must incorporate such capabilities.

OSA is ongoing standardization, the number of Change Requests produced by the authors of this paper alone [CR] prove that the standard is not completely mature yet. Assuming the parties involved in the standardization are willing to do so, this can improve very quickly as more implementations of the OSA specification and client applications are made. For the immediate future however interoperability and portability problems between different implementations can be expected.

The interaction between OSA client applications and IN services can cause problems if not addressed properly. Especially when it comes to call control type of functionality, there are some feature interaction types of problems between OSA client applications, and between client applications and IN services. However, these problems are not new and also exists in current IN platforms. While it is so much easier to create new OSA client applications, these problems will likely occur more often.

Focusing on the non-technical aspects of OSA standardization, criteria for this specification to be successfully adopted in the marketplace are that there are no major competing standards. The ongoing convergence of related standards such as Parlay, JAIN and TSAS [TSAS] is a step in the right direction. Another risk related to acceptance is that it will be considered too much a telecom standard and not an Internet standard, which would make it more difficult to gain acceptance in the Internet area. As with any standard, another risk is that it will miss required functionality, or that it takes too long to reach the right maturity level to guarantee portability and interoperability.

9   Conclusions

The OSA is a new approach for UMTS application provisioning on a public network that allows third parties to develop rich and interactive multimedia UMTS applications. Compared to current day IN services in current fixed or mobile network, services can be developed and deployed much faster (shorter time-to-market) and cheaper. This is because the OSA interfaces require much less detailed telecom specific expertise from the developer that uses them, because of the higher abstraction OSA offers, and because of the usage of object middleware (CORBA). Also the fact that the services are network technology independent makes it possible to create services that can run on different type of networks, and can migrate from one network technology to another. Since it will become much easier to develop new services, and those services can much easier be ported to different networks, of different operators and different vendors, it is expected that more specialized services will be deployed. Lucent will continue working on resolving the issues with, and considers OSA to be a major part of future, standards based, UMTS Service Platforms.

References

[3G TR 29.078]   3rd Generation Partnership Project; Technical Specification Group Core Network; *Customised Applications for Mobile network Enhanced Logic (CAMEL); CAMEL Application Part (CAP) specification* (3G TS 29.078 version 3.2.0)

[3G 23.127]   3rd Generation Partnership Project, Technical Specification Group and System Aspects. *Virtual Home Environment / Open Service Architecture (Release 1999).* 3GPP TS 23.127 V3.3.0 (2000-12)

[3G TR 29.998]   3rd Generation Partnership Project; Technical Specification Group Core Network; *Open Services Architecture Application Programming Interface - Part 2 (Release 1999)* (3G TR 29.998 version 3.2.0)

[Bakker]   Bakker J, McGoogan J, Opdyke W, Panken F, 2000, "Rapid Development and Delivery of Converged Services Using APIs", Bell Labs Tech. J., 5, 12-29

[Charging]   Lucent (Musa Unmehopa), Kick-off Discussion Paper for OSA Charging API, 3GPP TSG_CN WG5 N5-000302, http://www.3gpp.org/ftp/tsg_cn/WG5_osa/TSGN5_08_Scottsdale/Docs/N5-000302-charging-kick-off.zip

[CORBA FT]   OMG, *Fault Tolerant CORBA Specification*, http://www.omg.org, ptc/00-04-04

[CORBA]   OMG, *CORBA Specification version 2.4.1*

[CR]   Lucent (Musa Unmehopa), Change Requests to 3GPP CN WG5 for OSA Release 99, N5-000245, N5-000246, N5-000247, N5-000248, N5-000249, N5-000251, N5-000252, N5-000253, N5-000254, N5-000255, N5-000256

[Diakov]   Diakov, N.K., Batteram, H. J., Zandbelt, H., Sinderen, M. J., *Design and Implementation of a Framework for Monitoring Distributed Component Interactions*, Proceedings of the 7th International Workshop, IDMS'2000, Enschede, The Netherlands, October 17-20, 2000.

[Othman01]   Ossama Othman and Douglas C. Schmidt, *Optimizing Distributed system Performance via Adaptive Middleware Load Balancing*, ACM SIGPLAN Workshop on Optimization of Middleware and Distributed Systems (OM 2001), Snowbird, Utah, June 18, 2001.

[Parlay/JAIN]   Beddus S, Bruce G, David S, 2000, *Opening Up Networks with JAIN Parlay*, IEEE Comm. Mag., 38-4, 136-143

[Pluss01]   J.W. Hellenthal, F.J.M. Panken, M.Wegdam, *Validation of the Parlay API through prototyping*, IEEE Intelligent Network Workshop 2001 (IN2001), 6-8 May, Boston, USA.

[RFC1994]   IETF. *PPP Authentication Protocols – Challenge Handshake Authentication Protocol*. RFC 1994. August 1996

[Stretch]   Stretch, R., *OSA and other related issues*, BT Tech J., Vol. 19-1, January 2001.

[Torabi01]   M. Torabi, M.Unmehopa, *Service Control Architecture in IP Multimedia based 3G Networks (An OSA API Service Scenario)*, submitted to IEEE MWCN 2001, 14-17 Aug. 2001, Recife, Brazil

[TSAS]   OMG, *Telecom Service Access & Subscription,* http://www.omg.org, dtc/00-10-03

[Unmehopa01]   M. Unmehopa, M. Grech, *Using Open Service Access to Enable Mobile Internet Applications in UMTS Networks*, IEEE Second International Conference on 3G Mobile Communication Technologies, 26 - 28 March 2001, London, UK.

[Unmehopa02]   M. Unmehopa et. al., *The Support of Mobile Internet Applications in UMTS Networks through the Open Services Architecture*, (to be published) Bell Labs Technical Journal, Vol. 6, No. 2, July- Dec. 2001

[Yates]   Yates MJ, Boyd I, 2000, *The Parlay network API specification*, BT Tech J., Vol. 18-2, 57-64

On the End-User QoS-Awareness of a Distributed Service Environment[*]

I. Widya[1], R.E. Stap[2], L.J. Teunissen[3], and B.F. Hopman[4]

[1]CTIT University of Twente, P.O.Box 217, Enschede, the Netherlands
widya@cs.utwente.nl
[2]TNO-FEL Twente, Enschede, the Netherlands
stap@fel.tno.nl
[3]KPN Research, Groningen, the Netherlands
l.j.teunissen@kpn.com
[4]PTS Software, Bussum, the Netherlands
frank.hopman@pts.nl

Abstract. A lot of attention has been given to network quality of service and efforts to make layers on top of the network also QoS-aware increase noticeably. This paper explores QoS-aware service provisioning at a level close to end-user's perception. It shows how end-user oriented QoS requirements have been elaborated in a high level design onto QoS support of a distributed service platform and how realized QoS can be monitored. A GameHall has been used as the application context for which validation of the explored and applied concepts and models for QoS specification and monitoring have been exercised.

1 Introduction

Along with the functionality of an on-line service, the quality of the service determines the service usability and utility, both of them influencing the likelihood of use of the service. Provisioning of QoS may therefore be a significant success factor to distributed service environments and a service provider may benefit from this provisioning to distinguish its services from other service providers.

This paper addresses some of the QoS provisioning issues described in the literature, e.g. [Me98, Au98]. In particular, it addresses the issue of specification, establishment and feedback of QoS at a level close to the user's perception, for example in accordance with a specified service level agreement [Ve99]. This paper exemplifies a procedure for this provisioning in a distributed service environment, particularly, in the context of a GameHall demonstrator that runs on a distributed service platform [Ba99].

For the specification of QoS at different layered levels of the distributed service environment and for the mapping of the specified or derived QoS parameters across those levels, this paper applies a (nested) user-provider model for QoS specification that has been elaborated in the project AMIDST [Si98, He00]. This model, in turn, is based on the ISO QoS Framework [IS97]. Complexity of QoS mappings (see e.g. [Na95, Xu00, Si00]) is mostly avoided by a heuristic approach that only uses first order relevance between parameters of the different levels. This approach is feasible

---

[*] This work has been sponsored by the Dutch Ministry of Economic Affairs within the project FRIENDS.

M.J. van Sinderen and L.J.M. Nieuwenhuis (Eds.): PROMS 2001, LNCS 2213, pp. 222–237, 2001.
© Springer-Verlag Berlin Heidelberg 2001

within the reserved time span of the work and is sufficient for our demonstrator purposes. It simplifies QoS mapping considerably, i.e. it enables the use of mapping tables.

In the context of this work, the GameHall demonstrator is used as a vehicle to integrate the developed application oriented QoS framework into the service platform and to demonstrate the ability of this platform in differentiating resource allocations between the different types of games and end-user categories. In particular, the GameHall demonstrates the establishment and the monitoring of QoS. This monitoring is for the purpose of proactively informing the end-users on realized QoS to facilitate these users with service predictability [Bo99, Sa00] and the service accountability, which denotes the ability of the service to settle the benefit-cost factor up in accordance with realized performance.

This paper is organized as follows. Section 2 describes the business model of the demonstrator that provides the application domain context for the provisioning of QoS. Section 3 explains a procedure for QoS specification at interfaces and the mapping of QoS between these interfaces. Section 4 describes the provisioning and monitoring of QoS in the distributed service environment. Finally, Section 5 provides the conclusions of this work.

2 The Applied Business Model

This section describes the business model of the GameHall that has been used as the environment to exercise QoS provisioning, in particular the specification and the monitoring of QoS.

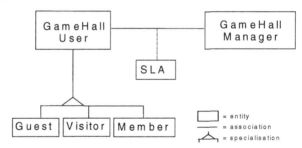

Fig. 1. The business model as a context for QoS provisioning

The GameHall offers to end-users different types of games, for example card-, chess- and car racing games. Like in the business model used in the Telecommunication Information Networking Architecture (TINA) [Ya97], the GameHall business model (Fig. 1) identifies the different stakeholders and expresses the relationship between these stakeholders. Each stakeholder has a different role in dealing with the use, control or provisioning of QoS. In the figure, the GameHall User represents a client and the GameHall manager is one of the representatives of the GameHall service provider.

In the model, users are categorized in different (sub-)roles. This yields different QoS requirements for the games in the GameHall. On one side, different requirements due to the different types and nature of the games and, on the other side, due to the different end-user roles. The Service Level Agreement (SLA) models the kind of relationship between the users and the provider, it will accommodate users satisfaction better since it specifies what users may expect [Ve99]. Moreover, the model is also used as a mean to make end-users aware of the different QoS facilities for different end-user roles, e.g. to provide fairness of charging.

As the GameHall is used as a context to elaborate the QoS framework that spans over user-oriented to system- and network-oriented QoS, we discuss this model further.

2.1 GameHall Users

Three user roles have been introduced in the GameHall demonstrator:
- *Guest*: a guest of the GameHall may try some games. QoS support for this role is limited and the options to play games at advanced levels are also restricted;
- *Visitor*: a visitor pays for the played games and therefore gets better facilities than non paying guest;
- *Member*: a user with a subscription and who's (playing) profile is stored in the GameHall. As a regular GameHall customer, this role typically needs and expects a higher game performance than the other two roles.

To accommodate the different QoS needs at user level, QoS of games are categorized in values like "gold', "silver", or "bronze". GameHall users either are provided with a fixed setting of QoS or may choose between alternative settings, which have been pre-selected by the GameHall manager in accordance with the SLA associated to the role of the user.

To satisfy the users even better, users will receive feedback of achieved QoS from the provider. In this demonstrator, feedback is given in the form of a traffic light, which stays green as long as the agreed QoS is realized. It turns to orange or red in case the quality of service degrades or drops completely.

2.2 GameHall Service Provider

Two service provider roles have been introduced, the GameHall manager and the GameHall deployer. At the applied level of granularity, the deployer is not visible in the model shown in Fig. 1. This due to the role of the deployer that at the applied level of abstraction has no direct association to the GameHall users, but complements the role of the manager.

- **GameHall manager**
  The GameHall manager has the responsibility of issues related to the SLA, for example the implementation of the business (commercial and marketing) policy for the GameHall. The manager instantiates and fine-tunes the QoS configurations of the games that have been defined by (possibly third party) GameHall deployers.

  The GameHall manager, for example, may apply a policy that gives members a higher serving priority than others. Paying users, moreover, may get better performance of selected games or get more reliable games than non-paying guests or members that only try new games.

- **GameHall deployer**
  The responsibility of the deployer is to define the constraints for QoS profiles, QoS specification and mapping with respect to the nature of the games and, if appropriate, to the technical restrictions or capacity of the provider. For example, the deployer specifies all *invariant* aspects of games with respect to QoS.

2.3 Service Level Agreements

A service level agreement is a mean to specify the relationship between the GameHall service provider and the end-users who have different membership roles. A definition for a service level agreement is for example [Ve99]:

"A service level agreement (SLA) is an explicit statement of the expectations and obligations that exist in a business relationship between two organisations: the service provider and the customer[1]."

Typically, an SLA contains [Ve99]:

- the type and nature of the service and the expected performance level of the service,
- the process of monitoring and reporting of realized service level,
- and many other aspects like management, other customer care and accounting aspects.

This paper elaborates on user-oriented QoS which settings are dependent on the role of the users and the type and nature of the games (Section 3). It also discusses a mechanism for monitoring delivered QoS (Section 4). Other customer care, management or accounting aspects are beyond the scope of this paper.

3 The Applied QoS Specification Framework

Establishment of QoS in a layered architecture includes the specification of QoS at an interface and the mapping down through the interfaces of the underlying layers until computing system or network resources can be determined for allocation. In this paper, we apply a user-provider model [Ha99, He00] to match at the interface the needed QoS by user entities to the QoS capabilities offered by the provider (Fig. 2).

The QoS interface model, shown in Fig. 2, originates from ISO QoS Framework [IS97] and has been elaborated in the project AMIDST [Si98]. User requirement in respect of QoS (abbr. as urQoS) represents the QoS of a user-to-user interaction. In this model, urQoS is in principle independent of the (middleware) provider that mediates the interaction between the peer users. The provider may however advertise its QoS capabilities in terms of QoS characteristics (denoted as midQoS in Fig. 2) and values or value ranges that it can support. Typically, a QoS characteristic is a quantifiable quality aspect of services, e.g. reliability or swiftness. In this paper, an aggregation of these characteristics and associated value ranges is called a QoS class. A provider may offer several QoS classes, each class optimised to a certain category of services, e.g., QoS classes suitable for chess up to car racing games.

---

[1] This paper does not distinguish between customer and end-user stakeholders.

3.1 QoS Specification Model at Interfaces

Specification of QoS at a user-provider interface therefore involves the translation of the required urQoS into a QoS class offered by a provider. To facilitate this, we use the concept QoS requirement [IS97] that specifies the qualifiers (e.g. maximum, mean) and the required values of the associated provider's characteristic. In this translation, a user entity may accept losses in accuracy of the translation or may choose between alternative QoS classes offered by one or more providers.

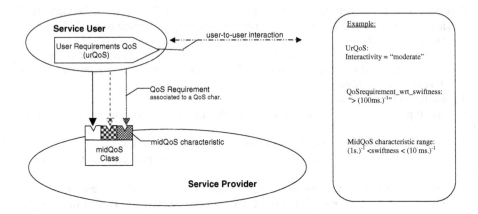

Fig. 2. User-provider model to specify QoS at interfaces

3.2 Layered QoS Model

In a layered architecture, a provider has to map the required midQoS characteristics and values mentioned earlier further downwards to QoS characteristics available at underlying interfaces (Fig. 3). In doing so, midQoS characteristics not only map "vertically" to lower level characteristics, e.g. QoS characteristics of local system components (sysQoS) and network elements (netQoS). In addition, some "horizontal" mapping may also be needed for peer capability matching, for example, to select and configure multimedia compression devices (e.g. MPEG-1 and MPEG-2) in a compatible manner. The triple headed arrow in the middleware layer in Fig. 3 models this multiparty mapping.

On the other hand, the double-headed arrow in the middleware layer models the peer-to-peer interactions that have to be QoS aware as well. These QoS needs before (multimedia) data is encoded and compressed are called media format level QoS and denoted as mfQoS in the figure. Furthermore, the QoS mapping in the layer may generate additionally the need for complementary peer-to-peer support such as retransmission protocols to increase reliability.

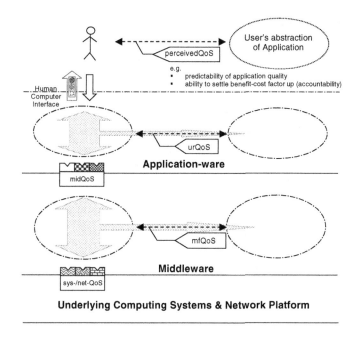

Fig. 3. Layered QoS Model for specification and monitoring

User-level QoS in the GameHall context:

As observed among others in [Bo99, Sa00, He00], QoS expected by users depends on the context of the use of the application. This so-called *task context* is characterised by the type of the application, the task of the invoked application for the user (i.e. the purpose of using the application) and the user role. In the GameHall demonstrator, the task context is characterised by the user role (i.e. guest, visitor or member), the type and nature of the game (e.g. a chess or a highly interactive car racing game) and the task (e.g. to try a game out or to play in a competition).

In our pursue to improve the attractiveness of the games in respect of QoS to the users, several articles from various disciplines have been studied:

- Models to predict the likelihood of use of distributed applications in a learning related context have been investigated in the educational science [Co00]. The so-called 3G model[2] of Kappetijn expresses this likelihood in terms of three aspects. Though not a fully appropriate translation, one of the aspects translates to benefit or pay-off. The other two aspects translate to ease of use and pleasure, attractiveness or one's engagement of use;

- In the area of stock investments, predictability of the performance of investment funds is an important aspect for investors. Investors also need an ability to settle up with these funds in accordance with the expectations and realized performance [Ba00];

---

[2] The 3G stand for the Dutch words "gewin", "gemak" and "genot".

- QoS studies in the human factors area among others identify feedback and also predictability as important QoS aspects for users [Bo99, Sa00].

Inspired by the previously mentioned studies, the GameHall demonstrator addresses the following task context dependent QoS aspects at user level (denoted by 'perceivedQoS' in Fig. 3):

- predictability of application quality:

   The demonstrator facilitates members to use a higher QoS setting compared to other user roles. On the other hand, paying users will be provided with more constant quality (e.g. higher reliability) than non-paying users. This GameHall policy is to better fulfill predictability of game quality as expected by end-users in respect to their task context.

- accountability that expresses the ability to settle up in accordance with realized QoS:

   In addition to the previously discussed policy, charges of used services will be adapted in case of drops in realized QoS. We believe that this ability to settle benefit-cost factor up will improve user satisfaction. However, one may argue whether this accountability is a quality characteristic or a kind of a "what-if" element of a QoS specification for the case that the commitment of the provider in respect to predictability is not met.

- task context dependent provider feedback:

   A QoS feedback mechanism will support the predictability and the ability to settle benefit-cost factor up. GameHall users will be facilitated by a monitoring component that displays a measure of realized QoS in the form of a traffic light positioned at the human computer interface HCI in Fig. 3. The setting of the traffic light depends on the task context of the user. That is, green signals for a GameHall guest and for a member generally mean different realization of QoS in respect to allocated computing system or network resources.

Applicationware QoS characteristics:

In this paper, we adopt the following urQoS dimensions introduced in [He00] and validate them for the GameHall case.

- *Availability*: UrQoS availability is the quality aspect of the peer-to-peer interaction of being present or ready for immediate use. In this paper, availability associates to both the instantiation and the use of a game, thus spanning over the whole lifetime of the game instantiation.

- *Fidelity*: UrQoS fidelity is the quality aspect of a peer-to-peer interaction of being good enough with respect to the task, such as the use of false colours to highlight important items. This urQoS dimension will not be elaborated further in the GameHall demonstrator.

- *Integrity*: UrQoS integrity is the quality aspect of the peer-to-peer interaction in maintaining the correctness of the interaction in respect to the source. In a car racing game, high integrity will preserve image resolution and synchronisation of the moving scene and the steer movements.

- *Interactivity*: UrQoS interactivity is the quality aspect of the peer-to-peer interaction of being responsive. In this paper, interactivity associates to the services (i.e. methods) of a game after instantiation of the game, and not to the responsiveness of the instantiation of the game itself (availability). It is clear that urQoS dimensions are not necessarily orthogonal.

- *Regulatory*: UrQoS regulatory is the quality aspect of the peer-to-peer interaction of being in conformance with the rules, the law, or the established usage in the application domain. In a GameHall, regulatory means the conformance to the rules of the games, for example, to ensure equal opportunity to win a game even in the case that the environment is heterogeneous.

Middleware QoS characteristics:

The QoS capabilities of a middleware provider that offers services to application components may be expressed in terms of classes of QoS characteristics, including the (ranges of) supported values. One may also specify QoS using a language for QoS that support specification of measurement units [Fr98]. The following list describes some of the midQoS characteristics introduced in [Ha99]:

- *accessibility*: MidQoS accessibility is the quality aspect of a service that represents the degree of being capable of serving a request. It may be expressed as a probability measure denoting the success rate or chance of a successful service instantiation at a point in time.

- *accuracy*: MidQoS accuracy is the quality aspect of a service that represents the degree of conformity to the true value, an ICT standard or a well-accepted custom (e.g. video accuracy value "VCR" or "studio-TV", which specification may refer to the CCIR.601 standard).

- *reliability*: MidQoS reliability is the quality aspect of a service that represents the degree of being capable of maintaining the service and service quality.

- Other described midQoS characteristics are *linkage unity* (the degree of parts being linked as a complex whole, e.g. synchronisation of multimedia), *swiftness* (the degree of how immediately or quickly something is done), and *urgency* (the degree of being important for immediate attention or processing).

Platform QoS characteristics:

QoS characteristics associated to the underlying platform are denoted as comQoS, netQoS and sysQoS. They represent the QoS aspects of the communication session layer (Fig. 4), the network platform and the computing system elements, respectively.

The applied distributed service platform, upon which the demonstrator runs contains a Load Balancer component that among others supports sysQoS characteristics like priority (i.e. the scheduling priority of a process in a computing node) and workload accessibility (i.e. the chance a request to schedule a game component in a computing node be accepted). The platform also supports comQoS characteristics associated to multimedia streams and is therefore closely related to mfQoS introduced in the layered model (Fig. 3), but defined at an intermediate level interface (Fig. 4). For video streams, the platform supports width and height dimensions of a frame, frame-rate, quantisation bits/pixel, colour-depth and delay.

Audio related comQoS characteristics supported are the number of audio channels, sampling frequency, quantisation, and delay. NetQoS characteristics are delay and bit-rate.

QoS Mapping:
For the demonstrator, we use a heuristic approach to by-pass the complexity of mapping of QoS characteristics across layers (see e.g. [Na95, Xu00, Si00] for QoS mappings). At user level, the GameHall manager typically determines the urQoS values of the games in accordance with its policies and service level agreement. Further, a simple benefit functions relates realized urQoS to the earlier mentioned traffic light that provides QoS feedback to users.

At the level of the middleware service, a subset of urQoS dimensions often relates to a subset of midQoS characteristics. An urQoS value may also map to a whole range of alternative values of midQoS characteristics forming a subspace in an offered QoS class. We have similar situations in the mapping of midQoS to netQoS and sysQoS characteristics, especially if special resources such as multimedia coding devices are involved.

Though these QoS mappings are generally M:N relations, we nevertheless apply translation tables that are mainly suitable for 1:N mappings. To enable this, the most dominant relation between the QoS parameters will only be taken into account. This paper does not address horizontal capability matching aspects nor the protocols that may be needed to complement QoS mappings such as retransmission protocols.

4 Implementation of the QoS Framework into the Demonstrator

This section discusses the incorporation of the QoS framework into the distributed service environment. First, the applied QoS specification and mapping procedure will be discussed. Then, the QoS extension of the service environment will be explained in brief. Thereafter, the monitoring mechanism to provide user feedback will be briefly described.

4.1 Implementation of QoS Specifications and Mappings

As was discussed earlier, the QoS settings of games depend on the task context and are constrained by the SLA. In the case of the demonstrator, we use tables to implement QoS specification at interfaces and to map QoS across layers.

It is the responsibility of the GameHall deployer to define the templates of the QoS specification tables, the constraints between the QoS values in the table cells, and the list of values that a GameHall manager can use in a succeeding configuration step. Table 1 exemplifies the constraints of urQoS dimensions of a chess game that can be played at different skill levels and players settings. The constraints are for example $A_i \leq A_{i+1}$; $C_i = \{$"only_once_semantic", $X_i\}$ with movement-to-speech synchronisation tolerance $X_i \geq X_{i+1}$ for $i = \{1,..,3\}$, and Z specifying an equal QoS setting for involved players for fairness of the play.

Table 1. Chess user requirements in the deployers' perspective.

CHESS Game		Availability	Interactivity	Fidelity	Integrity	Regulatory
with computer	Level 2	A_1	B_1	"don't care"	C_1	"don't care"
	Level 1	A_2	B_2	"don't care"	C_2	"don't care"
other user		A_3	B_3	"don't care"	C_3	Z
simul		A_4	B_4	"don't care"	C_4	Z

A GameHall manager has the responsibility to instantiate the templates in accordance with the SLA and its policy. Table 2 exemplifies the availability of the chess game for the different user roles. It shows what a user may expect in respect of playing quality. In this example, a guest player may only play against the computer at skill level 1. The table also shows that members may select between two QoS settings.

Table 2. Example QoS availability settings per role.

CHESS		Availability		
		Guest	Visitor	Member
with computer	Level 1	"ch_bronze"	"ch_bronze"	"ch_bronze_premier" or "ch_silver_premier"
	Level 2		"ch_bronze"	"ch_bronze_premier" or "ch_silver_premier"
other user			"ch_silver"	"ch_silver_premier" or "ch_gold_premier"
simul				"ch_gold_premier"

The availability values in Table 2 are partially ordered string typed values that may also be expressed using a QoS language, see e.g. [Fr98, He00]. These values map further downwards to midQoS characteristics like accessibility, reliability and swiftness of invocations (Table 3). As expected, QoS values at higher levels are more specific to the type of the game and task context, values at lower levels are typically more generic, that is, the prefix "ch_" specific for chess games can be omitted in the lower level values.

Table 3. Example availability to reliability and accessibility translation table.

CHESS Availability	Accessibility	Reliability
"ch_bronze"	"moderate"	"moderate"
"ch_bronze_premier"	"high"	"moderate"
"ch_silver"	"moderate"	"high"
"ch_silver_premier"	"high"	"high"
"ch_gold_premier"	"premier"	"premier"

Other QoS mappings can be elaborated in a similar way. One may indeed raise the question when mappings of string typed values ever ends or become concrete for the implementation. A downward mapping stops if it reaches values which interpretation have been specified in technical terms in a standard or are known from human factor studies (e.g. 44.1 KHz sampling rate, 16 bits/sample quantisation for uncompressed "CD" quality audio, 80 ms for a tolerable audio-video lip-synchronisation and 40 ms for a moderate lip-synchronisation [St93]).

4.2   QoS Extension of the Distributed Service Environment

This section briefly describes the high-level component architecture of the distributed service platform that has been extended with QoS. A time-sequence diagram related to the establishment of QoS for a game is used to explain the QoS extension of the platform.

As mentioned earlier, the distributed service platform is based on TINA [Ba99]. With respect to the layered QoS model (Fig. 3), the Service Session layer of the platform (Fig. 4) relates to the Application-ware layer in Fig. 3. The Communication and Connectivity Session layers relate to the Middleware layer and the Network layer (including the end-terminals) relates to the computing system and network platform in Fig. 3.

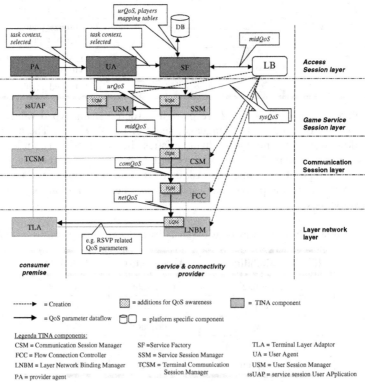

Fig. 4. Component architecture to provision a QoS service session

Some of the components in Fig. 4 are specific to the service platform [Ba99]. The database component DB contains information needed by the platform to provide the services to the users. It among others contains the user profiles and the QoS tables discussed earlier. The component LB is a load balancing component specific to the platform. This component does not only perform load balancing (including midQoS to sysQoS mappings), it also creates other TINA components, therefore, acting as a component factory. Though possibly not fully TINA complaint, these peculiarities are not significantly relevant in the context of this work that focus on QoS establishment and monitoring.

Moreover, the GameHall demonstrator is realized as one of the services of the distributed service environment, this enables accommodation of other demonstrators in the service environment. However, this means that a game is a sub-service of the GameHall service. Instantiation of a game will therefore by-pass several steps of the Access Session.

The QoS extensions are represented by different QoS Manager components (abbreviated as xQM with the prefix "x" = S, C, L, U standing for Session, Communication, Layer-network or User, respectively (Fig. 4)). These components are responsible for all QoS issues of the containing component. The call-outs that label the component interactions expose the conveyed QoS characteristic level. For clarity, the figure only depicts relevant components of a single party involved in the establishment of a multiparty service session.

Fig. 5 shows a time-sequence diagram of a game invocation after the instantiation of the GameHall service (i.e. after the user identified him/herself and received a list of games, including the settings in accordance to his/her role, and players who are also in the GameHall). This means that the service session User Application (ssUAP) and the User Agent (UA) of the GameHall service session have been instantiated.

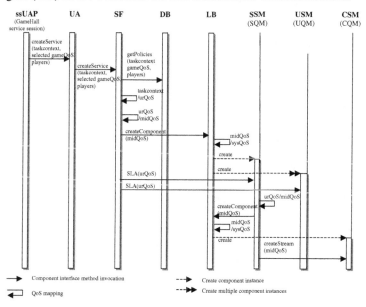

Fig. 5. Service session establishment in respect of QoS

A game session establishment procedure (see Fig. 5):

- In response to a user request for a game, the originating site ssUAP of the GameHall service session sends a createService request transparently via the Provider Agent (PA) to the UA. The request conveys the task context, the invited players (in case of a multi-party game) and the required game QoS in case a set of QoS settings are offered to the user.
- The UA forwards the request to the Service Factory (SF). The SF retrieves from the database (DB) component the urQoS dimensions and values, which are associated to the task context and the required game QoS, and the relevant urQoS/midQoS mapping tables. The SF uses these tables to compute the QoS settings of the components that will be created (Fig. 5).
- In the platform, the SF asks the Load Balancer (LB) to create the session layer components involved in the game, i.e. the Service Session Manager (SSM) and the User Session Manager (USM) of all parties. The LB component transforms the received midQoS parameters to sysQoS parameters that will be used to create the applicable components. In the user domain the PA creates the ssUAP of the game session. In the current version, creation of this ssUAP in the user premise is not yet QoS supported.
- The SF also informs (via SSM) the created USMs about the agreed urQoS to enable control of the traffic light (see also the section on QoS monitoring).
- For the establishment of QoS aware communication connections, the SSM maps the urQoS to midQoS parameters and provides these in the request to the LB to enable derivation of the sysQoS parameters and to create the CSM using these parameters. The CSM is responsible for the further processing of the midQoS parameters to a specific QoS aware network implementation, e.g. yielding an RSVP reserved stream that is supported by end-to-end QoS.

4.3   QoS Monitoring in the Distributed Service Environment

The main objective for the monitoring of the QoS performance is the implementation of the task context dependent feedback to the end-user. The following considerations have influenced the designed feedback mechanism:

- minimal monitoring-related interactions at the boundary between the user premises and the provider domain, therefore isolating provider 's measurement data flow within the provider's domain;
- reuse of components that receive QoS mapping tables during QoS establishment; and
- keep the design open for extensions in which a trusted third party performs (parts of) the monitoring.

As shown by the component architecture in Fig. 6 and the time-sequence diagram in Fig. 7, realized QoS performance information flows in the reversed direction of the signalling during the QoS establishment phase, traversing the components involved in the downwards QoS mapping. Method invocation is applied to transfer the information for the reasons listed above.

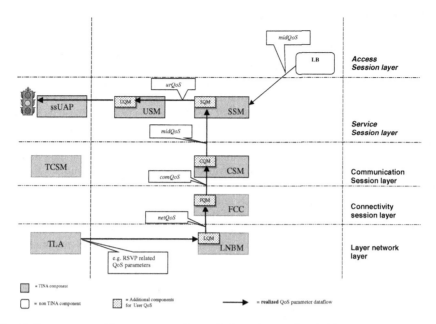

Fig. 6. Component architecture to monitor a QoS service session (with call-outs representing *realized* QoS values)

The figures also show the control of the traffic light by the UQM component of the USM. In particular, the differences in realized and required urQoS values, conditional to the type and nature of the game, the skills level selected and the user role, are equally weighted by a benefit function and then signalled to the traffic light. In case of not complying with the service level agreement, the provider may decrease a charging meter or adapt the QoS provisioning. The latter is however a challenging issue for further research.

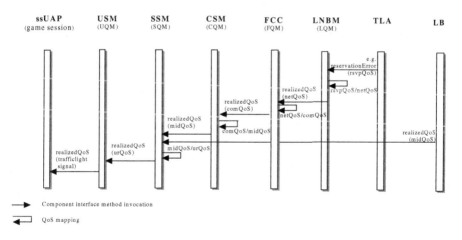

Fig. 7. Service session QoS monitor

5   Conclusions and Outlooks

In the context of a GameHall, we have exercised a QoS development trajectory starting from QoS specification at a level close to user's perception towards its high-level implementation onto a distributed service platform. To make this work feasible within the time-span of the collaboration project that develops the platform and the GameHall, we have explored and applied existing concepts and models for QoS specification and have used a heuristic design approach. This latter to avoid derivation or implementation of complicated M-to-N QoS mapping mechanisms. This work is to be considered as a validation exercise of the applied concepts and models and is a preliminary step to get experience to develop more advanced techniques for QoS specification and mechanisms for mapping of QoS.

The described model to specify QoS at interfaces has been successfully applied at several levels of the layered architecture of the service environment, at a level close to end-users' perception up to network-oriented levels. Within the layered framework, one may therefore apply similar techniques or mechanisms for QoS negotiation or mapping.

This paper works out user-oriented QoS issues which settings are dependent on the context of the users' task, determined by the role of the users, the purpose of the task and the type and nature of the games. It turns out that a lot of attention has to be put in task analysis in order to capture required QoS that should improve likelihood of service usage. To increase the satisfaction of the end-users, further (human factors) study has to be done on the relation between the required and the perceived QoS in accordance with the task context and established service level agreement.

Establishment of QoS in a layered architecture includes the specification of QoS at an interface and the mapping down through the interfaces of the underlying layers until computing system or network resources can be reserved. Several times we have experienced difficulties of QoS mappings, especially the reversed mapping of several QoS parameters to a QoS parameter one level higher, despite the simplified (table based) mapping approach applied. Further exploration of (research results of) M-to-N mappings, for example in combination with QoS specification languages, for the provisioning of end-user QoS is another interesting challenge.

This paper also discusses an elementary mechanism to monitor delivered QoS for end-users feedback. In the future, a third party that objectively appraises service performance may perform these monitoring of services. This approach also enables the benchmarking of services of different providers. This situation is anticipated, since the developed architecture distinguishes between provisioning and monitoring of services.

Other customer care issues, like accounting aspects and QoS control and management to maintain agreed QoS guarantees, are beyond the scope of this paper. Further study on the linkages between QoS policies, accounting and billing of delivered services is a necessity to enable commercial exploitation of QoS aware services.

References

[Au98]   C. Aurrecoechea, A.T. Campbell and L. Haw, "A Survey of QoS Architectures", Multimedia Systems Journal, Special Issue on QoS Architectures, May 1998;

[Ba99]   H.J. Batteram, J-L. Bakker, J.P.C. Verhoosel, and N.K. Diakov, "Design and Implementation of the MESH Services Platform", Proceedings of TINA'99 Conference, Oahu, Hawaii, April 1999;

[Ba00]   B. Bakker, "Een kroon op het fonds: nieuwe beleggingsfondsengids 2000 van Nyfer", in newspaper attachment "Geld Telt", NRC Handelsblad, Oct. 21st 2000 (in Dutch);

[Bo99]   A. Bouch and M.A. Sasse, "Network Quality of Service – An Integrated Perspective", Proc. RTAs '99, Vancouver, June 1999;

[Co00]   B. Collis and N. Pals, "A Model for Predicting an Individual's Use of a Telematics Application for a Learning-Related Purpose", International Journal of Educational Telecommunications, 6(1), pp. 63 – 103, 2000;

[Fr98]   S. Frølund and J. Koistinen, "Quality-of-service Specification in Distributed Object Systems", Distributed Systems Engineering, 5, 1998, pp. 179 – 202;

[Ha99]   A. van Halteren et al., "QoS architecture", Amidst project deliverable D.3.1.2, 1999, http://amidst.ctit.utwente.nl/workpackages/wp3/index.html;

[He00]   C. Hesselman, I. Widya, A.T. van Halteren, and L.J.M. Nieuwenhuis, "Middleware support for media-streaming establishment driven by user-oriented QoS requirements", Proceedings of the Interactive Distributed Multimedia Systems and Telecommunication Services (IDMS2000), Enschede, the Netherlands, Oct. 2000, pp. 158 – 171, Springer Verlag LNCS 1905;

[IS97]   ISO/IEC JTC1/SC21 N13236, "Information Technology – Quality of Service – Framework", Geneva, 1997;

[Me98]   J. de Meer and A. Hafid, "The Enterprise of QoS", tutorial presentation at the Middleware Conference, Sep. 1998, Lake District, U.K., http://www.fokus.gmd.de /research/cc/tip/employees/jdm/private/jdmPubList1998.html;

[Na95]   K. Nahrstedt and J.M. Smith, "The QoS Broker", IEEE Multimedia, 2(1), pp. 53 – 67, 1995;

[Sa00]   M.A. Sasse, "User-centred quality of service: why value is everything ..", slides at QofiS 2000, Berlin, Sep. 2000, http://www.fokus.gmd.de/events/qofis2000/slides /27ix00/s012-user-and-market/sasse.pdf;

[Si00]   F. Siqueira and V. Cahill, "Quartz: A QoS Architecture for Open Systems", The 20th IEEE Int. Conf. On Distributed Computing Systems, pp. 197 – 204, Taipei, Taiwan, April 2000;

[Si98]   M. van Sinderen, "AMIDST Application of Middleware in Services for Telematics", http://amidst.ctit.utwente.nl, 1998;

[St93]   R. Steinmetz, "Human Perception of Media Synchronization", IBM European Networking Center, IBM – Technical report no 43 9310, 1993;

[Ve99]   D. Verma, "Supporting Service Level Agreements on IP networks", Macmillan Technical Publications, ISBN 1-57870-146-5, 1999;

[Xu00]   D-Y. Xu, D-D. Wichadakul, and K. Nahrstedt, "Multimedia Service Configuration and Reservation in Heterogeneous Environments", The 20th IEEE Int. Conf. On Distributed Computing Systems, pp. 512 – 519, Taipei, Taiwan, April 2000;

Author Index

Lecture Notes in Computer Science

For information about Vols. 1–2118
please contact your bookseller or Springer-Verlag

Vol. 2161: F. Meyer auf der Heide (Ed.), Algorithms – ESA 2001. Proceedings, 2001. XII, 538 pages. 2001.

Vol. 2162: Ç. K. Koç, D. Naccache, C. Paar (Eds.), Cryptographic Hardware and Embedded Systems – CHES 2001. Proceedings, 2001. XIV, 411 pages. 2001.

Vol. 2163: P. Constantopoulos, I.T. Sølvberg (Eds.), Research and Advanced Technology for Digital Libraries. Proceedings, 2001. XII, 462 pages. 2001.

Vol. 2164: S. Pierre, R. Glitho (Eds.), Mobile Agents for Telecommunication Applications. Proceedings, 2001. XI, 292 pages. 2001.

Vol. 2165: L. de Alfaro, S. Gilmore (Eds.), Process Algebra and Probabilistic Methods. Proceedings, 2001. XII, 217 pages. 2001.

Vol. 2166: V. Matoušek, P. Mautner, R. Mouček, K. Taušer (Eds.), Text, Speech and Dialogue. Proceedings, 2001. XIII, 452 pages. 2001. (Subseries LNAI).

Vol. 2167: L. De Raedt, P. Flach (Eds.), Machine Learning: ECML 2001. Proceedings, 2001. XVII, 618 pages. 2001. (Subseries LNAI).

Vol. 2168: L. De Raedt, A. Siebes (Eds.), Principles of Data Mining and Knowledge Discovery. Proceedings, 2001. XVII, 510 pages. 2001. (Subseries LNAI).

Vol. 2170: S. Palazzo (Ed.), Evolutionary Trends of the Internet. Proceedings, 2001. XIII, 722 pages. 2001.

Vol. 2172: C. Batini, F. Giunchiglia, P. Giorgini, M. Mecella (Eds.), Cooperative Information Systems. Proceedings, 2001. XI, 450 pages. 2001.

Vol. 2173: T. Eiter, W. Faber, M. Truszczynski (Eds.), Logic Programming and Nonmonotonic Reasoning. Proceedings, 2001. XI, 444 pages. 2001. (Subseries LNAI).

Vol. 2174: F. Baader, G. Brewka, T. Eiter (Eds.), KI 2001: Advances in Artificial Intelligence. Proceedings, 2001. XIII, 471 pages. 2001. (Subseries LNAI).

Vol. 2175: F. Esposito (Ed.), AI*IA 2001: Advances in Artificial Intelligence. Proceedings, 2001. XII, 396 pages. 2001. (Subseries LNAI).

Vol. 2176: K.-D. Althoff, R.L. Feldmann, W. Müller (Eds.), Advances in Learning Software Organizations. Proceedings, 2001. XI, 241 pages. 2001.

Vol. 2177: G. Butler, S. Jarzabek (Eds.), Generative and Component-Based Software Engineering. Proceedings, 2001. X, 203 pages. 2001.

Vol. 2180: J. Welch (Ed.), Distributed Computing. Proceedings, 2001. X, 343 pages. 2001.

Vol. 2181: C. Y. Westort (Ed.), Digital Earth Moving. Proceedings, 2001. XII, 117 pages. 2001.

Vol. 2182: M. Klusch, F. Zambonelli (Eds.), Cooperative Information Agents V. Proceedings, 2001. XII, 288 pages. 2001. (Subseries LNAI).

Vol. 2184: M. Tucci (Ed.), Multimedia Databases and Image Communication. Proceedings, 2001. X, 225 pages. 2001.

Vol. 2185: M. Gogolla, C. Kobryn (Eds.), «UML» 2001 – The Unified Modeling Language. Proceedings, 2001. XIV, 510 pages. 2001.

Vol. 2186: J. Bosch (Ed.), Generative and Component-Based Software Engineering. Proceedings, 2001. VIII, 177 pages. 2001.

Vol. 2187: U. Voges (Ed.), Computer Safety, Reliability and Security. Proceedings, 2001. XVI, 261 pages. 2001.

Vol. 2188: F. Bomarius, S. Komi-Sirviö (Eds.), Product Focused Software Process Improvement. Proceedings, 2001. XI, 382 pages. 2001.

Vol. 2189: F. Hoffmann, D.J. Hand, N. Adams, D. Fisher, G. Guimaraes (Eds.), Advances in Intelligent Data Analysis. Proceedings, 2001. XII, 384 pages. 2001.

Vol. 2190: A. de Antonio, R. Aylett, D. Ballin (Eds.), Intelligent Virtual Agents. Proceedings, 2001. VIII, 245 pages. 2001. (Subseries LNAI).

Vol. 2191: B. Radig, S. Florczyk (Eds.), Pattern Recognition. Proceedings, 2001. XVI, 452 pages. 2001.

Vol. 2192: A. Yonezawa, S. Matsuoka (Eds.), Metalevel Architectures and Separation of Crosscutting Concerns. Proceedings, 2001. XI, 283 pages. 2001.

Vol. 2193: F. Casati, D. Georgakopoulos, M.-C. Shan (Eds.), Technologies for E-Services. Proceedings, 2001. X, 213 pages. 2001.

Vol. 2194: A.K. Datta, T. Herman (Eds.), Self-Stabilizing Systems. Proceedings, 2001. VII, 229 pages. 2001.

Vol. 2195: H.-Y. Shum, M. Liao, S.-F. Chang (Eds.), Advances in Multimedia Information Processing – PCM 2001. Proceedings, 2001. XIX, 1149 pages. 2001.

Vol. 2196: W. Taha (Ed.), Semantics, Applications, and Implementation of Program Generation. Proceedings, 2001. X, 219 pages. 2001.

Vol. 2197: O. Balet, G. Subsol, P. Torguet (Eds.), Virtual Storytelling. Proceedings, 2001. XI, 213 pages. 2001.

Vol. 2200: G.I. Davida, Y. Frankel (Eds.), Information Security. Proceedings, 2001. XIII, 554 pages. 2001.

Vol. 2201: G.D. Abowd, B. Brumitt, S. Shafer (Eds.), Ubicomp 2001: Ubiquitous Computing. Proceedings, 2001. XIII, 372 pages. 2001.

Vol. 2202: A. Restivo, S. Ronchi Della Rocca, L. Roversi (Eds.), Theoretical Computer Science. Proceedings, 2001. XI, 440 pages. 2001.

Vol. 2205: D.R. Montello (Ed.), Spatial Information Theory. Proceedings, 2001. XIV, 503 pages. 2001.

Vol. 2207: I.W. Marshall, S. Nettles, N. Wakamiya (Eds.), Active Networks. Proceedings, 2001. IX, 165 pages. 2001.

Vol. 2208: W.J. Niessen, M.A. Viergever (Eds.), Medical Image Computing and Computer-Assisted Intervention – MICCAI 2001. Proceedings, 2001. XXXV, 1446 pages. 2001.

Vol. 2209: W. Jonker (Ed.), Databases in Telecommunications II. Proceedings, 2001. VII, 179 pages. 2001.

Vol. 2210: Y. Liu, K. Tanaka, M. Iwata, T. Higuchi, M. Yasunaga (Eds.), Evolvable Systems: From Biology to Hardware. Proceedings, 2001. XI, 341 pages. 2001.

Vol. 2211: T.A. Henzinger, C.M. Kirsch (Eds.), Embedded Software. Proceedings, 2001. IX, 504 pages. 2001.

Vol. 2212: W. Lee, L. Mé, A. Wespi (Eds.), Recent Advances in Intrusion Detection. Proceedings, 2001. X, 205 pages. 2001.

Vol. 2213: M.J. van Sinderen, L.J.M. Nieuwenhuis (Eds.), Protocols for Multimedia Systems. Proceedings, 2001. XII, 239 pages. 2001.